D1263316

Introduction to Naval Architecture

Introduction to Naval Architecture

Third Edition

E. C. Tupper, BSc, CEng, RCNC, FRINA, WhSch

THE SOCIETY OF NAVAL ARCHITECTS AND MARINE ENGINEERS

Butterworth-Heinemann
Linacre House, Jordan Hill, Oxford OX2 8DP
A division of Reed Educational and Professional Publishing Ltd

Ⱥ A member of the Reed Elsevier plc group

OXFORD BOSTON JOHANNESBURG
MELBOURNE NEW DELHI SINGAPORE

First published as *Naval Architecture for Marine Engineers*, 1975
Reprinted 1978, 1981
Second edition published as *Muckle's Naval Architecture*, 1987
Third edition 1996

British Library Cataloguing in Publication Data
A catalogue record for this book is available from the British Library

ISBN 0-939773-21-X

Library of Congress Cataloguing in Publication Data
A catalogue record for this book is available from the Library of Congress

Published in the United States by
The Society of Naval Architects and Marine Engineers
601 Pavonia Avenue
Jersey City, New Jersey 07306

Composition by Genesis Typesetting, Rochester, Kent
Printed and bound in Great Britain

Contents

Preface to the third edition

One definition of wisdom is the thoughtful application of learning; insight; good sense; judgement. It can be said that this book aims to contribute to the reader's wisdom. It sets out to provide knowledge of the fundamentals of naval architecture so that the reader can define a ship form, calculate its draughts and displacement and check its stability. It seeks to give an understanding of other aspects of the ship such as the possible modes of structural failure and its manoeuvring and seakeeping performance. It presents information on the environment in which the ship has to operate, and describes the signs that might indicate pending trouble.

As with all branches of engineering, naval architecture is changing dramatically as a result of modern technology. Computers have made a big impact on the design, construction and operation of ships. New materials and changing world economics are bringing new ship types into commercial use or resulting in changes in more established types. Greater emphasis on protection of the environment has led to new regulations on waste disposal and the design of ships to minimize the harmful results of oil spillages and other accidents. There is now greater attention to safety of life at sea, not least as a result of the tragic loss of life in passenger ferries such as the *Estonia* and the *Herald of Free Enterprise*.

Because of the rate of change in the subject, new texts are required not only by those beginning a career in the profession but also by those already involved who wish to keep their knowledge up-dated. This book is intended only as an introduction to naval architecture. It sets out to educate those who need some knowledge of the subject in their work, such as sea-going engineers and those who work in design offices and production organizations associated with the maritime sector. It will help those who aspire to acquire a qualification in naval architecture up to about the incorporated engineer level. Most major design calculations are, today, carried out by computer. However, it is vital that the underlying principles are understood if computer programs are to be applied intelligently. It is this understanding which this book sets out to provide for the technician.

Apart from ships, many are involved in the exploitation of offshore energy resources, harvesting the riches of the sea or in leisure activities. Leisure is an increasingly important sector in the market, ranging from small boats to large yachts and ferries and even underwater passenger craft to show people the marvels of marine life. All marine structures must obey the same basic laws and remain effective in the harsh marine environment.

Many of those working in these fields will have had their basic training in a more general engineering setting. This volume presents the essential knowledge of naval architecture they need in a form which they should find easy to assimilate as part of a course of learning. Those who are already practitioners will find it useful as a reference text.

Acknowledgements

Many of the figures and most of the worked examples in this book are from *Muckle's Naval Architecture* which is the work this volume is intended to replace. A number of figures are taken from the publications of the Royal Institution of Naval Architects. They are reproduced by kind permission of the Institution and those concerned are indicated in the captions. I am very grateful to my son, Simon, for his assistance in producing the new illustrations.

1 Introduction

SHIPS

Ships are a vital element in the modern world. They still carry some 95 per cent of trade. In 1994 there were more than 80 000 ships each with a gross tonnage of 100 or more, representing a gross tonnage of over 450 million in total. Although aircraft have displaced the transatlantic liners, ships still carry large numbers of people on pleasure cruises and on the multiplicity of ferries operating in all areas of the globe. Ships, and other marine structures, are needed to exploit the riches of the deep.

Although one of the oldest forms of transport, ships, their equipment and their function, are subject to constant evolution. Changes are driven by changing patterns of world trade, by social pressures, by technological improvements in materials, construction techniques and control systems, and by pressure of economics. As an example, technology now provides the ability to build much larger, faster, ships and these are adopted to gain the economic advantages those features can confer.

NAVAL ARCHITECTURE

Naval architecture is a fascinating and demanding discipline. It is fascinating because of the variety of floating structures and the many compromises necessary to achieve the most effective product. It is demanding because a ship is a very large capital investment and because of the need to protect the people on board and the marine environment.

One has only to visit a busy port to appreciate the variety of forms a ship may take. This variation is due to the different demands placed on them and the conditions under which they operate. Thus there are fishing vessels ranging from the small local boat operating by day, to the ocean going ships with facilities to deep freeze their catches. There are vessels to harvest the other riches of the deep – for exploitation of energy sources, gas and oil, and extraction of minerals. There are oil tankers, ranging from small coastal vessels to giant supertankers. Other huge ships carry bulk cargoes such as grain, coal or ore. There are ferries for carrying passengers between ports which may be only a few kilometres or a hundred apart. There are the tugs for shepherding ships in port or for trans-ocean towing. Then there are the dredgers, lighters and pilot boats without which the port could not function. In a naval port there will be warships from huge aircraft carriers through cruisers and destroyers to frigates, patrol boats, mine countermeasure vessels and submarines.

Besides the variety of function there is variety in hull form. The vast majority of ships are single hull and rely upon their displacement to support their weight. In some applications multiple hulls are preferred because they provide large deck areas without excessive length. In other cases higher speeds may be achieved by using dynamic forces to support part of the weight when under way. Planing craft, surface effect ships and hydrofoil craft are examples. Air cushion craft enable shallow water to be negotiated and provide an amphibious capability. Some craft will be combinations of these specialist forms.

The variety is not limited to appearance and function. Different materials are used – steel, wood, aluminium and reinforced plastics of various types. The propulsion system used to drive the craft through the water may be the wind, but for most large craft is some form of mechanical propulsion. The driving power may be generated by diesels, steam turbine, gas turbine, some form of fuel cell or a combination of these. The power will be transmitted to the propulsion device through mechanical or hydraulic gearing or by using electric generators and motors as intermediaries. The propulsor itself will usually be some form of propeller, perhaps ducted, but may be water or air jet. There will be many other systems on board – means of manoeuvring the ship, electric power generation, hydraulic power for winches and other cargo handling systems.

A ship can be a veritable floating township with several thousand people on board and remaining at sea for several weeks. It needs electrics, air conditioning, sewage treatment plant, galleys, bakeries, shops, restaurants, cinemas, dance halls, concert halls and swimming pools. All these, and the general layout must be arranged so that the ship can carry out its intended tasks efficiently and economically. The naval architect has not only the problems of the building and town designer but a ship must float, move, be capable of surviving in a very rough environment and withstand a reasonable level of accident. It is the naval architect who 'orchestrates' the design, calling upon the expertise of many other professions in achieving the best compromise between many, often conflicting, requirements. The profession of naval architecture is a blend of science and art. Science is called upon to make sure the ship goes at the intended speed, is sufficiently stable and strong enough to withstand the rigours of the harsh environment in which it moves, and so on. The art is in getting a judicious blend of the many factors involved so as to produce a product that is not only aesthetically pleasing but is able to carry out its function with maximum effectiveness, efficiency and economy.

Naval architecture is a demanding profession because a ship is a major capital investment that takes many years to create and is expected to remain in service for perhaps twenty-five years or more. It is usually part of a larger transport system and must be properly integrated with the other elements of the overall system. The geography of, and facilities at, some ports will restrict the size of ship that can be accommodated and perhaps require it to carry special loading and discharging equipment. An example of this is the container ship. Goods can be placed in containers at the factory where they are produced. These containers are of certain standard dimensions and are taken by road, or rail, to a port with specialized handling equipment where they are loaded on board. At the port of destination they are offloaded on to land transport. The use of containers means that ships need spend far less time in port loading and unloading and the cargoes are more secure. Port fees are reduced and the ship is used more productively.

The designer must create the best possible ship to meet the operator's needs. In doing this he must know how the ship will be used and anticipate changes that may occur in those needs and usage over the years. Thus the design must be flexible. History shows that the most highly regarded ships have been those able to adapt with time.

Most important is the safety of ship, crew and environment. The design must be safe for normal operations and not be unduly vulnerable to mishandling or accident. No ship can be absolutely safe and a designer must take conscious decisions as to the level of risk judged acceptable in the full range of scenarios in which the ship can expect to find itself. There will always be a possibility that the conditions catered for will be exceeded and the risk of this and the potential consequences must be assessed and only accepted if they are judged unavoidable or acceptable. Acceptable, that is, by the owner, operator and the general public and not least by the designer who has ultimate responsibility. Even where errors on the part of others have caused an accident the designer should have considered such a possibility and taken steps to minimize the consequences. For instance, in the event of collision the ship must have a good chance of surviving or, at least, of remaining afloat long enough for passengers to be taken off safely. This brings with it the need for a whole range of life saving equipment. The heavy loss of life in the sinking of the *Estonia* in 1994 is a sad example of what can happen when things go wrong.

Cargo ships may carry materials which would damage the environment if released by accident. The consequences of large oil spillages are reported all too often. Other chemicals may pose an even greater threat. The bunker fuel in ships is a hazard and, in the case of ferries, the lorries on board may carry dangerous loads. Clearly those who design, construct and operate ships have a great responsibility to the community at large. If they fail to live up to the standards expected of them they are likely to be called to account[1].

Over the years the safety of life and cargo has prompted governments to lay down certain conditions that must be met by ships flying their flag, or using their ports. Because shipping is world wide there are also international rules to be obeyed. In the case of the United Kingdom the government department affected is the Department of Transport and its Marine Safety Agency. International control is through the International Maritime Organisation.

It is hoped that these few paragraphs have shown that naval architecture can be interesting and rewarding. The reader will find the various topics discussed in more detail in later chapters where the fundamental aspects of the subject are covered. The references at the end of each chapter indicate sources of further reading if it is desired to follow up any specific topic. A more advanced general textbook[2] can be consulted. This has many more references to assist the interested reader. For comments on references see the Appendix.

References

1. Rawson, K. J. (1989) Ethics and fashion in design. *TRINA*.
2. Rawson, K. J. and Tupper, E. C. (1994) *Basic Ship Theory*. Fourth Edition, Longman.

2 Definition and regulation

DEFINITION

A ship's hull form helps determine most of its main attributes; its stability characteristics; its resistance and therefore the power needed for a given speed; its seaworthiness; its manoeuvrability and its load carrying capacity. It is important, therefore, that the hull shape should be defined with some precision and unambiguously. To achieve this the basic descriptors used must be defined. Not all authorities use the same definitions and it is important that the reader of a document checks upon the exact definitions applying. Those used in this chapter cover those used by Lloyd's Register and the United Kingdom Ministry of Defence. Most are internationally accepted. Standard units and notation are discussed in the Appendix.

The geometry

A ship's hull is three dimensional and, except in a very few cases, is symmetrical about a fore and aft plane. Throughout this book a symmetrical hull form is assumed. The hull shape is defined by its intersection with three sets of mutually orthogonal planes. The horizontal planes are known as *waterplanes* and the lines of intersection are known as *waterlines*. The planes parallel to the middle line plane cut the hull in *buttock (or bow and buttock) lines*, the middle line plane itself defining the *profile*. The intersections of the athwartships planes define the *transverse sections*.

Three different lengths are used to define the ship (Figure 2.1). The *length between perpendiculars* (lbp), the *Rule length* of Lloyd's Register, is the distance measured along the summer load waterplane (the design waterplane in the case of warships) from the after to the fore perpendicular. The *after perpendicular* is taken as the after side of the rudder post, where fitted, or the line passing through the centreline of the rudder pintles. The *fore perpendicular* is the vertical line through the intersection of the forward side of the stem with the summer load waterline.

5

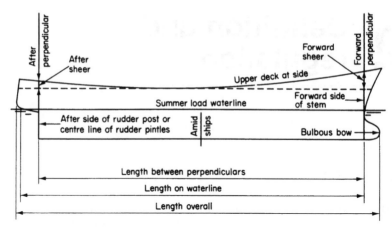

Figure 2.1 Principal dimensions

The *length overall* (loa) is the distance between the extreme points forward and aft measured parallel to the summer (or design) waterline. Forward the point may be on the raked stem or on a bulbous bow.

The *length on the waterline* (lwl) is the length on the waterline, at which the ship happens to be floating, between the intersections of the bow and after end with the waterline. If not otherwise stated the summer load (or design) waterline is to be understood.

The mid-point between the perpendiculars is called *amidships* or *midships*. The section of the ship at this point by a plane normal to both the summer waterplane and the centreline plane of the ship is called the *midship section*. It may not be the largest section of the ship. Unless otherwise defined the *beam* is usually quoted at amidships. The beam (Figure 2.2) most commonly quoted is the *moulded beam*, which is the greatest distance between the inside of plating on the two sides of the ship at the greatest width at the section chosen. The *breadth extreme* is measured to the outside of plating but will also take account of any overhangs or flare.

The ship *depth* (Figure 2.2) varies along the length but is usually quoted for amidships. As with breadth it is common to quote a *moulded depth*, which is from the underside of the deck plating at the ship's side to the top of the inner keel plate. Unless otherwise specified, the depth is to the uppermost continuous deck. Where a rounded gunwhale is fitted the convention used is indicated in Figure 2.2.

Sheer (Figure 2.1) is a measure of how much a deck rises towards the stem and stern. It is defined as the height of the deck at side above the deck at side amidships.

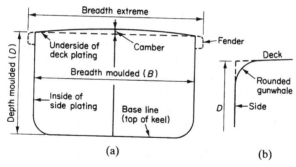

Figure 2.2 Breadth measurements

Camber or *round of beam* is defined as the rise of the deck in going from the side to the centre as shown in Figure 2.3. For ease of construction camber may be applied only to weather decks, and straight line camber often replaces the older parabolic curve.

The bottom of a ship, in the midships region, is usually flat but not necessarily horizontal. If the line of bottom is extended out to intersect the moulded breadth line (Figure 2.3) the height of this intersection above the keel is called the *rise of floor* or *deadrise*. Many ships have a flat keel and the extent to which this extends athwartships is termed the *flat of keel* or *flat of bottom*.

In some ships the sides are not vertical at amidships. If the upper deck beam is less than that at the waterline it is said to have *tumble home*, the value being half the difference in beams. If the upper deck has a greater beam the ship is said to have *flare*. All ships have flare at a distance from amidships.

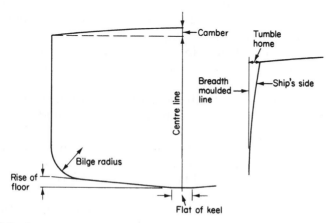

Figure 2.3 Section measurements

The *draught* of the ship at any point along its length is the distance from the keel to the waterline. If a *moulded draught* is quoted it is measured from the inside of the keel plating. For navigation purposes it is important to know the maximum draught. This will be taken to the bottom of any projection below keel such as a bulbous bow or sonar dome. If a waterline is not quoted the design waterline is usually intended. To aid the captain draught marks are placed near the bow and stern and remote reading devices for draught are often provided. The difference between the draughts forward and aft is referred to as the *trim*. Trim is said to be *by the bow* or *by the stern* depending upon whether the draught is greater forward or aft. Often draughts are quoted for the two perpendiculars. Being a flexible structure a ship will usually be slightly curved fore and aft. This curvature will vary with the loading. The ship is said to *hog* or *sag* when the curvature is concave down or up respectively. The amount of hog or sag is the difference between the actual draught amidships and the mean of the draughts at the fore and after perpendiculars.

Freeboard is the difference between the depth at side and the draught, that is it is the height of the deck above the waterline. The freeboard is usually greater at the bow and stern than at amidships. This helps create a drier ship in waves. Freeboard is important in determining stability at large angles (See Chapter 4).

Representing the hull form

The hull form is portrayed graphically by the *lines plan* or *sheer plan* (Figure 2.4). This shows the various curves of intersection between the hull and the three sets of orthogonal planes. Because the ship is symmetrical, by convention only one half is shown. The curves showing the intersections of the vertical fore and aft planes are grouped in the *sheer profile*; the waterlines are grouped in the *half breadth plan*; and the sections by transverse planes in the *body plan*. In merchant ships the transverse sections are numbered from aft to forward. In warships they are numbered from forward to aft although the forward half of the ship is still, by tradition, shown on the right hand side of the body plan. The distances of the various intersection points from the middle line plane are called *offsets*.

Clearly the three sets of curves making up the lines plan are inter-related as they represent the same three dimensional body. This inter-dependency is used in manual fairing of the hull form, each set being faired in turn and the changes in the other two noted. At the end of the iteration the three sets will be mutually compatible. Fairing is usually now carried out by computer. Indeed the form itself is often

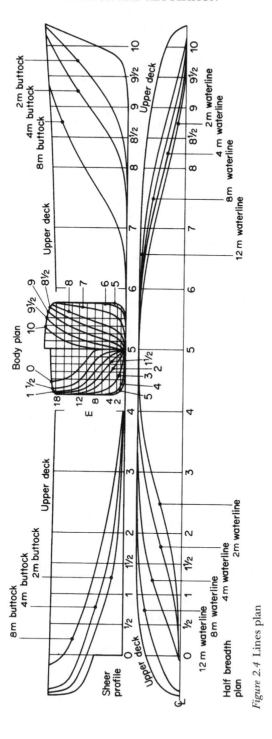

Figure 2.4 Lines plan

generated directly from the early design processes in the computer. Manual fairing is done first in the design office on a reduced scale drawing. To aid production the lines used to be laid off, and re-faired, full scale on the floor of a building known as the mould loft. Many shipyards now use a reduced scale, say one-tenth, for use in the building process. For computer designed ships the computer may produce the set of offsets for setting out in the shipyard or, more likely, it will provide computer tapes to be used in computer aided manufacturing processes.

In some ships, particularly carriers of bulk cargo, the transverse cross section is constant for some fore and aft distance near amidships. This portion is known as the *parallel middle body*.

Where there are excrescences from the main hull, such as shaft bossings or a sonar dome, these are treated as *appendages* and faired separately.

Hull characteristics

Having defined the hull form it is possible to derive a number of characteristics which have significance in determining the general performance of the ship. As a floating body, a ship in equilibrium will displace its own weight of water. This is explained in more detail in Chapter 4. Thus the volume of the hull below the design load waterline must represent a weight of water equal to the weight of the ship at its designed load. This *displacement*, as it is called, can be defined as:

$$\Delta = \rho g \nabla$$

where ρ = the density of the water in which the ship is floating
       g = the acceleration due to gravity
       ∇ = the underwater volume

It should be noted that displacement is a force and will be measured in newtons.

For flotation, stability, and hydrodynamic performance generally, it is this displacement, expressed either as a volume or a force, that is of interest. For rule purposes Lloyd's Register also use a *moulded displacement* which is the displacement within the moulded lines of the ship between perpendiculars.

It is useful to have a feel for the fineness of the hull form. This is provided by a number of *form coefficients* or *coefficients of fineness*. These are defined as follows, where ∇ is the volume of displacement:

Block coefficient $C_B = \dfrac{\nabla}{L_{pp}BT}$

where L_{pp} is length between perpendiculars
        B is the extreme breadth underwater
        T is the mean draught.

Corresponding to their moulded displacement Lloyd's Register use a block coefficient based on the moulded displacement and the Rule length. This will not be used in this book.

Coefficient of fineness of waterplane, $C_{WP} = \dfrac{A_W}{L_{WL}B}$

where A_W is waterplane area
        L_{WL} is the waterline length
        B is the extreme breadth of the waterline.

Midship section coefficient, $C_M = \dfrac{A_M}{BT}$

where A_M is the midship section area
        B is the extreme underwater breadth amidships.

Longitudinal prismatic coefficient, $C_p = \dfrac{\nabla}{A_M L_{pp}}$

Vertical prismatic coefficient, $C_{VP} = \dfrac{\nabla}{A_W T}$

It will be noted that these are ratios of the volume of displacement to various circumscribing rectangular or prismatic blocks, or of an area to the circumscribing rectangle. In the above, use has been made of displacement and not the moulded dimensions. This is because the coefficients are used in the early design stages and the displacement dimensions are more likely to be known. Practice varies, however, and moulded dimensions may be needed in applying some classification societies' rules.

The values of these coefficients can provide useful information about the ship form. The block coefficient indicates whether the form is full or fine and whether the waterlines will have large angles of inclination to the middle line plane at the ends. The angle at the bow is termed the *angle of entry* and influences resistance. A large value of vertical prismatic coefficient will indicate body sections of U-form, a low value will indicate V-sections. A low value of midship section coefficient indicates a high rise of floor with rounded bilges. It will be associated with a higher prismatic coefficient.

Displacement and tonnage

Displacement

A ship's *displacement* significantly influences its behaviour at sea. Displacement is a force and is expressed in newtons but the term *mass displacement* can also be used.

Deadweight

Although influencing its behaviour, displacement is not a direct measure of a ship's carrying capacity, that is, its earning power. To measure capacity *deadweight* and *tonnage* are used.

The *deadweight*, or *deadmass* in terms of mass, is the difference between the load displacement up to the minimum permitted freeboard and the *lightweight* or light displacement. The lightweight is the weight of the hull and machinery so the deadweight includes the cargo, fuel, water, crew and effects. The term *cargo deadweight* is used for the cargo alone. A table of deadweight against draught, for fresh and salt water, is often provided to a ship's master in the form of a *deadweight scale*.

Tonnage

Ton is derived from *tun*, which was a wine cask. The number of tuns a ship could carry was a measure of its capacity. Thus tonnage is a volume measure, not a weight measure, and for many years the standard ton was taken as 100 cubic feet. Two 'tonnages' are of interest to the international community – one to represent the overall size of a vessel and one to represent its carrying capacity. The former can be regarded as a measure of the difficulty of handling and berthing and the latter of earning ability. Because of differences between systems adopted by different countries, in making allowances say for machinery spaces, etc., there were many anomalies. Sister ships could have different tonnages merely because they flew different flags. It was to remove these anomalies and establish an internationally approved system that the International Convention on Tonnage Measurement of Ships, was adopted in 1969[1]. It came into force in 1982 and became fully operative in 1994. The Convention was held under the auspices of the International Maritime Organisation to produce a universally recognised system for tonnage measurement. It provided for the independent calculation of gross and net tonnages and has been discussed in some detail by Wilson[2].

The two parameters of gross and net tonnage are used. *Gross tonnage* is based on the volume of all enclosed spaces. *Net tonnage* is the volume of the cargo space plus the volume of passenger spaces multiplied by a coefficient to bring it generally into line with previous calculations of tonnage. Each is determined by a formula.

Gross tonnage $(GT) = K_1 V$

$$\text{Net tonnage } (NT) = K_2 V_c \left(\frac{4T}{3D}\right)^2 + K_3 \left(N_1 + \frac{N_2}{10}\right)$$

where:

V = total volume of all enclosed spaces of the ship in cubic metres

$K_1 = 0.2 + 0.02 \log_{10} V$

V_c = total volume of cargo spaces in cubic metres

$K_2 = 0.2 + 0.02 \log_{10} V_c$

$K_3 = 1.25 \dfrac{GT + 10\,000}{10\,000}$

D = moulded depth amidships in metres

T = moulded draught amidships in metres

N_1 = number of passengers in cabins with not more than eight berths

N_2 = number of other passengers

$N_1 + N_2$ = total number of passengers the ship is permitted to carry.

In using these formulae:

(1) When $N_1 + N_2$ is less than 13, N_1 and N_2 are to be taken as zero.
(2) The factor $(4T/3D)^2$ is not to be taken as greater than unity and the term $K_2 V_c (4T/3D)^2$ is not to be taken as less than $0.25\,GT$.
(3) NT is not to be less than $0.30\,GT$.
(4) All volumes included in the calculation are measured to the inner side of the shell or structural boundary plating, whether or not insulation is fitted, in ships constructed of metal.

Volumes of appendages are included but spaces open to the sea are excluded.

(5) *GT* and *NT* are stated as dimensionless numbers. The word ton is no longer used.

Other tonnages

Special tonnages are calculated for ships operating through the Suez and Panama Canals. They are shown on separate certificates and charges for the use of the canals are based on them.

REGULATION

There is a lot of legislation concerning ships, much of it concerned with safety matters and the subject of international agreements. For a given ship the application of this legislation is the responsibility of the government of the country in which the ship is registered. In the United Kingdom it is the concern of the Department of Transport and its executive agency, the *Marine Safety Agency* (MSA). Authority comes from the Merchant Shipping Acts. The MSA was formerly the Surveyor General's Organisation. It is responsible for the implementation of the UK Government's strategy for marine safety and prevention of pollution from ships. Its four primary activities are related to marine standards, surveys and certification, inspection and enforcement and keeping a register of shipping and seamen. Some of the survey and certification work has been delegated to classification societies and other recognized bodies.

Some of the matters that are regulated in this way are touched upon in other chapters, including subdivision of ships, carriage of grain and dangerous cargoes. Tonnage measurement has been discussed above. The other major area of regulation is the freeboard demanded and this is covered by the *Load Line Regulations*.

Load lines

An important insurance against damage in a merchant ship is the allocation of a *statutory freeboard*. The rules governing this are somewhat complex but the intention is to provide a simple visual check that a laden ship has sufficient *reserve of buoyancy* for its intended service.

The load line is popularly associated with the name of Samuel Plimsoll who introduced a bill to Parliament to limit the draught to which a ship could be loaded. This reflects the need for some minimum watertight volume of ship above the waterline. That is a minimum freeboard to provide a reserve of buoyancy when a ship moves through waves, to ensure an adequate range of stability and enough bouyancy following damage to keep the ship afloat long enough for people to get off.

Freeboard is measured downwards from the *freeboard deck* which is the uppermost complete deck exposed to the weather and sea, the deck and the hull below it having permanent means of watertight closure. A lower deck than this can be used as the freeboard deck provided it is permanent and continuous fore and aft and athwartships. A basic freeboard is given in the Load Line Regulations, the value depending upon ship length and whether it carries liquid cargoes only in bulk. This basic freeboard has to be modified for the block coefficient, length to depth ratio, the sheer of the freeboard deck and the extent of superstructure. The reader should consult the latest regulations for the details for allocating freeboard. They are to be found in the Merchant Shipping (Load Line) Rules.

When all corrections have been made to the basic freeboard the figure arrived at is termed the *Summer freeboard*. This distance is measured down from a line denoting the top of the freeboard deck at side and a second line is painted on the side with its top edge passing through the centre of a circle, Figure 2.5.

To allow for different water densities and the severity of conditions likely to be met in different seasons and areas of the world, a series of extra lines are painted on the ship's side. Relative to the Summer

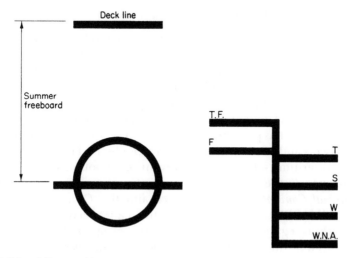

Figure 2.5 Load line markings

freeboard, for a Summer draught of T, the other freeboards are as follows:

(1) The Winter freeboard is $T/48$ greater.
(2) The Winter North Atlantic freeboard is 50mm greater still.
(3) The Tropical freeboard is $T/48$ less.
(4) The Fresh Water freeboard is $\Delta/40t$ cm less, where Δ is the displacement in tonne and t is the tonnes per cm immersion.
(5) The Tropical Fresh Water freeboard is $T/48$ less than the Fresh Water freeboard.

Passenger ships

As might be expected ships designated as passenger ships are subject to very stringent rules. A passenger ship is defined as one carrying more than twelve passengers. It is issued with a *Passenger Certificate* when it has been checked for compliance with the regulations. Various maritime nations had rules for passenger ships before 1912 but it was the loss of the *Titanic* in that year that focused international concern on the matter. An international conference was held in 1914 but it was not until 1932 that the International Convention for the Safety of Life at Sea was signed by the major nations. The Convention has been reviewed at later conferences in the light of experience. The Convention covers a wide range of topics including watertight subdivision, damaged stability, fire, life saving appliances, radio equipment, navigation, machinery and electrical installations.

The International Maritime Organisation (IMO)

The first international initiative in safety was that following the loss of the *Titanic*. In 1959 a permanent body was set up under the aegis of the United Nations to deal with the safety of life at sea. It is based in London and now represents some 150 maritime nations. It has an Assembly which meets every two years and between assemblies the organization is administered by a Council. Its technical work is conducted by a number of committees. It has promoted the adoption of some thirty conventions and protocols and of some seven hundred codes and recommendations related to maritime safety and the prevention of pollution. Amongst the conventions are the *Safety of Life at Sea Convention* (SOLAS) and the *International Convention on Load Lines,* and the *Convention on Marine Pollution* (MARPOL). The benefits that can accrue from satellites particularly as regards the transmission and receipt of distress messages, were covered by the *International Convention on the International Maritime Satellite Organisation* (INMARSAT).

Classification societies

There are many classification societies around the world including the American Bureau of Shipping of the USA, Bureau Veritas of France, Det Norske Veritas of Norway, Germanischer Lloyd of Germany, Nippon Kaiji Kyokai of Japan and Registro Italiano Navale of Italy. The work of the classification societies is exemplified by *Lloyd's Register* (LR) of London which was founded in 1760 and is the oldest society. It classes some 6700 ships totalling about 96 million in gross tonnage. When a ship is built to LR class it must meet the requirements laid down by the society for design and build. LR demands that the materials, structure, machinery and equipment are of the required quality. Construction is surveyed to ensure proper standards of workmanship are adhered to. Later in life, if the ship is to retain its class, it must be surveyed at regular intervals. The scope and depth of these surveys reflect the age and service of the ship. Thus, through classification, standards of safety, quality and reliability are set and maintained. Classification applies to ships and floating structures extending to machinery and equipment such as propulsion systems, liquefied gas containment systems and so on.

Lloyd's is international in character and is independent of government but has delegated powers to carry out many of the statutory functions mentioned earlier. Lloyd's carry out surveys and certification on behalf of more than 130 national administrations. They carry out statutory surveys covering the international conventions on load lines, cargo ship construction, safety equipment, pollution prevention, grain loading, etc., and issue International Load Line Certificates, Passenger Ship Safety Certificates and so on. The actual registering of ships is carried out by the government organization. Naturally owners find it easier to arrange registration of their ships with a government, and to get insurance cover, if the ship has been built and maintained in accordance with the rules of a classification society. The classification societies co-operate through the *International Association of Classification Societies* (IACS).

Lloyd's Register must not be confused with Lloyd's of London, the international insurance market, which is a quite separate organization although it had similar origins.

SUMMARY

It has been seen how a ship's principal geometric features can be defined and characterized. It will be shown in the next chapter how the parameters can be calculated and they will be called into use in later chapters. The concept and calculation of gross and net tonnage have been covered. The regulations concerning minimum freeboard values and the roles of the classification societies and government bodies have been outlined.

References

1. Final Act and Recommendations of the International Conference on Tonnage Measurement of Ships, 1969, and International Convention on Tonnage Measurement of Ships, 1969. HMSO publication, Miscellaneous No6 (1970) Cmmd.4332.
2. Wilson, E. (1970) The International Conference on Tonnage Measurement of Ships. *TRINA*.

3 Ship form calculations

It has been seen that the three dimensional hull form can be represented by a series of curves which are the intersections of the hull with three sets of mutually orthogonal planes. The naval architect is interested in the areas and volumes enclosed by the curves and surfaces so represented. To find the centroids of the areas and volumes it is necessary to obtain their first moments about chosen axes. For some calculations the moments of inertia of the areas are needed. This is obtained from the second moment of the area, again about chosen axes. These properties could be calculated mathematically, by integration, if the form could be expressed in mathematical terms. This is not easy to do precisely and approximate methods of integration are usually adopted, even when computers are employed. These methods rely upon representing the actual hull curves by ones which are defined by simple mathematical equations. In the simplest case a series of straight lines are used.

APPROXIMATE INTEGRATION

One could draw the shape, the area of which is required, on squared paper and count the squares included within it. If mounted on a uniform card the figure could be balanced on a pin to obtain the position of its centre of gravity. Such methods would be very tedious but illustrate the principle of what is being attempted. To obtain an area it is divided into a number of sections by a set of parallel lines. These lines are usually equally spaced but not necessarily so.

TRAPEZOIDAL RULE

If the points at which the parallel lines intersect the area perimeter are joined by straight lines, the area can be represented approximately by the summation of the set of trapezia so formed. The generalized

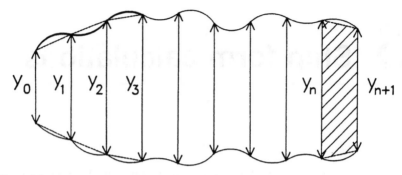

Figure 3.1

situation is illustrated in Figure 3.1. The area of the shaded trapezium is:

$$A_n = \tfrac{1}{2}h_n(y_n + y_{n+1})$$

Any area can be divided into two, each with part of its boundary a straight line. Such a line can be chosen as the axis about which moments are taken. This simplifies the representation of the problem as in Figure 3.2 which also uses equally spaced lines, called *ordinates*. The device is very apt for ships, since they are symmetrical about their

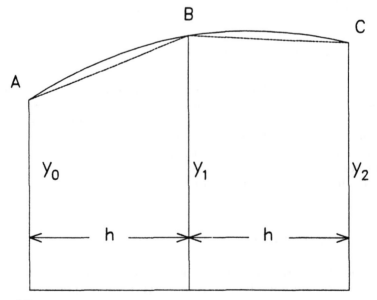

Figure 3.2

middle line planes, and areas such as waterplanes can be treated as two halves.

Referring to Figure 3.2, the curve ABC has been replaced by two straight lines, AB and BC with ordinates y_0, y_1 and y_2 distance h apart. The area is the sum of the two trapezia so formed:

$$\text{Area} = \frac{h(y_0 + y_1)}{2} + \frac{h(y_1 + y_2)}{2} = \frac{h(y_0 + 2y_1 + y_2)}{2}$$

The accuracy with which the area under the actual curve is calculated will depend upon how closely the straight lines mimic the curve. The accuracy of representation can be increased by using a smaller interval h. Generalizing for n+1 ordinates the area will be given by:

$$\text{Area} = \frac{h(y_0 + 2y_1 + 2y_2 + \ldots + 2y_{n-1} + y_n)}{2}$$

In many cases of ships' waterplanes it is sufficiently accurate to use ten divisions with eleven ordinates but it is worth checking by eye whether the straight lines follow the actual curves reasonably accurately. Because warship hulls tend to have greater curvature they are usually represented by twenty divisions with twenty-one ordinates. To calculate the volume of a three dimensional shape the areas of its cross sectional areas at equally spaced intervals can be calculated as above. These areas can then be used as the new ordinates in a *curve of areas* to obtain the volume.

SIMPSON'S RULES

The trapezoidal rule, using straight lines to replace the actual ship curves, has limitations as to the accuracy achieved. Many naval architectural calculations are carried out using what are known as Simpson's rules. In Simpson's rules the actual curve is represented by a mathematical equation of the form:

$$y = a_0 + ax_1 + a_2 x^2 + a_3 x^3$$

The curve, shown in Figure 3.3, is represented by three equally spaced ordinates y_0, y_1 and y_2. It is convenient to choose the origin to be at the base of y_1 to simplify the algebra but the results would be the same

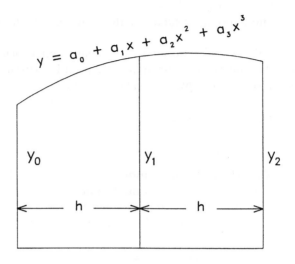

Figure 3.3

wherever the origin is taken. The curve extends from $x = -h$ to $x = +h$ and the area under it is:

$$A = \int_{-h}^{+h} (a_0 + a_1 x + a_2 x^2 + a_3 x^3)\,dx$$

$$= \left[a_0 x + a_1 x^2/2 + a_2 x^3/3 + a_3 x^4/4 \right]_{-h}^{+h}$$

$$= 2a_0 h + 2a_2 h^3/3$$

Now: $y_0 = a_0 - a_1 h + a_2 h^2 - a_3 h^3$
$y_1 = a_0$
$y_2 = a_0 + a_1 h + a_2 h^2 + a_3 h^3$

It would be convenient to be able to express the area of the figure as a simple sum of the ordinates each multiplied by some factor to be determined. Assuming that A can be represented by:

$$A = Fy_0 + Gy_1 + Hy_2,$$

then:

$$A = (F + G + H)a_0 - (F - H)a_1 h + (F + H)a_2 h^2 - (F - H)a_3 h^3$$

$$= 2a_0 h + 2a_2 h^3/3$$

These equations give:

$$F = H = h/3 \quad \text{and} \quad G = 4h/3$$

Hence:

$$A = \frac{h}{3}(y_0 + 4y_1 + y_2)$$

This is *Simpson's First Rule* or *3 Ordinate Rule*.

This rule can be generalized to any figure defined by an odd number of evenly spaced ordinates, by applying the First Rule to ordinates 0 to 2, 2 to 4, 4 to 6 and so on, and then summing the resulting answers. This provides the rule for n + 1 ordinates:

$$A = \frac{h}{3}(y_0 + 4y_1 + 2y_2 + 4y_3 + 2y_4 + 4y_5 \ldots + 4y_{n-1} + y_n)$$

For many ship forms it is adequate to divide the length into ten equal parts using eleven ordinates. When the ends have significant curvature greater accuracy can be obtained by introducing intermediate ordinates in those areas, as shown in Figure 3.4. The figure gives the

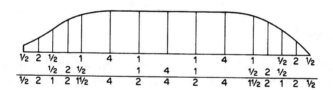

Figure 3.4

Simpson multipliers to be used for each consecutive area defined by three ordinates. The total area is given by:

$$A = \frac{h}{3}(\tfrac{1}{2}y_0 + 2y_1 + y_2 + 2y_3 + 1\tfrac{1}{2}y_4 + 4y_5 + 2y_6 + 4y_7 + 2y_8 + 4y_9$$
$$+ 1\tfrac{1}{2}y_{10} + 2y_{11} + y_{12} + 2y_{13} + \tfrac{1}{2}y_{14})$$

where y_1, y_3, y_{11} and y_{13} are the extra ordinates.

The method outlined above for calculating areas can be applied to evaluating any integral. Thus it can be applied to the first and second

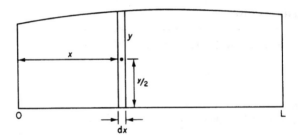

Figure 3.5

moments of area. Referring to Figure 3.5, these moments about the y-axis, that is the axis through O, are given by:

First moment $= \int xy\,dx$ about the y-axis

$= \int \frac{1}{2}y^2\,dx$ about the x-axis

Second moment $= \int x^2 y\,dx$ about the y-axis $= I_y$

$= \int \frac{1}{4}y^3\,dx$ about the x-axis $= I_x$

The calculations, if done manually, are best set out in tabular form.

Example 3.1

Calculate the area between the curve, defined by the ordinates below, and the x-axis. Calculate the first and second moments of area about the x- and y-axes and the position of the centroid of area.

x	0	1	2	3	4	5	6	7	8
y	1	1.2	1.5	1.6	1.5	1.3	1.1	0.9	0.6

Solution
There are 9 ordinates spaced one unit apart. The results can be calculated in tabular fashion as in Table 3.1.

Hence:

$$\text{Area} = \frac{29.8}{3} = 9.93\,\text{m}^2$$

Table 3.1

x	y	SM	$F(A)$	xy	$F(M_y)$	x^2y	$F(I_y)$	y^2	$F(M_x)$	y^3	$F(I_x)$
0	1.0	1	1.0	0	0	0	0	1.0	1.0	1.0	1.0
1	1.2	4	4.8	1.2	4.8	1.2	4.8	1.44	5.76	1.728	6.912
2	1.5	2	3.0	3.0	6.0	6.0	12.0	2.25	4.50	3.375	6.750
3	1.6	4	6.4	4.8	19.2	14.4	57.6	2.56	10.24	4.096	16.384
4	1.5	2	3.0	6.0	12.0	24.0	48.0	2.25	4.50	3.375	6.750
5	1.3	4	5.2	6.5	26.0	32.5	130.0	1.69	6.76	2.197	8.788
6	1.1	2	2.2	6.6	13.2	39.6	79.2	1.21	2.42	1.331	2.662
7	0.9	4	3.6	6.3	25.2	44.1	176.4	0.81	3.24	0.729	2.916
8	0.6	1	0.6	4.8	4.8	38.4	38.4	0.36	0.36	0.216	0.216
Totals			29.8		111.2		546.4		38.78		52.378

$$\text{First moment about } y\text{-axis} = \frac{111.2}{3} = 37.07\,\text{m}^3$$

$$\text{Centroid from } y\text{-axis} = \frac{37.07}{9.93} = 3.73\,\text{m}$$

$$\text{First moment about } x\text{-axis} = 0.5 \times \frac{38.78}{3} = 6.463\,\text{m}^3$$

$$\text{Centroid from } x\text{-axis} = \frac{6.463}{9.93} = 0.65\,\text{m}$$

$$\text{Second moment about } y\text{-axis} = \frac{546.4}{3} = 182.13\,\text{m}^4$$

$$\text{Second moment about } x\text{-axis} = 0.25 \times \frac{52.378}{3} = 4.36\,\text{m}^4$$

The second moment of an area is always least about an axis through its centroid. If the second moment of an area, A, about an axis x from its centroid is I_x and I_{xx} is that about a parallel axis through the centroid:

$$I_{xx} = I_x - Ax^2$$

In the above example the second moments about axes through the centroid and parallel to the x-axis and y-axis, are respectively:

$$I_{xx} = 4.36 - 9.93(0.65)^2 = 0.16 \, \text{m}^4$$

$$I_{yy} = 182.13 - 9.93(3.73)^2 = 43.97 \, \text{m}^4$$

Where there are large numbers of ordinates the arithmetic in the table can be simplified by halving each Simpson multiplier and then doubling the final summations so that:

$$A = \frac{2h}{3} \left(\tfrac{1}{2}y_0 + 2y_1 + y_2 + \ldots + 2y_n + \tfrac{1}{2}y_{n+1} \right)$$

Other rules can be deduced for figures defined by unevenly spaced ordinates or by different numbers of evenly spaced ordinates. The rule for four evenly spaced ordinates becomes:

$$A = \frac{3h}{8} \left(y_0 + 3y_1 + 3y_2 + y_3 \right)$$

This is known as *Simpson's Second Rule*. It can be extended to cover 7, 10, 13, etc., ordinates, becoming:

$$A = \frac{3h}{8} \left(y_0 + 3y_1 + 3y_2 + 2y_3 + 3y_4 + \ldots + 3y_{n-1} + y_n \right)$$

A special case is where the area between two ordinates is required when three are known. If, for instance, the area between ordinates y_0 and y_1 of Figure 3.3 is needed:

$$A_1 = \frac{h}{12} \left(5y_0 + 8y_1 - y_2 \right)$$

This is called *Simpson's 5, 8 minus 1 Rule* and it will be noted that if it is applied to both halves of the curve then the total area becomes:

$$A = \frac{h}{3} \left(y_0 + 4y_1 + y_2 \right)$$

as would be expected.

Unlike others of Simpson's rules the 5, 8, −1 cannot be applied to moments. A corresponding rule for moments, derived in the same way as those for areas, is known as *Simpson's 3, 10 minus 1 Rule* and gives the moment of the area bounded by y_0 and y_1 about y_0, as:

$$M = \frac{h^2}{24} \left(3y_0 + 10y_1 - y_2 \right)$$

If in doubt about the multiplier to be used, a simple check can be applied by considering the area or moment of a simple rectangle.

TCHEBYCHEFF'S RULES

In arriving at Simpson's rules, equally spaced ordinates were used and varying multipliers for the ordinates deduced. The equations concerned can equally well be solved to find the spacing needed for ordinates if the multipliers are to be unity. For simplicity the curve is assumed to be centred upon the origin, $x = 0$, with the ordinates arranged symmetrically about the origin. Thus for an odd number of ordinates the middle one will be at the origin. Rules so derived are known as *Tchebycheff rules* and they can be represented by the equation:

$$A = \frac{\text{Span of curve on } x\text{-axis} \times \text{Sum of ordinates}}{\text{Number of ordinates}}$$

Thus for a curve spanning two units, $2h$, and defined by three ordinates:

$$A = \frac{2h}{3} (y_0 + y_1 + y_2)$$

The spacings required of the ordinates are given in Table 3.2.

Table 3.2

Number of ordinates	Spacing each side of origin ÷ the half length				
2	0.5773				
3	0	0.7071			
4	0.1876	0.7947			
5	0	0.3745	0.8325		
6	0.2666	0.4225	0.8662		
7	0	0.3239	0.5297	0.8839	
8	0.1026	0.4062	0.5938	0.8974	
9	0	0.1679	0.5288	0.6010	0.9116
10	0.0838	0.3127	0.5000	0.6873	0.9162

GENERAL

It has been shown[1] that:

1. Odd ordinate Simpson's rules are preferred as they are only marginally less accurate than the next higher even number rule.
2. Even ordinate Tchebycheff rules are preferred as they are as accurate as the next highest odd ordinate rule.
3. A Tchebycheff rule with an even number of ordinates is rather more accurate than the next highest odd number Simpson rule.

POLAR CO-ORDINATES

The rules discussed above have been illustrated by figures defined by a set of parallel ordinates and this is most convenient for waterplanes. For transverse sections a problem can arise at the turn of bilge unless closely spaced ordinates are used in that area. An alternative is to adopt polar co-ordinates radiating from some convenient pole, O, on the centreline. Figure 3.6.

$$\text{Area of the half section} = \frac{1}{2} \int_0^{180} r^2 \, d\theta$$

If the section shape is defined by a number of radial ordinates at equal angular intervals the area can be determined using one of the

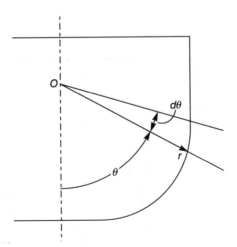

Figure 3.6 Polar co-ordinates

approximate integration methods. Since the deck edge is a point of discontinuity one of the radii should pass through it. This can be arranged by careful selection of O for each transverse section.

SUMMARY

It has been shown how areas and volumes enclosed by typical ship curves and surfaces, toether with their moments, can be calculated by approximate methods. These methods can be applied quite widely in engineering applications other than naval architecture. They provide the means of evaluating the various integrals called up by the theory outlined in the following chapters.

Reference

1. Miller, N. S. (1963–4) The accuracy of numerical integration in ship calculations. *TIESS*.

4 Flotation and stability

A rigid body floating freely on the surface of a fluid has six degrees of freedom, three of translation and three of rotation. For disturbances from a state of equilibrium, the naval architect refers to the movements in the six degrees as follows:

Fore and aft translation is termed *surge.*
Transverse translation is termed *sway.*
Vertical translation is termed *heave.*
Rotation about a fore and aft axis is termed *heel* or *roll.*
Rotation about a transverse axis is termed *trim* or *pitch.*
Rotation about a vertical axis is termed *yaw.*

The terms heel and trim are used in static or quasi-static conditions. Roll and pitch are used in the dynamic situation which is dealt with under seakeeping.

Having suffered a disturbance the body is said to be in stable, neutral or unstable equilibrium if, when the disturbance is removed, it returns to its original position, stays where it is or continues to depart further from its original attitude, respectively. Correspondingly it is said to possess positive, neutral or negative stability. A body floating freely on the surface of a fluid must be stable in heave since the buoyany force must equal weight as explained later. It will also have neutral stability for surge, sway and yaw. The naval architect is concerned primarily with bodies floating in water but the results are applicable to any fluid.

EQUILIBRIUM OF A BODY FLOATING IN STILL WATER

A body floating freely in still water experiences a downward force acting on it due to gravity. If the body has a mass m, this force will be mg and is known as the *weight.* Since the body is in equilibrium there must be a force of the same magnitude and in the same line of action as the weight but opposing it. Otherwise the body would move. This opposing force is generated by the hydrostatic pressures which act on the body,

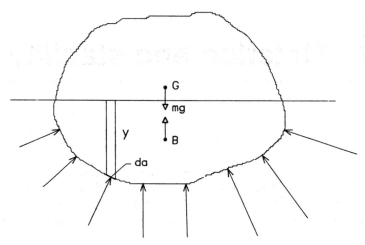

Figure 4.1 Floating body

Figure 4.1. These act normal to the body's surface and can be resolved into vertical and horizontal components. The sum of the vertical components must equal the weight. The horizontal components must cancel out otherwise the body would move sideways. The gravitational force *mg* can be imagined as concentrated at a point G which is the centre of mass, commonly known as the *centre of gravity*. Similarly the opposing force can be imagined to be concentrated at a point B.

Consider now the hydrostatic forces acting on a small element of the surface, d*a*, a depth *y* below the surface.

Pressure = density × gravitational acceleration × depth = $\rho g y$

The normal force on an element of area d*a* = $\rho y g \, da$

If φ is the angle of inclination of the body's surface to the horizontal then the vertical component of force is:

$(\rho g y da) \cos \varphi = \rho g$(volume of vertical element)

Integrating over the whole volume the total vertical force is:

$\rho g \nabla$ where ∇ is the immersed volume of the body.

This is also the weight of the displaced water. It is this vertical force which 'buoys up' the body and it is known as the *buoyancy force* or simply *buoyancy*. The point, B, through which it acts is the centroid of volume of the displaced water and is known as the *centre of buoyancy*.

Since the buoyancy force is equal to the weight of the body, $m = \rho\nabla$

In other words the mass of the body is equal to the mass of the water displaced by the body. This can be visualized in simple physical terms. Consider the underwater portion of the floating body to be replaced by a weightless membrane filled to the level of the free surface with water of the same density as that in which the body is floating. As far as the water is concerned the membrane need not exist, there is a state of equilibrium and the forces on the skin must balance out.

Underwater volume

Once the ship form is defined the underwater volume can be calculated by the rules discussed in Chapter 3. If the immersed areas of a number of sections throughout the length of a ship are calculated a

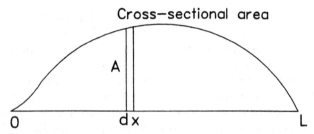

Figure 4.2 Cross-sectional area curve

sectional area curve can be drawn as in Figure 4.2. The underwater volume is:

$$\nabla = \int A \, dx$$

If immersed cross-sectional areas are calculated to a number of waterlines parallel to the design waterline, then the volume up to each can be determined and plotted against draught as in Figure 4.3. The volume corresponding to any given draught T can be picked off, provided the waterline at T is parallel to those used in deriving the curve.

A more general method of finding the underwater volume, known as the *volume of displacement,* is to make use of *Bonjean* curves. These are curves of immersed cross-sectional areas plotted against draught for each transverse section. They are usually drawn on the ship profile as in

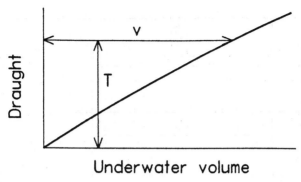

Figure 4.3 Volume curve

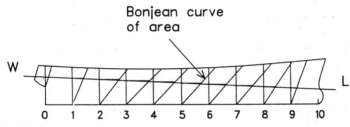

Figure 4.4 Bonjean curves

Figure 4.4. Suppose the ship is floating at waterline WL. The immersed areas for this waterline are obtained by drawing horizontal lines, shown dotted, from the intercept of the waterline with the middle line of a section to the Bonjean curve for that section. Having the areas for all the sections, the underwater volume and its longitudinal centroid, its centre of buoyancy, can be calculated.

When the displacement of a ship was calculated manually, it was customary to use what was called a *displacement sheet*. A typical layout is shown in Figure 4.5. The displacement from the base up to, in this case, the 5 m waterline was determined by using Simpson's rule applied to half ordinates measured at waterlines 1 m apart and at sections taken at every tenth of the length. The calculations were done in two ways. Firstly the areas of sections were calculated and integrated in the fore and aft direction to give volume. Then areas of waterplanes were calculated and integrated vertically to give volume. The two volume values, A and B in the figure, had to be the same if the arithmetic had been done correctly, providing a check on the calculation. The displacement sheet was also used to calculate the vertical and longitudinal positions of the centre of buoyancy. The calculations are now done by computer.

Section	Simpson's multipliers	Levers from amidships	Waterlines above base (metres)														Sum of products of sectional areas	Simpson's multipliers	Volume products	Levers from amidships	Moments about amidships
			0.0		0.5		1.0		2.0		3.0		4.0		5.0						
			½		2		1½		4		2		4		1						
			Half-ordinate	Area product	Half-ordinate	Area product	Half-ordinate	Area product	Half-ordinate	Area product	Half-ordinate	Area product	Half-ordinate	Area product	Half-ordinate	Area product					
0	1	5																1		5	
1	4	4																4		4	
2	2	3																2		3	
3	4	2																4		2	
4	2	1																2		1	
5	4	0																4		0	$M_{A\otimes}$
6	2	1																2		1	
7	4	2																4		2	
8	2	3																2		3	
9	4	4																4		4	
10	1	5																1		5	
Total products of water-plane areas																			A		$M_{F\otimes}$
Simpson's multipliers				½		2		1½		4		2		4		1					
Volume products																	B				
Levers above base				0		½		1		2		3		4		5					
Moments about base																	M_Y				

Figure 4.5 Displacement sheet

STABILITY AT SMALL ANGLES

The concept of the stability of a floating body can be explained by considering it to be inclined from the upright by an external force which is then removed. In Figure 4.6 a ship floats originally at waterline W_0L_0 and after rotating through a small angle at waterline W_1L_1.

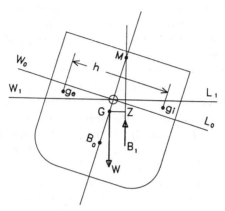

Figure 4.6 Small angle stability

The inclination does not affect the position of G, the ship's centre of gravity, provided no weights are free to move. The inclination does, however, affect the underwater shape and the centre of buoyancy moves from B_0 to B_1. This is because a volume, v, repesented by W_0OW_1, has come out of the water and an equal volume, represented by L_0OL_1, has been immersed.

If g_e and g_i are the centroids of the emerged and immersed wedges and $g_eg_i = h$, then:

$$B_0B_1 = \frac{v \times h}{\nabla}$$

where ∇ is the total volume of the ship.

In general a ship will trim slightly when it is inclined at constant displacement. For the present this is ignored but it means that strictly B_0, B_1, g_e etc., are the projections of the actual points on to a transverse plane.

The buoyancy acts upwards through B_1 and intersects the original vertical at M. This point is termed the *metacentre* and for small inclinations can be taken as fixed in position. The weight $W = mg$ acting downwards and the buoyancy force, of equal magnitude, acting upwards are not in the same line but form a couple $W \times GZ$, where GZ is the perpendicular on to B_1M drawn from G. As shown this couple will restore the body to its original position and in this condition the body is said to be in stable equilibrium. $GZ = GM \sin\varphi$ and is called the *righting lever* or *lever* and GM is called the *metacentric height*. For a given position of G, as M can be taken as fixed for small inclinations, GM will be constant for any particular waterline. More importantly, since G can vary with the loading of the ship even for a given displacement, BM will be constant for a given waterline. In Figure 4.6 M is above G, giving positive stability, and GM is regarded as positive in this case.

If, when inclined, the new position of the centre of buoyancy, B_1, is directly under G, the three points M, G and Z are coincident and there is no moment acting on the ship. When the disturbing force is removed the ship will remain in the inclined position. The ship is said to be in neutral equilibrium and both GM and GZ are zero.

A third possibility is that, after inclination, the new centre of buoyancy will lie nearer to the centreline than G. There is then a moment $W \times GZ$ which will take the ship further from the vertical. In this case the ship is said to be unstable and it may heel to a considerable angle or even capsize. For unstable equilibrium M is below G and both GM and GZ are considered negative.

The above considerations apply to what is called the *initial stability* of the ship, that is when the ship is upright or very nearly so. The criterion of initial stability is the metacentric height. The three conditions can be summarized as:

M above G	GM and GZ positive	stable
M at G	GM and GZ zero	neutral
M below G	GM and GZ negative	unstable

Transverse metacentre

The position of the metacentre is found by considering small inclinations of a ship about its centreline, Figure 4.7. For small angles, say 2 or 3 degrees, the upright and inclined waterlines will intersect at O on the centreline. The volumes of the emerged and immersed wedges must be equal for constant displacement.

For small angles the emerged and immersed wedges at any section, W_0OW_1 and L_0OL_1, are approximately triangular. If y is the half-

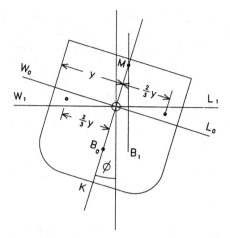

Figure 4.7 Transverse metacentre

ordinate of the original waterline at the cross-section the emerged or immersed section area is:

$$\tfrac{1}{2}y \times y \tan\varphi = \tfrac{1}{2}y^2\varphi$$

for small angles, and the total volume of each wedge is:

$$\int \tfrac{1}{2}y^2\varphi \, dx$$

integrated along the length of the ship.

This volume is effectively moved from one side to the other and for triangular sections the transverse movement will be $4y/3$ giving a total transverse shift of buoyancy of:

$$\int \tfrac{1}{2}y^2\varphi \, dx \times 4y/3 = \varphi \int 2y^3/3 \, dx$$

since φ is constant along the length of the ship.

The expression within the integral sign is the second moment of area, or the moment of inertia, of a waterplane about its centreline. It may be denoted by I, whence the transverse movement of buoyancy is:

$$I\varphi, \text{ and } \nabla \times BB_1 = I\varphi$$

so that $BB_1 = I\varphi/\nabla$ where ∇ is the total volume of displacement.

Referring to Figure 4.7 for the small angles being considered $BB_1 = BM\varphi$ and $BM = I/\nabla$. Thus the height of the metacentre above the centre of buoyancy is found by dividing the second moment of area of the waterplane about its centreline by the volume of displacement. The height of the centre of buoyancy above the keel, KB, is the height of the centroid of the underwater volume above the keel, and hence the height of the metacentre above the keel is:

$$KM = KB + BM$$

The difference between KM and KG gives the metacentric height, GM.

Transverse metacentre for simple geometrical forms

Vessel of rectangular cross section
Consider the form in Figure 4.8 of breadth B and length L floating at draught T. If the cross section is uniform throughout its length, the volume of displacement = LBT.

The second moment of area of waterplane about the centreline = $LB^3/12$. Hence:

$$BM = \frac{LB^3}{12LBT} = B^2/12T$$

Height of centre of buoyancy above keel, $KB = T/2$ and the height of metacentre above the keel is:

$$KM = T/2 + B^2/12T$$

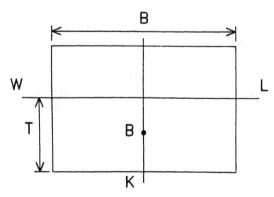

Figure 4.8 Rectangular section vessel

The height of the metacentre depends upon the draught and beam but not the length. At small draught relative to beam, the second term predominates and at zero draught KM would be infinite.

To put some figures to this consider the case where B is 15 m for draughts varying from 1 to 6 m. Then:

$$KM = \frac{T}{2} + \frac{15^2}{12T} = 0.5T + \frac{18.75}{T}$$

KM values for various draughts are shown in Table 4.1 and KM and KB are plotted against draught in Figure 4.9. Such a diagram is called a *metacentric diagram*. KM is large at small draughts and falls rapidly with increasing draught. If the calculations were extended KM would reach a minimum value and then start to increase. The draught at which KM is minimum can be found by differentiating the equation for KM with respect to T and equating to zero. That is, KM is a

Table 4.1

d	$0.5d$	$18.75d$	KM
1	0.5	18.75	19.25
2	1.0	9.37	10.37
3	1.5	6.25	7.75
4	2.0	4.69	6.69
5	2.5	3.75	6.25
6	3.0	3.12	6.12

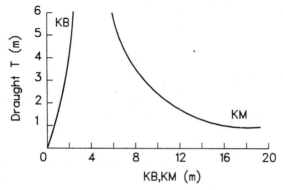

Figure 4.9 Metacentric diagram

minimum at T given by:

$$\frac{\mathrm{d}KM}{\mathrm{d}T} = \tfrac{1}{2} - \frac{B^2}{12T^2} = 0, \text{ giving } T^2 = \frac{B^2}{6} \text{ or } T = \frac{B}{\sqrt{6}}$$

In the example KM is a minimum when the draught is 6.12 m.

Vessel of constant triangular section

Consider a vessel of triangular cross section floating apex down, the breadth at the top being B and the depth D. The breadth of the waterline at draught T is given by:

$$b = (T/D) \times B$$
$$I = (L/12) \times [(T/D) \times B]^3$$
$$\nabla = L \times (T/D) \times B \times T/2$$
$$BM = I/\nabla = B^2 T/6D^2$$
$$KB = 2T/3$$
$$KM = 2T/3 + B^2 T/6D^2$$

In this case the curves of both KM and KB against draught are straight lines starting from zero at zero draught.

Vessel of circular cross section
Consider a circular cylinder of radius R and centre of section O, floating with its axis horizontal. For any waterline, above or below O, and for any inclination, the buoyancy force always acts through O. That is, KM is independent of draught and equal to R. The vessel will be stable or unstable depending upon whether KG is less than or greater than R.

Metacentric diagrams

The positions of B and M have been seen to depend only upon the geometry of the ship and the draughts at which it is floating. They can therefore be determined without knowledge of the loading of the ship that causes it to float at those draughts. A *metacentric diagram*, in which KB and KM are plotted against draught, is a convenient way of defining the positions of B and M for a range of waterplanes parallel to the design or load waterplane.

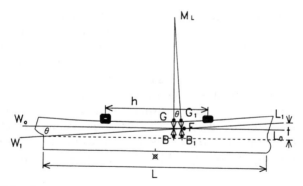

Figure 4.10 Trim changes

Trim

Suppose a ship, floating at waterline W_0L_0 (Figure 4.10), is caused to trim slightly, at constant displacement, to a new waterline W_1L_1 intersecting the original waterplane in a transverse axis through F.

The volumes of the immersed and emerged wedges must be equal so, for small θ :

$$\int 2\, y_f(x_f\theta)\, dx = \int 2\, y_a(x_a\theta)\, dx$$

where y_f and y_a are the waterplane half breadths at distances x_f and x_a from F.

This is the condition that F is the centroid of the waterplane and F is known as the *centre of flotation*. For small trims at constant displacement a ship trims about a transverse axis through the centre of flotation.

If a small weight is added to a ship it will sink and trim until the extra buoyancy generated equals the weight and the centre of buoyancy of the added buoyancy is vertically below the centre of gravity of the added weight. If the weight is added in the vertical line of the centre of flotation then the ship sinks bodily with no trim as the centre of buoyancy of the added layer will be above the centroid of area of the waterplane. Generalizing this a small weight placed anywhere along the length can be regarded as being initially placed at F to cause sinkage and then moved to its actual position, causing trim. In other words, it can be regarded as a weight acting at F and a trimming moment about F.

Longitudinal stability

The principles involved are the same as those for transverse stability but for longitudinal inclinations, the stability depends upon the distance between the centre of gravity and the longitudinal metacentre. In this case the distance between the centre of buoyancy and the longitudinal metacentre will be governed by the second moment of area of the waterplane about a transverse axis passing through its centroid. For normal ship forms this quantity is many times the value for the second moment of area about the centreline. Since BM_L is obtained by dividing by the same volume of displacement as for transverse stability, it will be large compared with BM_T and often commensurate with the length of the ship. It is thus virtually impossible for an undamaged conventional ship to be unstable when inclined about a transverse axis.

$$KM_L = KB + BM_L = KB + I_L/\nabla$$

where I_L is the second moment of the waterplane area about a transverse axis through its centroid, the centre of flotation.

If the ship in Figure 4.10 is trimmed by moving a weight, w, from its initial position to a new position h forward, the trimming moment will be wh. This will cause the centre of gravity of the ship to move from G to G_1 and the ship will trim causing B to move to B_1 such that:

$$GG_1 = wh/W$$

and B_1 is vertically below G_1

The trim is the difference in draughts forward and aft. The change in trim angle can be taken as the change in that difference divided by the longitudinal distance between the points at which the draughts are measured. From Figure 4.10:

$$\tan \theta = t/L = GG_1/GM_L = wh/WGM_L$$

from which:

$$wh = t \times W \times GM_L/L$$

This is the moment that causes a trim t, so the moment to cause unit change of trim is:

$$WGM_L/L$$

This *moment to change trim*, MCT, one unit is a convenient figure to quote to show how easy a ship is to trim. The value in SI units would be 'moment to change trim one metre'. This can be quite a large quantity and it might be preferred to work with the 'moment to change trim one centimetre' which would be $W \times GM_L/100L$. In Imperial units the *moment to change trim one inch* is usually quoted. In this latter case the units must be watched. If W is in tonft and L and GM_L are in feet then:

$$\text{Moment to change trim one inch, MCT 1 in} = \frac{W \times GM_L}{12L}$$

The value of MCT is very useful in calculating the draughts at which a ship will float for a given condition of loading. Suppose it has been ascertained that the weight of the ship is W and the centre of gravity is x forward of amidships and that at that weight with a waterline parallel to the design waterline it would float at a draught T with the centre of buoyancy y forward of amidships. There will be a moment $W(y-x)/\text{MCT}$ taking it away from a waterline parallel to the design one. The ship trims about the centre of flotation and the draughts at any point along the length can be found by simple ratios.

Example 4.1

A ship of mass 5000 tonnes, 98m long, floats at draughts of 5.5 m forward and 6.2 m aft, being measured at the extreme ends. The longitudinal metacentric height is 104 m and the centre of flotation is 2.1 m aft of amidships. Determine the moment to change trim 1 cm and the new end draughts when a mass of 85 tonnes, which is already on board, is moved 30 m forward.

Solution

$$\text{MCT 1 cm} = \frac{W \times GM_L}{100L}$$

$$= \frac{5000 \times 9.81 \times 104}{100 \times 98} \text{ where } g = 9.81 \text{ m/s}^2$$

$$= 520.5 \text{ MNm}$$

As the mass is already on board there will be no bodily sinkage. The change of trim is given by the trimming moment divided by MCT.

$$\text{Change in trim} = \frac{85 \times 9.81 \times 30}{520.5}$$

$$= 48.1 \text{ cm by the bow.}$$

The changes in draught will be:

$$\text{Forward} = 48.1 \times \frac{(98/2) + 2.1}{98} = 25.1\,\text{cm}$$

$$\text{Aft} \quad = 48.1 \times \frac{(98/2) - 2.1}{98} = 23.0\,\text{cm}$$

The new draughts become 5.751 m forward and 5.97 m aft.

Hydrostatic curves

It has been shown how the displacement, position of B, M and F can be calculated. It is customary to obtain these quantities for a range of waterplanes parallel to the design waterplane and plot them against draught, draught being measured vertically. Such sets of curves are called *hydrostatic curves*, Figure 4.11.

The curves in the figure show moulded and extreme displacement. The former was mentioned in Chapter 2. It is the latter, normally shown simply as the displacement curve and which allows for displacement outside the perpendiculars, and bossings, bulbous bows, etc., which is relevant to the discussion of flotation and stability. Clearly the additions to the moulded figure can have a measurable effect upon displacement and the position of B.

It will be noted that the curves include one for the increase in displacement for unit increase in draught. If a waterplane has an area

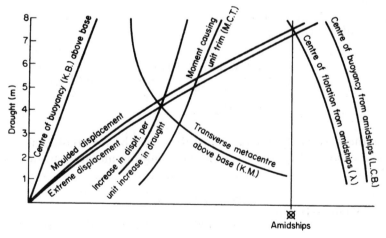

Figure 4.11 Hydrostatic curves

A, then the increase in displaced volume for unit increase in draught at that waterplane is $1 \times A$. The increase in displacement will be $\rho g A$. In SI units for $\rho = 1025 \, \text{kg/m}^3$ and $g = 9.81 \, \text{m/s}^2$ increase in displacement per metre increase in draught is:

$$1025 \times 9.81 \times 1 \times A = 10\,055A \text{ newtons.}$$

In imperial units the value quoted was usually the added *tons per inch immersion*, TPI. As it was assumed that $35 \, \text{ft}^3$ of sea water weighed 1 ton, for A in ft^2:

$$\text{TPI} = \frac{A}{35 \times 12} = \frac{A}{420}$$

The increase in displacement per unit increase in draught is useful in approximate calculations when weights are added to a ship. Since its value varies with draught it should be applied with care.

Hydrostatic curves are useful for working out the draughts and the initial stability, as represented by GM, in various conditions of loading. This is done for all normal working conditions of the ship and the results supplied to the master.

Fully submerged bodies

A fully submerged body presents a special case. Firstly there is no waterplane and therefore no metacentre. The forces of weight and displacement will always act vertically through G and B respectively. Stability then will be the same for inclination about any axis. It will be positive if B is above G. Secondly a submarine or submersible is an elastic body and will compress as the depth of submergence increases. Since water is effectively incompressible, there will be a reducing buoyancy force. Thus the body will experience a net downward force that will cause it to sink further so that the body is unstable in depth variation. In practice the decrease in buoyancy must be compensated for by pumping water out from internal tanks or by forces generated by the control surfaces, the hydroplanes. Care is needed when first submerging to arrange that weight and buoyancy are very nearly the same. If the submersible moves into water of a different density there will again be an imbalance in forces due to the changed buoyancy force. There is no 'automatic' compensation such as a surface vessel experiences when the draught adjusts in response to density changes.

Problems in trim and stability

Determination of displacement from observed draughts

Suppose draughts at the perpendiculars are T_a and T_f as in Figure 4.12. The mean draught will be $T = (T_a + T_f)/2$ and a first approximation to the displacement could be obtained by reading off the corresponding displacement, Δ, from the hydrostatic curves. In general, $W_0 L_0$ will not be parallel to the waterlines for which the hydrostatics were computed. If waterline $W_1 L_1$, intersecting $W_0 L_0$ at amidships, is parallel to the design waterline then the displacement read from the hydrostatics for draught T is in fact the displacement to $W_1 L_1$. It has been seen that because ships are not symmetrical fore and aft they trim about F. As shown in Figure 4.12, the displacement to $W_0 L_0$ is less than that to $W_1 L_1$, the difference

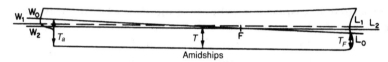

Figure 4.12

being the layer $W_1 L_1 L_2 W_2$ where $W_2 L_2$ is the waterline parallel to $W_1 L_1$ through F on $W_0 L_0$. If λ is the distance of F forward of amidships then the thickness of layer $= \lambda \times t/L$ where $t = T_a - T_f$.

If i is the increase in displacement per unit increase in draught:

Displacement of layer $= \lambda \times ti/L$ and the actual displacement

$$= \Delta - \lambda \times ti/L$$

Whether the correction to the displacement read off from the hydrostatics initially is positive or negative depends upon whether the ship is trimming by the bow or stern and the position of F relative to amidships. It can be determined by making a simple sketch.

If the ship is floating in water of a different density to that for which the hydrostatics were calculated a further correction is needed in proportion to the two density values, increasing the displacement if the water in which ship is floating is greater than the standard.

This calculation for displacement has assumed that the keel is straight. It is likely to be curved, even in still water, so that a draught taken at amidships may not equal $(d_a + d_f)/2$ but have some value d_m giving a deflection of the hull, δ. If the ship sags the above calculation would underestimate the volume of displacement. If it hogs it would overestimate the volume. It is reasonable to assume the deflected profile of the ship is parabolic, so that the deflection at any point distant x from amidships is $\delta[1 - (2x/L)^2]$, and hence:

$$\text{Volume correction} = \int b\delta\,[1 - (2x/L)^2]\ \mathrm{d}x$$

where b is the waterline breadth.

Unless an expression is available for b in terms of x this cannot be integrated mathematically. It can be evaluated by approximate integration using the ordinates for the waterline.

Longitudinal position of the centre of gravity
Suppose a ship is floating in equilibrium at a waterline $W_0 L_0$ as in Figure 4.13 with the centre of gravity distant x from amidships, a distance yet to be determined. The centre of buoyancy B_0 must be directly beneath G. Now assume the ship brought to a waterline $W_1 L_1$ parallel to those used for the hydrostatics, which cuts off the correct

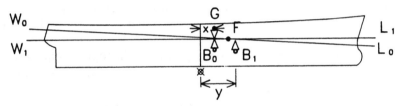

Figure 4.13

displacement. The position of the centre of buoyancy will be at B_1, distant y from amidships, a distance that can be read from the hydrostatics for waterline $W_1 L_1$. It follows that if t was the trim, relative to $W_1 L_1$, when the ship was at $W_0 L_0$:

$$\Delta(y - x) = t \times (\text{moment to cause unit trim}) \text{ and:}$$

$$x = y - \frac{t \times \text{MCT}}{\Delta}$$

giving the longitudinal centre of gravity.

Direct determination of displacement and position of G
The methods described above for finding the displacement and longitudinal position of G are usually sufficiently accurate when the trim

is small. To obtain more accurate results and for larger trims the Bonjean curves can be used. If the end draughts, distance L apart, are observed then the draught at any particular section can be calculated, since:

$$T_x = T_a - (T_a - T_f) \frac{x}{L}$$

where x is the distance from where T_a is measured.

These draughts can be corrected for hog or sag if necessary. The calculated draughts at each section can be set up on the Bonjean curves and the immersed areas read off. The immersed volume and position of the centre of buoyancy can be found by approximate integration. For equilibrium, the centre of gravity and centre of buoyancy must be in the same vertical line and the position of the centre of gravity follows. Using the density of water in which the ship is floating, the displacement can be determined.

Heel due to moving weight

In Figure 4.14 a ship is shown upright and at rest in still water. If a small weight w is shifted transversely through a distance h, the centre of gravity of the ship, originally at G, moves to G_1 such that $GG_1 = wh/W$. The ship will heel through an angle φ causing the centre of buoyancy to move to B_1 vertically below G_1 to restore equilibrium. It will be seen that:

$$\frac{GG_1}{GM} = \tan \varphi \quad \text{and} \quad \tan \varphi = \frac{wh}{W \times GM}$$

This applies whilst the angle of inclination remains small enough for M to be regarded as a fixed point.

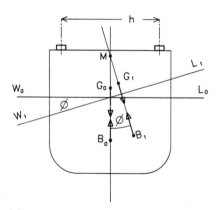

Figure 4.14 Moving weight

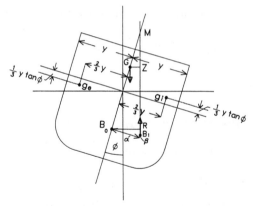

Figure 4.15 Wall-sided ship

Wall-sided ship

It is interesting to consider a special case when a ship's sides are vertical in way of the waterline over the whole length. It is said to be wall-sided, see Figure 4.15. The vessel can have a turn of bilge provided it is not exposed by the inclination of the ship. Nor must the deck edge be immersed. Because the vessel is wall-sided the emerged and immersed wedges will have sections which are right-angled triangles of equal area. Let the new position of the centre of buoyancy B_1 after inclination through φ be α and β relative to the centre of buoyancy position in the upright condition. Then using the notation shown in the figure:

$$\text{Transverse moment of volume shift} = \int \frac{y}{2} \times y \tan \varphi \, dx \times \frac{4y}{3}$$

$$= \int \frac{2}{3} y^3 \tan \varphi \, dx$$

$$= \tan \varphi \int \frac{2}{3} y^3 dx$$

$$= I \tan \varphi$$

where I is the second moment of area of the waterplane about the centreline. Therefore

$$\alpha = I \tan \varphi / V = B_0 M \tan \varphi \text{ since } B_0 M = \frac{I}{V}$$

Similarly the vertical moment of volume shift is:

$$\int \tfrac{1}{2} y^2 \tan \varphi \times \tfrac{2}{3} y \tan \varphi \; \mathrm{d}x = \int \frac{y^3}{3} \tan^2 \varphi \; \mathrm{d}x = \frac{I}{2} \tan^2 \varphi$$

and:

$$\beta = \tfrac{1}{2} I \tan^2 \varphi / \nabla = \tfrac{1}{2} B_0 M \tan^2 \varphi$$

From the figure it will be seen that:

$$
\begin{aligned}
B_0 R &= \alpha \cos \varphi + \beta \sin \varphi \\
&= B_0 M \tan \varphi \cos \varphi + \tfrac{1}{2} B_0 M \tan^2 \varphi \sin \varphi \\
&= \sin \varphi \, (B_0 M + \tfrac{1}{2} B_0 M \tan^2 \varphi)
\end{aligned}
$$

Now $\quad$
$$
\begin{aligned}
GZ &= B_0 R - B_0 G \sin \varphi \\
&= \sin \varphi \, (B_0 M - B_0 G + \tfrac{1}{2} B_0 M \tan^2 \varphi) \\
&= \sin \varphi \, (GM + \tfrac{1}{2} B_0 M \tan^2 \varphi)
\end{aligned}
$$

This is called the *wall-sided formula*. It is often reasonably accurate for full forms up to angles as large as 10°. It will not apply if the deck edge is immersed or the bilge emerges. It can be regarded as a refinement of the simple expression $GZ = GM \sin \varphi$.

Influence on stability of a freely hanging weight
Consider a weight w suspended freely from a point h above its centroid. When the ship heels slowly the weight moves transversely and takes up a new position, again vertically below the suspension point. As far as the ship is concerned the weight seems to be located at the suspension point. Compared to the situation with the weight fixed, the ship's centre of gravity will be effectively reduced by GG_1 where:

$$GG_1 = wh/W$$

This can be regarded as a loss of metacentric height of GG_1.

Weights free to move in this way should be avoided but this is not always possible. For instance, when a weight is being lifted by a shipboard crane, as soon as the weight is lifted clear of the deck or quayside its effect on stability is as though it were at the crane head. The result is a rise in G which, if the weight is sufficiently large, could cause a stability problem. This is important to the design of heavy lift ships.

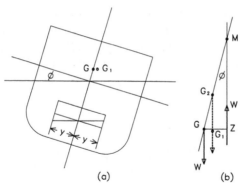

Figure 4.16 Fluid free surface

Effect of liquid free surfaces
A ship in service will usually have tanks which are partially filled with
liquids. These may be the fuel and water tanks the ship is using or may
be tanks carrying liquid cargoes. When such a ship is inclined slowly
through a small angle to the vertical the liquid surface will move so as
to remain horizontal. In this discussion a quasi-static condition is
considered so that slopping of the liquid is avoided. Different
considerations would apply to the dynamic conditions of a ship rolling.
For small angles, and assuming the liquid surface does not intersect the
top or bottom of the tank, the volume of the wedge that moves is:

$\int \frac{1}{2} y^2 \, \varphi \, dx$, integrated over the length, l, of the tank.

Assuming the wedges can be treated as triangles, the moment of
transfer of volume is:

$$\int \tfrac{1}{2} y^2 \, \varphi \, dx \times \frac{4y}{3} = \varphi \int \tfrac{2}{3} y^3 \, dx = \varphi I_1$$

where I_1 is the second moment of area of the liquid, or free, surface.
The moment of mass moved $= \rho_f \varphi I_1$, where ρ_f is the density of the liquid
in the tank. The centre of gravity of the ship will move because of this
shift of mass to a position G_1 and:

$$GG_1 = \rho_f g \varphi I_1 / W = \rho_f g \varphi I_1 / \rho g \nabla = \rho_f \varphi \nabla_1 / \rho \nabla$$

where ρ is the density of the water in which the ship is floating and V
is the volume of displacement.

The effect on the transverse movement of the centre of gravity is to reduce GZ by the amount GG_1 as in Figure 4.16(b). That is, there is an effective reduction in stability. Since $GZ = GM \sin \varphi$ for small angles, the influence of the shift of G to G_1 is equivalent to raising G to G_2 on the centre line so that $GG_1 = GG_2 \tan \varphi$ and the righting moment is given by:

$$W(GM \sin \varphi - GG_2 \cos \varphi \tan \varphi) = W(GM - GG_2) \sin \varphi$$

Thus the effect of the movement of the liquid due to its free surface, is equivalent to a rise of GG_2 of the centre of gravity, the 'loss' of GM being:

$$\text{Free surface effect } GG_2 = \rho_f I_1 / \rho \nabla$$

Another way of looking at this is to draw an analogy with the loss of stability due to the suspended weight. The water in the tank with a free surface behaves in such a way that its weight force acts through some point above the centre of the tank and height I_1/v above the centroid of the fluid in the tank, where v is the volume of fluid. In effect the tank has its own 'metacentre' through which its fluid weight acts. The fluid weight is $\rho_f v$ and the centre of gravity of the ship will be effectively raised through GG_2 where:

$$W \times GG_2 = \rho \nabla \times GG_2 = (\rho_f v)(I_1/v) = \rho_f I_1$$
and
$$GG_2 = \rho_f I_1 / \rho \nabla \text{ as before.}$$

This loss is the same whatever the height of the tank in the ship or its transverse position. If the loss is sufficiently large, the metacentric height becomes negative and the ship heels over and may even capsize. It is important that the free surfaces of tanks should be kept to a minimum. One way of reducing them is to subdivide wide tanks into two or more narrow ones. In Figure 4.17 a double bottom tank is shown with a central division fitted.

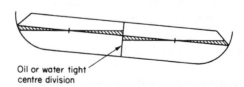

Oil or water tight
centre division

Figure 4.17 Tank subdivision

If the breadth of the tank is originally B, the width of each of the two tanks, created by the central division, is $B/2$. Assuming the tanks have a constant section, and have a length, l, the second moment of area without division is $lB^3/12$. With centre division the sum of the second moments of area of the two tanks is $(l/12)(B/2)^3 \times 2 = lB^3/48$

That is, the introduction of a centre division has reduced the free surface effect to a quarter of its original value. Using two bulkheads to divide the tank into three equal width sections reduces the free surface to a ninth of its original value. Thus subdivision is seen to be very effective and it is common practice to subdivide the double bottom of ships. The main tanks of ships carrying liquid cargoes must be designed taking free surface effects into account and their breadths are reduced by providing centreline or wing bulkheads.

Free surface effects should be avoided where possible and where unavoidable must be taken into account in the design. The operators must be aware of their significance and arrange to use the tanks in ways intended by the designer.

The inclining experiment

As the position of the centre of gravity is so important for initial stability it is necessary to establish it accurately. It is determined initially by calculation by considering all weights making up the ship – steel, outfit, fittings, machinery and systems – and assessing their individual centres of gravity. From these data can be calculated the displacement and centre of gravity of the light ship. For particular conditions of loading the weights of all items to be carried must then be added at their appropriate centres of gravity to give the new displacement and centre of gravity. It is difficult to account for all items accurately in such calculations and it is for this reason that the lightship weight and centre of gravity are measured experimentally.

The experiment is called the *inclining experiment* and involves causing the ship to heel to small angles by moving known weights known distances tranversely across the deck and observing the angles of inclination. The draughts at which the ship floats are noted together with the water density. Ideally the experiment is conducted when the ship is complete but this is not generally possible. There will usually be a number of items both to go on and to come off the ship (e.g. staging, tools etc.). The weights and centres of gravity of these must be assessed and the condition of the ship as inclined corrected.

A typical set up is shown in Figure 4.18. Two sets of weights, each of w, are placed on each side of the ship at about amidships, the port and starboard sets being h apart. Set 1 is moved a distance h to a position

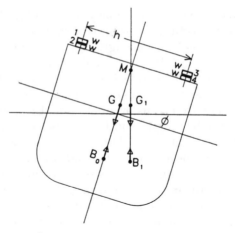

Figure 4.18 Inclining experiment

alongside sets 3 and 4. G moves to G_1 as the ship inclines to a small angle and B moves to B_1. It follows that:

$$GG_1 = \frac{wh}{W} = GM \tan \varphi \quad \text{and} \quad GM = wh \cot \varphi / W$$

φ can be obtained in a number of ways. The commonest is to use two long pendulums, one forward and one aft, suspended from the deck into the holds. If d and l are the shift and length of a pendulum respectively, $\tan \varphi = d/l$.

To improve the accuracy of the experiment, several shifts of weight are used. Thus, after set 1 has been moved, a typical sequence would be to move successively set 2, replace set 2 in original position followed by set 1. The sequence is repeated for sets 3 and 4. At each stage the angle of heel is noted and the results plotted to give a mean angle for unit applied moment. When the metacentric height has been obtained, the height of the centre of gravity is determined by subtracting *GM* from the value of *KM* given by the hydrostatics for the mean draught at which the ship was floating. This *KG* must be corrected for the weights to go on and come off. The longitudinal position of B, and hence G, can be found using the recorded draughts.

To obtain accurate results a number of precautions have to be observed. First the experiment should be conducted in calm water with little wind. Inside a dock is good as this eliminates the effects of tides and currents. The ship must be floating freely when records are taken so any mooring lines must be slack and the brow must be lifted clear. All weights must be secure and tanks must be empty or pressed full to avoid free surface effects. If the ship does not return to its original position when the inclining weights are restored it is an indication that a weight has moved in the ship, or that fluid has moved from one tank to another, possibly through a leaking valve. The number of people on board must be kept to a minimum, and those present must go to defined positions when readings are taken. The pendulum bobs are damped by immersion in a trough of water.

The draughts must be measured accurately at stem and stern, and must be read at amidships if the ship is suspected of hogging or sagging. The density of water is taken by hydrometer at several positions around the ship and at several depths to give a good average figure. If the ship should have a large trim at the time of inclining it might not be adequate to use the hydrostatics to give the displacement and the longitudinal and vertical positions of B. In this case detailed calculations should be carried out to find these quantities for the inclining waterline.

The Merchant Shipping Acts require every new passenger ship to be inclined upon completion and the elements of its stability determined.

Stability when docking or grounding

When a ship is partially supported by the ground, or dock blocks, its stability will be different from that when floating freely. The example of a ship docking is used here. The principles are the same in each case although when grounding the point of contact may not be on the centreline and the ship will heel as well as change trim.

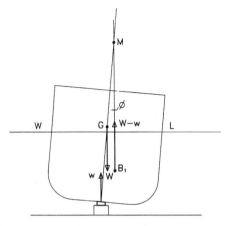

Figure 4.19 Docking

Usually a ship has a small trim by the stern as it enters dock and as the water is pumped out it first sits on the blocks at the after end. As the water level drops further the trim reduces until the keel touches the blocks over its entire length. It is then that the force on the sternframe, or after cut-up, will be greatest. This is usually the point of most critical stability as at that point it becomes possible to set side shores in place to support the ship.

Suppose the force at the time of touching along the length is w, and that it acts a distance $\bar{x}$ aft of the centre of flotation. Then, if t is the change of trim since entering dock:

$$w\bar{x} = t(\text{MCT})$$

The value of w can be found using the value of MCT read from the hydrostatics. This MCT value should be that appropriate to the actual waterline at the instant concerned and the density of water. As the mean draught will itself be dependent upon w an approximate value can be found using the mean draught on entering dock followed by a second calculation when this value of w has been used to calculate a new mean draught. Referring now to Figure 4.19, the righting moment acting on the ship, assuming a very small heel, is:

$$\begin{aligned}
\text{Righting moment} &= (W - w)\,GM \sin \varphi - wKG \sin \varphi \\
&= [\,WGM - w(GM - KG)\,] \sin \varphi \\
&= (WGM - wKM) \sin \varphi \\
&= \left(GM - \frac{w}{W}\,KM \right) W \sin \varphi
\end{aligned}$$

Should the expression inside the brackets become negative the ship will be unstable and may tip over.

Example 4.2

Just before entering drydock a ship of 5000 tonnes mass floats at draughts of 2.7 m forward and 4.2 m aft. The length between perpendiculars is 150 m and the water has a density of 1025 kg/m^3. Assuming the blocks are horizontal and the hydrostatic data given are constant over the variation in draught involved, find the force on the heel of the sternframe, which is at the after perpendicular, when the ship is just about to settle on the dockblocks, and the metacentric height at that instant.

Hydrostatic data: $KG = 8.5$ m, $KM = 9.3$ m, MCT 1 m = 105 MNm, LCF = 2.7 m aft of amidships.

Solution

Trim lost when touching down = $4.2 - 2.7 = 1.5$ m

Distance from heel of sternframe to LCF = $\dfrac{150}{2} - 2.7 = 72.3$ m

Moment applied to ship when touching down = $w \times 72.3$

Trimming moment lost by ship when touching down = $1.5 \times 105 = 157.5$ MN m

Hence, thrust on keel, $w = \dfrac{157.5}{72.3} = 2.18$ MN

Loss of GM when touching down = $(w/W)\ KM$

$$= \frac{2.18 \times 10^3 \times 9.3}{5000 \times 9.81}$$

$$= 0.41 \text{ m}$$

Metacentric height when touching down = $9.3 - 8.5 - 0.41$

$$= 0.39 \text{ m}$$

LAUNCHING

The launch is an occasion in the ship's life when the buoyancy, stability, and strength, must be studied with care. If the ship has been built in a dry dock the 'launch' is like an undocking except that the ship is only partially complete and the weights built in must be carefully assessed to establish the displacement and centre of gravity position. Large ships are quite often nowadays built in docks but in the more general case the ship is launched down inclined ways and one end, usually the stern, enters the water first. The analysis may be complicated by the launching ways being curved in the longitudinal direction to increase the rate of buoyancy build up in the later stages.

An assessment must be made of the weight and centre of gravity position at the time of launch. The procedure then adopted is to move a profile of the ship progressively down a profile of the launch ways, taking account of the launching cradle. This cradle is specially strengthened at the forward end as it is about this point, the so-called *fore poppet*, that the ship eventually pivots. At that point the force on the fore poppet is very large and the stability can be critical. As the ship

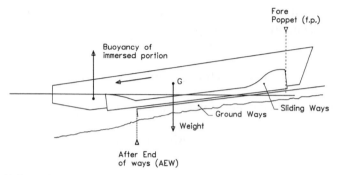

Figure 4.20 Launching

enters the water the waterline at various distances down the ways can be
noted on the profile. From the Bonjean curves the immersed sectional
areas can be read off and the buoyancy and its longitudinal centre
computed. The ship will continue in this fashion until the moment of
weight about the fore poppet equals that of the moment of buoyancy
about the same position.

The data are usually presented as a series of curves, the *launching
curves*, as in Figure 4.21.

The curves plotted are the weight which will be constant; the
buoyancy which increases as the ship travels down the ways; the
moment of weight about the fore poppet which is also effectively
constant; the moment of buoyancy about the fore poppet; the moment
of weight about the after end of the ways; and the moment of buoyancy
about the after end of the ways.

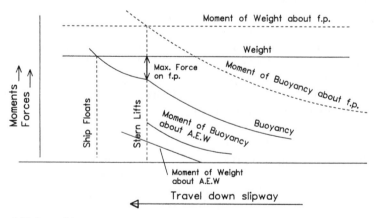

Figure 4.21 Launching curves

The maximum force on the fore poppet will be the difference between the weight and the buoyancy at the moment the ship pivots about the fore poppet which occurs when the moment of buoyancy equals the moment of weight about the fore poppet. The ship becomes fully waterborne when the buoyancy equals the weight. To ensure the ship does not tip about the after end of the ways, the moment of buoyancy about that point must always be greater than the moment of weight about it. If the ship does not become waterborne before the fore poppet reaches the after end of the ways it will drop at that point. This is to be avoided if possible. If it cannot be avoided there must be sufficient depth of water to allow the ship to drop freely allowing for the dynamic 'overshoot'. The stability at the point of pivoting can be calculated in a similar way to that adopted for docking. There will be a high hogging bending moment acting on the hull girder which must be assessed. The forces acting are also needed to ensure the launching structures are adequately strong.

The ship builds up considerable momentum as it slides down the ways. This must be dissipated before the ship comes to rest in the water. Typically chains and other energy absorbing devices are brought into action during the latter stages of travel. Tugs are on hand to manoeuvre the ship once afloat in what are usually very restricted waters.

STABILITY AT LARGE ANGLES OF INCLINATION

Atwood's formula

So far only a ship's *initial stability* has been considered. That is for small inclinations from the vertical. When the angle of inclination is greater than, say, 4 or 5 degrees, the point, M, at which the vertical through the inclined centre of buoyancy meets the centreline of the ship, can no longer be regarded as a fixed point. Metacentric height is no longer a suitable measure of stability and the value of the *righting arm, GZ*, is used instead.

Assume the ship is in equilibrium under the action of its weight and buoyancy with $W_0 L_0$ and $W_1 L_1$ the waterlines when upright and when inclined through φ respectively. These two waterlines will cut off the same volume of buoyancy but will not, in general, intersect on the centreline but at some point S.

A volume represented by $W_0 S W_1$ has emerged and an equal volume, represented by $L_0 S L_1$ has been immersed. Let this volume be v. Using the notation in Figure 4.22, the horizontal shift of the centre of buoyancy, is given by:

$$B_0 R = v \times h_e h_i / \nabla \quad \text{and} \quad GZ = B_0 R - B_0 G \sin \varphi$$

This expression for *GZ* is often called *Atwood's formula*.

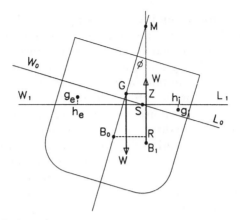

Figure 4.22 Atwood's formula

Curves of statical stability

By evaluating v and $h_e\,h_i$ for a range of angles of inclination it is possible to plot a curve of GZ against φ. A typical example is Figure 4.23. GZ increases from zero when upright to reach a maximum at A and then decreases becoming zero again at some point B. The ship will capsize if the applied moment is such that its lever is greater than the value of GZ at A. It becomes unstable once the point B has been passed. *OB* is known as the *range of stability*. The curve of GZ against φ is termed the *GZ curve* or *curve of statical stability*.

Because ships are not wall-sided, it is not easy to determine the position of S and so find the volume and centroid positions of the emerged and immersed wedges. One method is illustrated in Figure 4.24. The ship is first inclined about a fore and aft axis through O on the centreline. This leads to unequal volumes of emerged and

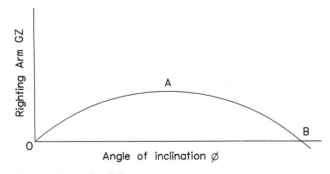

Figure 4.23 Curve of statical stability

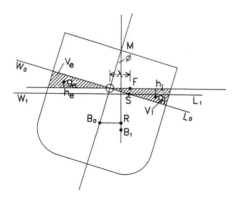

Figure 4.24

immersed wedges which must be compensated for by a bodily rise or
sinkage. In the case illustrated the ship rises. Using subscripts e and i
for the emerged and immersed wedges respectively, the geometry of
Figure 4.24 gives:

$$B_0 R = \frac{v_e(h_e O) + v_i(h_i O) - \lambda(v_i - v_e)}{\nabla}$$

and:

$$GZ = B_0 R - B_0 G \sin \varphi$$
$$= \frac{v_e(h_e O) + v_i(h_i O) - \lambda(v_i - v_e)}{\nabla} - B_0 G \sin \varphi$$

For very small angles GZ still equates to $GM \varphi$, so the slope of the GZ
curve at the origin equals the metacentric height. That is $GM = dGZ/d\varphi$ at $\varphi = 0$. It is useful in drawing a GZ curve to erect an ordinate
at $\varphi = 1$ rad, equal to the metacentric height, and joining the top of
this ordinate to the origin to give the slope of the GZ curve at the
origin.

The wall-sided formula, derived earlier, can be regarded as a special
case of Atwood's formula. For the wall-sided ship:

$$GZ = \sin \varphi (GM + \tfrac{1}{2} B_0 M \tan^2 \varphi)$$

If the ship has a positive GM it will be in equilibrium when GZ is zero,
that is:

$$0 = \sin \varphi (GM + \tfrac{1}{2} B_0 M \tan^2 \varphi)$$

This equation is satisfied by two values of φ. The first is $\sin \varphi = 0$, or $\varphi = 0$. This is the case with the ship upright as is to be expected. The second value is given by:

$$GM + \tfrac{1}{2}B_0 M \tan^2 \varphi = 0 \quad \text{or} \quad \tan^2 \varphi = -2GM/B_0 M$$

With both GM and $B_0 M$ positive there is no solution to this meaning that the upright position is the only one of equilibrium. This also applies to the case of zero GM, it being noted that in the upright position the ship has stable, not neutral, equilibrium due to the term in $B_0 M$.

When, however, the ship has a negative GM there are two possible solutions for φ in addition to that of zero, which in this case would be a position of unstable equilibrium. These other solutions are at φ either side of the upright φ being given by:

$$\tan \varphi = \left(\frac{2GM}{B_0 M}\right)^{0.5}$$

The ship would show no preference for one side or the other. Such an angle is known as an *angle of loll*. The ship does not necessarily capsize although if φ is large enough the vessel may take water on board through side openings. The GZ curve for a ship lolling is shown in Figure 4.25.

If the ship has a negative GM of 0.08 m, associated with a $B_0 M$ of 5 m, φ, which can be positive or negative, is:

$$\varphi = \tan^{-1}\left(\frac{2 \times 0.08}{5}\right)^{0.5} = \tan^{-1} 0.179 = 10.1°$$

This shows that small negative GM can lead to significant loll angles. A ship with a negative GM will loll first to one side and then the other in response to wave action. When this happens the master should investigate why the stability is so poor.

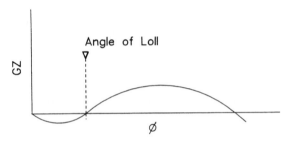

Figure 4.25 Angle of loll

Metacentric height in the lolled condition

Continuing with the wall-side assumption, if φ_1 is the angle of loll, the value of GM for small inclinations about the loll position, will be given by the slope of the GZ curve at that point. Now:

$$GZ = \sin \varphi \ (GM + \tfrac{1}{2} B_0 M \tan^2 \varphi)$$

$$\frac{dGZ}{d\varphi} = \cos \varphi \ (GM + \tfrac{1}{2} B_0 M \tan^2 \varphi) + \sin \varphi \ B_0 M \tan \varphi \sec^2 \varphi$$

substituting φ_1 for φ gives $dGZ/d\varphi = 0 + B_0 M \tan^2\varphi_1/\cos \varphi_1 = -2GM/\cos \varphi_1$.

Unless φ_1 is large, the metacentric height in the lolled position will be effectively numerically twice that in the upright position although of opposite sign.

Cross curves of stability

Cross curves of stability are drawn to overcome the difficulty in defining waterlines of equal displacement at various angles of heel.

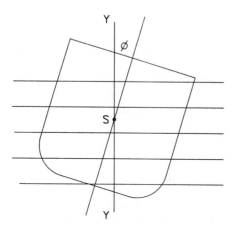

Figure 4.26

Figure 4.26 shows a ship inclined to some angle φ. Note that S is not the same as in Figure 4.24. By calculating, for a range of waterlines, the displacement and perpendicular distances, SZ, of the centroids of these volumes of displacement from the line YY through S, curves such as those in Figure 4.27 can be drawn. These curves are known as *cross*

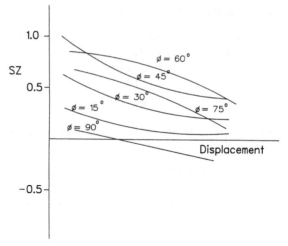

Figure 4.27 Cross curves of stability

curves of stability and depend only upon the geometry of the ship and not upon its loading. They therefore apply to all conditions in which the ship may operate.

Deriving curves of statical stability from the cross curves

For any desired displacement of the ship, the values of *SZ* can be read from the cross curves. Knowing the position of G for the desired loading enables *SZ* to be corrected to *GZ* by adding or subtracting *SG* sin φ, when G is below or above S respectively.

Features of the statical stability curve

There are a number of features of the *GZ* curve which are useful in describing a ship's stability. It has already been shown that the slope of the curve at the origin is a measure of the initial stability *GM*. The maximum ordinate of the curve multiplied by the displacement equals the largest steady heeling moment the ship can sustain without capsizing. Its value and the angle at which it occurs are both important. The value at which *GZ* becomes zero, or 'disappears', is the largest angle from which a ship will return once any disturbing moment is removed. This angle is called the *angle of vanishing stability*. The range of angle over which *GZ* is positive is termed the *range of stability*.

Important factors in determining the range of stability are freeboard and reserve of buoyancy.

The angle of deck edge immersion varies along the length of the ship. However, often it becomes immersed over a reasonable length within a small angle band. In such cases the GZ curve will exhibit a point of inflexion at that angle. It is the product of displacement and GZ that is important in most cases, rather than GZ on its own.

Example 4.3

The angles of inclination and corresponding righting lever for a ship at an assumed KS of 6.5 m are:

Inclination (°)	0	15	30	45	60	75	90
Righting lever (m)	0	0.11	0.36	0.58	0.38	−0.05	−0.60

In a particular loaded condition the displacement mass is made up of:

Item	Mass (tonnes)	KG (m)
Lightship	4200	6.0
Cargo	9100	7.0
Fuel	1500	1.1
Stores	200	7.5

Plot the curve of statical stability for this loaded condition and determine the range of stability.

Solution
The height of the centre of gravity is first found by taking moments about the keel:

$$(4200 + 9100 + 1500 + 200) \, KG = (4200 \times 6.0) + (9100 \times 7.0)$$
$$+ (1500 \times 1.1) + (200 \times 7.5)$$

$$KG = \frac{25\,200 + 63\,700 + 1650 + 1500}{15\,000} = 6.14 \, \text{m}$$

Since G is below S the actual righting lever values are given by:

$$GZ = SZ + SG \sin \varphi \quad \text{and} \quad SG = 6.5 - 6.14 = 0.36 \, \text{m}$$

The GZ values for the various angles of inclination can be determined in tabular form as in Table 4.2. By plotting GZ against inclination the range of stability is found to be 82°.

Table 4.2

Inclination (°)	sin φ	SG sin φ m	SZ m	GZ m
0	0	0	0	0
15	0.259	0.093	0.11	0.203
30	0.500	0.180	0.36	0.540
45	0.707	0.255	0.58	0.835
60	0.866	0.312	0.38	0.692
75	0.966	0.348	−0.05	0.298
90	1.000	0.360	−0.60	−0.240

Transverse movement of weight

Sometimes a weight moves permanently across the ship. Perhaps a piece of cargo has not been properly secured and moves when the ship rolls. If the weight of the item is w and it moves horizontally through a distance h, there will be a corresponding horizontal shift of the ship's centre of gravity, $GG_1 = wh/W$, where W is the weight of the ship, Figure 4.28. The value of GZ is reduced by $GG_1 \cos \varphi$ and the modified righting arm = $GZ - (wh/W) \cos \varphi$.

Unlike the case of the suspended weight, the weight will not in general return to its original position when the ship rolls in the opposite direction. If it doesn't the righting lever, and righting moment, are reduced for inclinations to one side and increased for angles on the

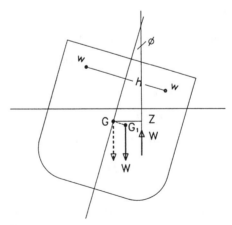

Figure 4.28 Transverse weight shift

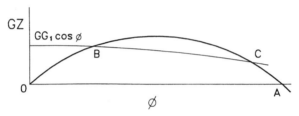

Figure 4.29 Modified *GZ* curve

other side. If $GG_1 \cos \varphi$ is plotted on the stability curve, Figure 4.29, for the particular condition of loading of the ship, the two curves intersect at B and C. B gives the new equilibrium position of the ship in still water and C the new angle of vanishing stability. The range of stability and the maximum righting arm are greatly reduced on the side to which the ship lists. For heeling to the opposite side the values are increased but it is the worse case that is of greater concern and must be considered. Clearly every precaution should be taken to avoid shifts of cargo.

Bulk cargoes

A related situation can occur in the carriage of dry bulk cargoes such as grain, ore and coal. Bulk cargoes settle down when the ship goes to sea so that holds which were full initially, have void spaces at the top. All materials of this type have an *angle of repose*. If the ship rolls to a greater angle than this the cargo may move to one side and not move back later. Consequently there can be a permanent transfer of weight to one side resulting in a permanent list with a reduction of stability on that side. In the past many ships have been lost from this cause.

Figure 4.30 shows a section through the hold of a ship carrying a bulk cargo. When the cargo settles down at sea its centre of gravity is at g. If the ship rolls the cargo could take up a new position shown by the inclined line, causing some weight, w, to move horizontally by h_1 and vertically by h_2. As a result the ship's G will move:

$$\frac{wh_1}{\Delta} \text{ to one side,} \quad \text{and} \quad \frac{wh_2}{\Delta} \text{ higher}$$

The modified righting arm becomes:

$$G_1 Z_1 = GZ - \frac{w}{\Delta} [h_1 \cos \varphi + h_2 \sin \varphi]$$

where *GZ* is the righting arm before the cargo shifted.

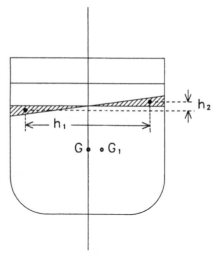

Figure 4.30 Cargo shift

Compared with the stability on initial loading there will have been a slight improvement due to the settling of the cargo.

Preventing shift of bulk cargoes

Regulations have existed for some time to minimize the movement of bulk cargoes and, in particular, grain. First, when a hold is filled with grain in bulk it must be trimmed so as to fill all the spaces between beams and at the ends and sides of holds.

Also centreline bulkheads and shifting boards are fitted in the holds to restrict the movement of grain. They have a similar effect to divisions in liquid carrying tanks in that they reduce the movement of cargo. Centreline bulkheads and shifting boards were at one time required to extend from the tank top to the lowest deck in the holds and from deck to deck in 'tween deck spaces. The present regulations require that the shifting boards or divisions extend downwards from the underside of deck or hatch covers to a depth determined by calculations related to an assumed heeling moment of a filled compartment.

The centreline bulkheads are fitted clear of the hatches, and are usually of steel. Besides restricting cargo movement they can act as a line of pillars supporting the beams if they extend from the tank top to the deck. Shifting boards are of wood and are placed on the centreline in way of hatches. They can be removed when bulk cargoes are not carried.

Even with centreline bulkheads and shifting boards spaces will appear at the top of the cargo as it settles down. To help fill these spaces feeders are fitted to provide a head of grain which will feed into the empty spaces. Hold feeders are usually formed by trunking in part of the hatch in the 'tween decks above. Feeder capacity must be 2 per cent of the volume of the space it feeds. Precautions such as those outlined above permit grain cargoes to be carried with a high degree of safety.

DYNAMICAL STABILITY

So far stability has been considered as a static problem. In reality it is a dynamic one. One step in the dynamic examination of stability is to study what is known as a ship's *dynamical stability*. The work done in heeling a ship through an angle $\delta\varphi$ will be given by the product of the displacement, GZ at the instantaneous angle and $\delta\varphi$. Thus the area under the GZ curve, up to a given angle, is proportional to the energy needed to heel it to that angle. It is a measure of the energy it can absorb from wind and waves without heeling too far. This energy is solely potential energy because the ship is assumed to be heeled slowly. In practice a ship can have kinetic energy of roll due to the action of wind and waves. This is considered in the next section.

Example 4.4

Using the tabulated values of GZ from the previous example, determine the dynamical stability of the vessel at 60° inclination.

Solution
The dynamical stability is given by:

$$\int \Delta GZ\, d\varphi = \Delta \int GZ\, d\varphi$$

This integral can be evaluated, as in Table 4.3, using Simpson's 1,4,1 rule and the ordinate heights from Table 4.2.

$$\text{The area under the curve to } 60° = \frac{15}{57.3} \times \frac{1}{3} \times 5.924$$

$$= 0.517 \text{ mrads}$$

Dynamical stability $= 15\,000 \times 9.81 \times 0.517 = 76.08$ MNm.

Table 4.3

Inclination (°)	GZ m	Simpson's multiplier	Area product
0	0	1	0
15	0.203	4	0.812
30	0.540	2	1.080
45	0.835	4	3.340
60	0.692	1	0.692
		Summation	= 5.924

Influence of wind on stability

In a beam wind the force generated on the above water surface of the ship is resisted by the hydrodynamic force produced by the slow sideways movement of the ship through the water. The wind force may be taken to act through the centroid of the above water area and the hydrodynamic force as acting at half draught, Figure 4.31. For ships with high freeboard the variation of wind speed with height may be worth allowing for (see Chapter 5). For all practical purposes the two forces can be assumed equal.

Let the vertical distance between the lines of action of the two forces be h and the projected area of the above water form be A. To a first order as the ship heels, both h and A will be reduced in proportion to $\cos \varphi$.

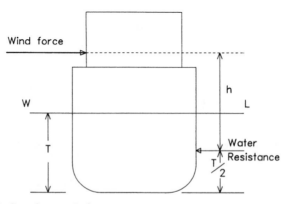

Figure 4.31 Heeling due to wind

The wind force will be proportional to the square of the wind velocity, V_w, and can be written as:

$$\text{wind force} = kAV_w^2 \cos \varphi$$

where k is an empirical constant. The moment will be:

$$M = kAhV_w^2 \cos^2 \varphi$$

The curve of wind moment can be plotted with the ΔGZ curve as in Figure 4.32. If the wind moment builds up or is applied slowly the ship will heel to an angle represented by A and in this condition the range of stability will be from A to B. The problem would then be analogous to that of the shifted weight. On the other hand, if the moment is applied suddenly, say by a gust of wind, the amount of energy applied to the ship as it heeled to A would be represented by the area DACO. The ship would only absorb energy represented by area OAC and the remaining energy would carry it beyond A to some angle F such that area AEF = area DAO. Should F be beyond B the ship will capsize, assuming the wind is still acting.

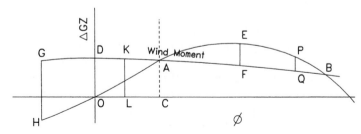

Figure 4.32

A severe case for a rolling ship is if it is inclined to its maximum angle to windward and about to return to the vertical when the gust hits it. Suppose this position is represented by GH in Figure 4.32. The ship would already have sufficient energy to carry it to some angle past the upright, say KL in the figure. Due to damping this would be somewhat less than the initial windward angle. The energy put into the ship by the wind up to angle L is now represented by the area GDKLOH. The ship will continue to heel until this energy is absorbed, perhaps reaching angle Q.

Angle of heel due to turning

When a ship is turning under the action of its rudder, the rudder holds the hull at an angle of attack relative to the direction of advance. The hydrodynamic force on the hull, due to this angle, acts towards the centre of the turning circle causing the ship to turn. Under the action of the rudder and hull forces the ship will heel to an angle that can be determined in a similar way to the above.

STABILITY STANDARDS

It has been demonstrated how a ship's transverse stability can be defined and calculated. Whilst the longitudinal stability can be evaluated according to the same principles, it is not critical for normal ship forms as the longitudinal stability is so much greater than the transverse. This may not be true for unconventional forms such as off-shore platforms. The stability of planing craft, hydrofoils and surface effect craft also require special analysis because the forces supporting the weight of the craft, which will determine their stability, are at least partly dynamic in origin. In what follows attention is focused on transverse stability of intact conventional monohulls. Stability in the damaged state will be dealt with later.

The designer must decide very early on in the design process what level of stability needs to be provided. Clearly some stability is needed or else the ship will not float upright, but loll to one side or the other. In theory a very small positive metacentric height would be enough to avoid this. In practice more is needed to allow for differing loading conditions, bad weather, growth in the ship during service and so on. If the ship is to operate in very cold areas, allowance must be made for possible icing up of superstructure, masts and rigging.

The designer, then, must decide what eventualities to allow for in designing the ship and the level of stability needed to cope with each. Typically modern ships are designed to cope with:

(1) the action of winds, up to say 100 kts;
(2) the action of waves in rolling a ship;
(3) the heel generated in a high speed turn;
(4) lifting heavy weights over the side, noting that the weight is effectively acting at the point of suspension;
(5) the crowding of passengers to one side.

Standards for USN warships have been stated[1] as have the standards adopted by Japan[2] and for passenger ships[3]. These last may be summarized as:

(1) The areas under the *GZ* curve shall not be less than 0.055 m rad up to 30°; not less than 0.09 m rad up to 40° or up to the downflooding angle and not less than 0.03 m rad between these two angles.
(2) *GZ* must be greater than 0.20 m at 30°.
(3) Maximum *GZ* must occur at an angle greater than 30°.
(4) Metacentric height must be at least 0.15 m.

Loading conditions

Possible loading conditions of a ship are calculated and information is supplied to the master. It is usually in the form of a profile of the ship indicating the positions of all loads on board, a statement of the end draughts, the trim of the ship and the metacentric height. Stability information in the form of curves of statical stability is often supplied. The usual loading conditions covered are:

(1) the lightship;
(2) fully loaded departure condition with homogeneous cargo;
(3) fully loaded arrival condition with homogeneous cargo;
(4) ballast condition;
(5) other likely service conditions.

A trim and stability booklet is prepared for the ship showing all these conditions of loading. Nowadays the supply of much of this data is compulsory and, indeed, is one of the conditions for the assignment of a freeboard.

Other data supplied include hydrostatics, cross curves of stability and plans showing the position, capacity and position of centroids for all spaces on board. These are to help the master deal with non-standard conditions.

FLOODING AND DAMAGED STABILITY

So far only the stability of an intact ship has been considered. In the event of collision, grounding or just springing a leak, water can enter the ship. If unrestricted, this flooding would eventually cause the ship to founder, that is sink bodily, or capsize, that is turn over. To reduce the probability of this, the hull is divided into a series of watertight compartments by means of bulkheads. In action, warships are expected to take punishment from the enemy so damage stability is clearly an important consideration in their design. However, damage is a possibility for any ship.

Bulkheads cannot ensure complete safety in the event of damage. If the hull is opened up over a sufficient length several compartments can be flooded. This was the case in the tragedy of the *Titanic.* Any flooding can cause a reduction in stability and if this reduction becomes great enough the ship will capsize. Even if the reduction does not cause capsize it may lead to an angle of heel at which it is difficult, or impossible, to launch lifeboats. The losses of buoyancy and stability due to flooding are considered in the following sections.

Sinkage and trim when a compartment is open to the sea

Suppose a forward compartment is open to the sea, Figure 4.33. The buoyancy of the ship between the containing bulkheads is lost and the ship settles in the water until it picks up enough buoyancy from the rest of the ship to restore equilibrium. At the same time the position of the LCB moves and the ship must trim until G and B are again in a vertical line. The ship which was originally floating at waterline $W_0 L_0$ now floats at $W_1 L_1$. Should $W_1 L_1$ be higher at any point than the deck at which the bulkheads stop (the *bulkhead deck*) it is usually assumed that the ship would be lost as a result of the water pressure in the damaged compartment forcing off the hatches and leading to unrestricted flooding fore and aft. In practice the ship might still remain afloat for a considerable time.

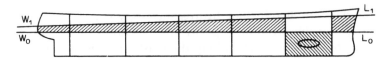

Figure 4.33 Compartment open to the sea

Most compartments in a ship contain items which will reduce the volume of water that can enter. Even 'empty' spaces usually have frames or beams in them. At the other extreme some spaces may already be full of ballast water or fuel. The ratio of the volume that is floodable to the total volume is called the *permeability* of the space. Formulae for calculating permeabilities for merchant ships are laid down in the Merchant Ship (Construction) Rules. Typical values are presented in Table 4.4. Although not strictly accurate, the same values of permeability are usually applied as factors when assessing the area and inertias of the waterplane in way of damage.

Table 4.4

Space	Permeability (%)	
Watertight compartment	97	(warship)
	95	(merchant ship)
Accommodation spaces	95	(passengers or crew)
Machinery compartments	85	
Cargo holds	60	
Stores	60	

It is not easy to calculate the damaged waterline and successive approximation is necessary. One reason is that the assumptions of small changes will not apply. There are two common approaches: the *lost buoyancy method* and the *added weight method.*

Lost buoyancy method
First the volume of the damaged compartment, Figure 4.34, up to the original waterplane, and the area of waterplane lost, are calculated making allowance for the permeability. Suppose the area of original waterplane is A and the area lost is μa, where μ is the permeability. Let the lost volume of buoyancy be μv. A first approximation to the parallel sinkage suffered is given by:

$$z = \frac{\mu v}{A - \mu a}$$

A second approximation will almost certainly be needed because of the variations in waterplane area with draught. This can be made by taking the characteristics of a waterplane at sinkage $z/2$. The longitudinal centre of flotation and the moment to change trim can be calculated

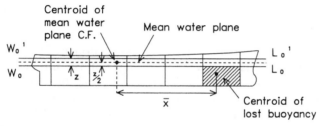

Figure 4.34 Lost bouyancy method

for this intermediate waterplane, again allowing for the permeability. Using subscript m to denote the values for the intermediate waterplane:

$$\text{sinkage} = \frac{\mu v}{A_m} \quad \text{and} \quad \text{trim} = \frac{\mu v \bar{x}}{\text{MCT}_m}$$

where $\bar{x}$ is the centroid of the lost volume from the CF.

The new draughts can be calculated from the sinkage and trim. A further approximation can be made if either of these is very large, or the results can be checked from first principles using the Bonjean curves allowing for the flooding and permeability.

In the lost buoyancy method the position of G remains unaltered unless the damage has been so severe as to remove structure or equipment from the ship.

Added weight method

In this method the water entering the damaged compartment is regarded as an added weight. Permeability would have to be allowed for in assessing this weight, and allowance must be made for the free surface of the water that has entered, but all the hydrostatic data used are those for the intact ship. Initially the calculation can proceed as for any added weight, but when the new waterline is established allowance must be made for the extra water that would enter the ship up to that waterplane. Again a second iteration may be needed and the calculation is repeated until a sufficiently accurate answer is obtained.

In the description of both methods it is assumed that the compartment that has been breached extends above the original and the final waterlines. If it does not then the actual floodable volumes must be used, and the assumed waterplane characteristics amended accordingly. It will be clear that it is highly desirable for the ship to have reasonable amounts of potential buoyancy above the intact waterplane as a 'reserve'. This is termed *reserve of buoyancy.*

Example 4.5

A vessel of constant rectangular cross section is 60 m long and 10 m wide. It floats at a level keel draught of 3 m and has a centre of gravity 2.5 m above the keel. Determine the fore and aft draughts if an empty, full width, fore-end compartment 8 m long is opened to the sea. For simplicity a permeability of 100 per cent is assumed.

Solution

Lost buoyancy method

Area of intact waterplane, $A = 52 \times 10 = 520\,\text{m}^2$
Volume of lost buoyancy, $v = 8 \times 10 \times 3 = 240\,\text{m}^3$
Parallel sinkage, $z = 240/520 = 0.46\,\text{m}$

The vessel now trims about the new centre of flotation, F_1 from amidships. Taking moments about amidships, and using subscript 1 to denote damaged values:

$$(60 \times 10 \times 0) - (8 \times 10 \times 26) = [(60 \times 10) - (8 \times 10)]F_1,$$

giving $F_1 = -4\,\text{m}$

That is, the centre of flotation is 4 m aft of amidships or 30 m aft of the centroid of the damaged compartment.

$$KB_1 = \frac{T_1}{2} = \frac{3 + 0.46}{2} = 1.73\,\text{m}$$

$$B_1 M_L = \frac{I_L}{\nabla} = \frac{1}{12} \times \frac{52^3 \times 10}{60 \times 10 \times 3} = 65.10\,\text{m}$$

$KG = 2.50\,\text{m}$ (constant)

$GM_L = 1.73 + 65.10 - 2.5 = 64.33\,\text{m}$

Hence $\text{MCT}\,1\,\text{m} = W \times GM_L/L$

$$= \frac{60 \times 10 \times 3 \times 1.025 \times 9.81 \times 64.33}{60}$$

$$= 19\,406\,\text{kNm}$$

$$\text{Trim} = \frac{\rho g v \bar{x}}{\text{MCT}\,1\text{m}} = \frac{1.025 \times 9.81 \times 240 \times 30}{19\,406} = 3.73\,\text{m}$$

Thus draught aft $= 3 + 0.46 - \dfrac{26 \times 3.73}{60} = 1.84\,\text{m}$

draught forward $= 3 + 0.46 + \dfrac{34 \times 3.73}{60} = 5.57\,\text{m}$

Added mass method

Mass added at 3 m draught = $8 \times 10 \times 3 \times 1.025$

$$= 246 \text{ tonne } [364.9]$$

Parallel sinkage $= \dfrac{246}{1.025 \times 60 \times 10} = 0.4 \text{ m } [0.593]$

New displacement mass $= 60 \times 10 \times 3.4 \times 1.025$

$$= 2091 \text{ tonne } [2210]$$

$KB_1 = \dfrac{3.4}{2} = 1.7 \text{ m } [1.797]$

$BM_1 = \dfrac{I_L}{\nabla} = \dfrac{1}{12} \times \dfrac{(60^3 - 8^3) \times 10}{60 \times 10 \times 3.4} = 88.0 \text{ m } [83.3]$

$KG_1 = \dfrac{(60 \times 10 \times 3 \times 1.025 \times 2.5) + (246 \times 1.5)}{2091}$

$$= 2.38 \text{ m } [2.45]$$

MCT 1 m $= \dfrac{2091 \times 9.81 \times (1.7 + 88.0 - 2.38)}{60}$

$$= 29\,850 \text{ kNm } [29860]$$

Trim $= \dfrac{246 \times 9.81 \times 26}{29\,850} = 2.10 \text{ m } [3.12]$

Thus draught aft $= \dfrac{3 + 0.4 - 2.10}{2} = 2.35 \text{ m}$

and

draught forward $= \dfrac{3 + 0.4 + 2.10}{2} = 4.45 \text{m}$

A second calculation considering the mass of water entering at 4.45 m draught forward will give a trim of 3.12 m and draughts of 2.03 m aft and 5.15 m forward. Results of the intermediate steps in the calculation are given in [] above. A third calculation yields draughts of 1.88 m aft and 5.49 m forward.

In this case, since a rectangular body is involved the draughts can be deduced directly by simple calculation using the lost buoyancy approach and treating the underwater fore and aft sections as trapezia. The body effectively becomes a rectangular vessel 60 m long (but with buoyancy only over the aftermost 52 m) by 10 m wide with an LCG 30 m from one end and the LCB 26 m from aft. It will trim by the bow until the LCB is 30 m from aft. It will be found that the draught aft = 1.863 m and the draught 52 m forward of the after end = 5.059 m. The draught right forward will be:

$$1.863 + (5.059 - 1.863) \times \frac{60}{52} = 5.551 \text{ m.}$$

Stability in the damaged condition

Consider first the lost buoyancy method and the metacentric height. The effect of the loss of buoyancy in the damaged compartment is to remove buoyancy (volume v) from a position below the original waterline to some position above this waterline so that the centre of buoyancy will rise. If the vertical distance between the centroids of the lost and gained buoyancy is bb_1 the rise in centre of buoyancy = $\mu v bb_1 / \nabla$. BM will decrease because of the loss of waterplane inertia in way of the damage. If the damaged inertia is I_d, $BM_d = I_d/\nabla$. The value of KG remains unchanged so that the damaged GM, which may be more, but is generally less, than the intact GM is:

$$\text{damaged } GM = GM(\text{intact}) + \frac{\mu v bb_1}{\nabla} - \frac{I_d}{\nabla}$$

If the added weight method is used then the value of KG will change and the height of M can be found from the hydrostatics for the intact ship at the increased draught. The free surface of the water in the damaged compartment must be allowed for.

Asymmetrical flooding

When there are longitudinal bulkheads in the ship there is the possibility of the flooding not extending right across the ship causing the ship to heel. In deciding whether a longitudinal bulkhead will be breached it is usually assumed that damage does not penetrate more than 20 per cent of the breadth of the ship. Taking the case illustrated in Figure 4.35 and using the added weight approach, the ship will heel until:

$$\rho g \, \nabla GM \sin \varphi = \mu \, \rho g v z \quad \text{or} \quad \sin \varphi = \frac{\mu v z}{\nabla GM}$$

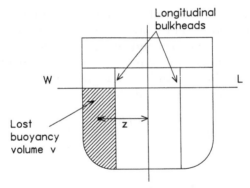

Figure 4.35 Asymmetrical flooding

As with the calculation for trim, this first angle will need to be corrected for the additional weight of water at the new waterline, and the process repeated if necessary.

Large heels should be avoided and usually means are provided to flood a compartment on the opposite side of the ship. This is termed *counterflooding*. The ship will sink deeper in the water but this is usually a less dangerous situation than that posed by the heel.

Floodable length

So far the consequences of flooding a particular compartment have been studied. The problem can be looked at the other way by asking what length of ship can be flooded without loss of the ship. Loss is generally accepted to occur when the damaged waterline is tangent to the bulkhead deck line at side. The *bulkhead deck* is the uppermost weathertight deck to which transverse watertight bulkheads are carried. A margin is desirable and the limit is taken when the

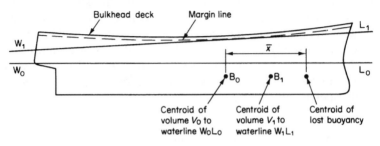

Figure 4.36

waterline is tangent to a line drawn 76 mm (3 inches) below the bulkhead deck at side. This line is called the *margin line*. The *floodable length* at any point along the length of the ship is the length, with that point as centre, which can be flooded without immersing any part of the margin line when the ship has no list.

Take the ship shown in Figure 4.36 using subscripts 0 and 1 to denote the intact ship data for the intact and damaged waterlines. Loss of buoyancy $= V_1 - V_0$ and this must be at such a position that B_1 moves back to B_0 so that B is again below G. Hence:

$$\bar{x} = \frac{V_1 \times B_0 B_1}{V_1 - V_0}$$

This then gives the centroid of the lost buoyancy and, knowing $(V_1 - V_0)$ it is possible to convert this into a length of ship that can be flooded. The calculation would be one of reiteration until reasonable figures are obtained.

The calculations can be repeated for a series of waterlines tangent to the margin line at different positions along the length. This will lead to a curve of floodable length as in Figure 4.37. The ordinate

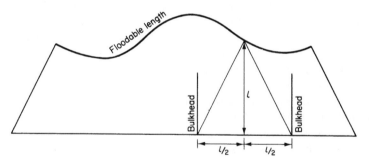

Figure 4.37 Floodable length

at any point represents the length which can be flooded with the centre at the point concerned. Thus if l is the floodable length at some point the positions of bulkheads giving the required compartment length are given by setting off distances $l/2$ either side of the point. The lines at the ends of the curves, called the *forward and after terminals* will be at an angle $\tan^{-1}2$ to the base if the base and ordinate scales are the same.

The permeabilities of compartments will affect the floodable length and it is usual to work out average permeability figures for the machinery spaces and for each of the two regions forward and aft.

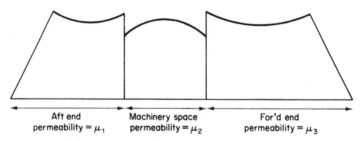

Figure 4.38 Floodable length with permeability

This leads to three curves for the complete ship as shown in Figure 4.38. The condition that a ship should be able to float with any one compartment open to the sea is a minimum requirement for ocean going passenger ships. The Merchant Shipping Regulations set out formulae for calculating permeabilities and a *factor of subdivision* which must be applied to the floodable length curves giving *permissible length*. The permissible length is the product of the floodable length and the factor of subdivision. The factor of subdivision depends upon the length of the ship and a *criterion of service numeral* or more simply *criterion numeral*. This numeral represents the criterion of service of the ship and takes account of the number of passengers, the volumes of the machinery and accommodation spaces and the total ship volume. It decreases in a regular and continuous manner with the ship length and factors related to whether the ship carries predominantly cargo or passengers. Broadly, the factor of subdivision ensures that one, two or three compartments can be flooded before the margin line is immersed leading to what are called *one-, two- or three-compartment ships*. That is, compartment standard is the inverse of the factor of subdivision. In general terms the factor of subdivision decreases with length of ship and is lower for passenger ships than cargo ships.

SUMMARY

The reader has been introduced to the methods for calculating the draughts at which a ship will float, and its stability for both initial stability and stability at large angles of inclination. Standards for stability have been discussed. Both the intact and the damaged states have been covered. These are fundamental concepts in the design and operation of ships. A more detailed discussion on stability at about this level, with both worked and set examples, is to be found in Derrett.[4]

References

1. Sarchin, T. H. and Goldberg, L. L. (1962) Stability and buoyancy criteria for US naval surface warships. *TSNAME*.
2. Yamagata, M. (1959) Standard of stability adopted in Japan. *TRINA*.
3. Merchant Shipping (Passenger Ship Construction) Regulations 1984, amended 1990 and 1992.
4. Derrett, D. R. (1994) *Ship Stability for Masters and Mates*. Butterworth-Heinemann.

5 The environment

Apart from submerged submarines, ships operate on the interface between air and water. The properties of both fluids are important.

BASIC PROPERTIES

Water

Water is effectively incompressible so its density does not vary with depth as such. Density of water does vary with temperature and salinity as does its kinematic viscosity. The density of sea water increases with increasing salinity. The figures in Table 5.1 are based on a standard salinity of 3.5 per cent.

Table 5.1 Water properties

Temperature (°C)	Density (kg/m^3)		Kinematic viscosity (m^2/s $\times$ 10^6)	
	Fresh water	Salt water	Fresh water	Salt water
0	999.8	1028.0	1.787	1.828
10	999.6	1026.9	1.306	1.354
20	998.1	1024.7	1.004	1.054
30	995.6	1021.7	0.801	0.849

The naval architect has traditionally used approximate figures in calculations. These have included taking a mass density of fresh water as 62.2 lb/ft^3 (36 cubic feet per ton) and of sea water as 64 lb/ft^3 (35 cubic feet per ton). The corresponding 'preferred' values in SI units are 1.000 tonne/m^3 and 1.025 tonne/m^3 respectively.

Air
At standard barometric pressure and temperature, with 70 per cent humidity air has been taken as having a mass of $0.08\,\text{lb/ft}^3$ (13 cubic feet per lb). The corresponding preferred SI figure is $1.28\,\text{kg/m}^3$.

Temperatures
The ambient temperatures of sea and air a ship is likely to meet in service determine the amount of air conditioning and insulation to be provided besides affecting the power produced by machinery. Extreme air temperatures of 52°C in the tropics in harbour and 38°C at sea, have been recorded: also −40°C in the Arctic in harbour and −30°C at sea. Less extreme values are taken for design purposes and typical design figures for warships, in degrees Celsius, are as in Table 5.2.

Table 5.2 Design temperatures

Area of world	Average max. summer temperature			Average min. winter temperature		
	Air		Sea	Air		Sea
	DB	WB		DB	WB	
Extreme tropic	34.5	30	33			
Tropics	31	27	30			
Temperate	30	24	29			
Temperate winter				−4	−	2
Sub Arctic winter				−10	−	1
Arctic/Antarctic winter				−29	−	−2

Notes   1. Temperatures in degrees Celsius.
2. Water temperatures measured near the surface in deep water.

WIND

Unfortunately for the ship designer and operator the air and the sea are seldom still. Strong winds can add to the resistance a ship experiences and make manoeuvring difficult. Beam winds will make a ship heel and winds create waves. The wave characteristics depend upon the wind's *strength*, the time for which it acts, its *duration* and the distance over which it acts, its *fetch*. The term *sea* is applied to waves generated locally by a wind. When waves have travelled out of the

Table 5.3 Beaufort scale

Number/description	Limits of speed	
	(knots)	(m/s)
0 Calm	1	0.3
1 Light air	1 to 3	0.3 to 1.5
2 Light breeze	4 to 6	1.6 to 3.3
3 Gentle breeze	7 to 10	3.4 to 5.4
4 Moderate breeze	11 to 16	5.5 to 7.9
5 Fresh breeze	17 to 21	8.0 to 10.7
6 Strong breeze	22 to 27	10.8 to 13.8
7 Near gale	28 to 33	13.9 to 17.1
8 Gale	34 to 40	17.2 to 20.7
9 Strong gale	41 to 47	20.8 to 24.4
10 Storm	48 to 55	24.5 to 28.4
11 Violent storm	56 to 63	28.5 to 32.6
12 Hurricane	64 and over	32.7 and over

generation area they are termed *swell*. The wave form depends also upon depth of water, currents and local geographical features. Unless otherwise specified the waves referred to in this book are to be taken as fully developed in deep water.

The strength of a wind is classified in broad terms by the *Beaufort Scale*, Table 5.3.

Due to the interaction between the wind and sea surface, the wind velocity varies with height. Beaufort wind speeds are based on the wind speed at a height of 6 m. At half this height the wind speed will be about 10 per cent less than the nominal and at 15 m will be 10 per cent greater. The higher the wind speed the less likely it is to be exceeded. In the North Atlantic, for instance, a wind speed of 10 knots is likely to be exceeded for 60 per cent of the time, 20 knots for 30 per cent and 30 knots for only 10 per cent of the time.

WAVES

An understanding of the behaviour of a vessel in still water is essential but a ship's natural environment is far from still, the main disturbing forces coming from waves.

To an observer the sea surface looks very irregular, even confused. For many years it defied any attempt at mathematical definition. The essential nature of this apparently random surface was understood by R. E. Froude who, in 1905,[1] postulated that irregular wave systems are only a compound of a number of regular systems, individually of comparatively small amplitude, and covering a range of periods. Further he stated that the effect of such a compound wave system on a ship would be 'more or less the compound of the effects proper to the individual units composing it'. This is the basis for all modern studies of waves and ship motion. Unfortunately the mathematics were not available in 1905 for Froude to apply his theory. That had to wait until the early 1950s.

Since the individual wave components are regular it is necessary to study the properties of regular waves.

Regular waves

A uni-directional regular wave would appear constant in shape with time and resemble a sheet of corrugated iron of infinite width. As it passes a fixed point a height recorder would record a variation with time that would be repeated over and over again. Two wave shapes are of particular significance to the naval architect, the *trochoidal wave* and the *sinusoidal wave.*

The trochoidal wave

By observation the crests of ocean waves are sharper than the troughs. This is a characteristic of trochoidal waves and they were taken as an approximation to ocean waves by early naval architects in calculating longitudinal strength. The section of the wave is generated by a fixed point within a circle when that circle rolls along and under a straight line, Figure 5.1.

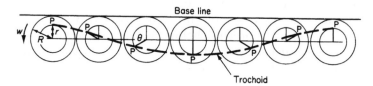

Figure 5.1 Trochoidal wave

The crest of the wave occurs when the point is closest to the straight line. The wavelength, λ, is equal to the distance the centre of the circle moves in making one complete rotation, that is $\lambda = 2\pi R$. The waveheight is $2r = h_w$. Consider the x-axis as horizontal and passing though the centre of the circle, and the z-axis as downwards with origin at the initial position of the centre of the circle. If the circle now rolls through θ, the centre of the circle will move $R\theta$ and the wave generating point, P, has co-ordinates:

$$x = R\theta - r \sin \theta$$

$$z = r \cos \theta$$

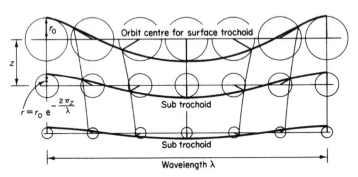

Figure 5.2 Sub-trochoids

Referring to Figure 5.2, the following mathematical relationships can be shown to exist:

(1) The velocity of the wave system, $C = \left(\dfrac{g\lambda}{2\pi} \right)^{0.5}$.

(2) The still water surface will be at $z = \dfrac{r_0^2}{2R}$ reflecting the fact that the crests are sharper than the troughs.

(3) Particles in the wave move in circular orbits.

(4) Surfaces of equal pressure below the wave surface are trochoidal. These subsurface amplitudes reduce with depth so that, at z below the surface, the amplitude is:

$$r = r_0 \exp \frac{-z}{R} = r_0 \exp \frac{-(2\pi z)}{\lambda}.$$

(5) This exponential decay is very rapid and there is little movement at depths of more than about half the wavelength.

Wave pressure correction

The water pressure at the surface of the wave is zero and at a reasonable depth, planes of equal pressure will be horizontal. Hence the pressure variation with depth within the wave cannot be uniform along the

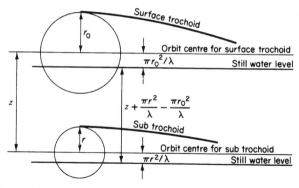

Figure 5.3 Pressure in wave

length of the wave. The variation is due to the fact that the wave particles move in circular orbits. It is a dynamic effect, not one due to density variations. It can be shown that the pressure at a point z below the wave surface is the same as the hydrostatic pressure at a depth z', where z' is the distance between the mean, still water, axis of the surface trochoid and that for the subsurface trochoid through the point considered.

Now
$$z' = z - \frac{\pi}{\lambda}[r_0^2 - r^2]$$

$$= z - \frac{r_0^2}{2R}[1 - r^2/r_0^2] = z - \frac{r_0^2}{2R}[1 - \exp(-2z/R)]$$

To obtain the forces acting on the ship in the wave the usual hydrostatic pressure based on depth must be corrected in accordance with this relationship. This correction is generally known as the *Smith effect.* Its effect is to increase pressure below the trough and reduce it below the crest for a given absolute depth.

The sinusoidal wave
Trochoidal waveforms are difficult to manipulate mathematically and irregular waves are analysed for their sinusoidal components. Taking the x-axis in the still water surface, the same as the mid-height of the wave, and z-axis vertically down, the wave surface height at x and time t can be written as:

$$z = \frac{H\sin(qx + \omega t)}{2}$$

In this equation q is termed the *wave number* and $\omega = 2\pi/T$ is known as the *wave frequency*. T is the *wave period*. The principal characteristics of the wave, including the *wave velocity*, C, are:

$$C = \frac{\lambda}{T} = \frac{\omega}{q}$$

$$T^2 = \frac{2\pi\lambda}{g}$$

$$\omega^2 = \frac{2\pi g}{\lambda}$$

$$C^2 = \frac{g\lambda}{2\pi}$$

As with trochoidal waves water particles in the wave move in circular orbits, the radii of which decrease with depth in accordance with:

$$r = \tfrac{1}{2}H \exp(-qz)$$

From this it is seen that for depth $\lambda/2$ the orbit radius is only $0.02H$ which can normally be ignored.

The average total energy per unit area of wave system is $\rho g H^2/8$, the potential and kinetic energies each being half of this figure. The energy of the wave system is transmitted at half the speed of advance of the waves. The front of the wave system moves at the speed of energy transmission so the component waves, travelling at twice this speed, will 'disappear' through the wave front.

For more information on sinusoidal waves, including proofs of the above relationships, the reader should refer to a standard text.[2,3]

Irregular wave systems

The irregular wave surface can be regarded as the compound of a large number of small waves. Each component wave will have its own length and height. If they were all travelling in the same direction the irregular pattern would be constant across the breadth of the wave, extending to infinity in each direction. Such a sea is said to be a *long crested irregular system* and is referred to as *one-dimensional*, the one dimension being frequency. In the more general case the component waves will each be travelling in a different direction. In that case the sea surface resembles a series of humps and hollows with any apparent crests being of short length. Such a system is said to be a *short crested irregular wave system* or a *two-dimensional system*, the dimensions being frequency and direction. Only the simpler, long crested system will be considered in this book. For briefness it will be called an irregular wave system.

Evidence, based on both measured and visual data at a number of widely separated locations over the North Atlantic, leaves little doubt that mean wave heights have increased over the past 30 years or more at a rate of the order of about 1.5 per cent per annum.[4,5] Indications that extreme wave heights may also have increased slightly are noted but the evidence for this is not conclusive. One possible cause for the increase in the mean height is increasing storm frequency giving waves less time to decay between storms. The fresh winds then act upon a surface with swell already present. This increase in mean wave height has important implications for the naval architect, particularly as in many cases a new design is based upon comparison with existing, successful, designs. The data given in this chapter does not allow for this increase. With the increasing use of satellites to provide wave data the effect should become clearer with time.

Describing an irregular wave system
A typical wave profile, as recorded at a fixed point, is shown in Figure 5.4. The wave heights could be taken as vertical distances between successive crests and troughs, and the wavelength measured between successive crests, as shown.

Figure 5.4 Wave record

If λ_a and T_a are the average distance and time interval in seconds between crests, it has been found that, approximately:

$$\lambda_a = 2gT_a^2/6\pi = 1.04\ T_a^2\ \text{m},$$
and
$$T_a = 0.285\ V_w \text{ in seconds if } V_w \text{ is wind speed in knots.}$$

If the wave heights measured are arranged in order of reducing magnitude the mean height of the highest third of the waves is called the *significant wave height*. This is often quoted and an observer tends to assess the height of a set of waves as being close to this figure. A general

Table 5.4 Sea state code

Code	Description of sea	Significant wave height (m)
0	Calm (glassy)	0
1	Calm (rippled)	0 to 0.10
2	Smooth (wavelets)	0.10 to 0.50
3	Slight	0.50 to 1.25
4	Moderate	1.25 to 2.50
5	Rough	2.50 to 4.00
6	Very rough	4.00 to 6.00
7	High	6.00 to 9.00
8	Very high	9.00 to 14.00
9	Phenomenal	Over 14

description of a sea state, related to significant wave height is given by the *sea state code*, Table 5.4, which is quite widely accepted although an earlier code will sometimes still be encountered.

The wave height data from Figure 5.4 can be plotted as a histogram showing the frequency of occurrence of wave heights within selected bands, as in Figure 5.5. A similar plot could be produced for wave length. In such plots the number of records in each interval is usually expressed as a percentage of the total number in the record so that the total area under the curve is unity.

A distribution curve can be fitted to the histogram as shown. For long duration records or for samples taken over a period of time a *normal* or *Gaussian distribution* is found to give a good approximation. The curve is expressed as:

$$p(h) = \sigma^{-1}(2\pi)^{-0.5}\exp\frac{-(h - \overline{h})^2}{2\sigma^2}$$

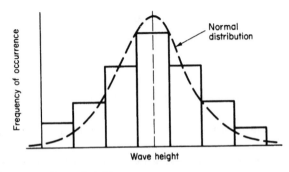

Figure 5.5 Histogram of wave height

where:

$p(h)$ = the height of curve, the frequency of occurrence
h = wave height
$\overline{h}$ = mean wave height from record
σ = standard deviation

Where data are from a record of say 30 minutes duration, during which time conditions remain reasonably steady, a *Rayleigh distribution* is found to be a better fit. The equation for this type of distribution is:

$$p(h) = \frac{2h}{E} \exp \frac{-h^2}{E}$$

where:

$E = \dfrac{1}{N} \Sigma h^2$ = mean value of h^2, N being the total number of observations.

In these expressions $p(h)$ is a probability density, the area under the curve being unity because it is certain that the variable will take some value of h. The area under the curve between two values of h represents the probability that the waveheight will have a value within that range. Integrating the curve leads to a *cumulative probability distribution*. The ordinate at some value h on this curve represents the probability that the waveheight will have a value less than or equal to h.

For more information on these and other probability distributions the reader should refer to a textbook on statistics.

Energy spectra

One of the most powerful means of representing an irregular sea and, incidentally, a ship's responses as will be discussed in Chapter 6, is the concept of an energy spectrum. The components of the sea can be found by Fourier analysis and the elevation of the sea surface at any point and time can be represented by:

$$h = \Sigma h_n \cos (\omega_n + \varepsilon_n)$$

where h_n, ω_n and ε_n are the height, circular frequency and arbitrary phase angle of the nth wave component.

The energy per unit area of surface of a regular wave system is proportional to half the square of the wave height. The energy therefore, of the nth component will be proportional to $h_n^2/2$, and the total energy of the composite system given by:

$$\text{Total energy} \propto \frac{\Sigma\, h_n^2}{2}$$

Within a small interval, $\delta\omega$, the energy in the waves can be represented by half the square of the mean surface elevation in that interval. Plotting this against ω, Figure 5.6, gives what is termed an *energy spectrum*. The ordinate of the spectrum is usually denoted by $S(\omega)$. Since the ordinate represents the energy in an interval whose units are $1/s$ its units will be $(\text{height})^2\,(\text{seconds})$. $S(\omega)$ is called the *spectral density*.

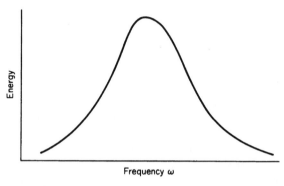

Figure 5.6 Energy spectrum

Some interesting general wave characteristics can be deduced from the area under the spectrum. If this is m_o, and the distribution of wave amplitude is Gaussian, then the probability that the magnitude of the wave amplitude at a random instant, will exceed some value ζ is:

$$p(\zeta) = 1 - \text{erf}\, \frac{\zeta}{(2m_o)^{0.5}}$$

In this expression erf is the *error function* which will be found in standard mathematical tables.

However, wave observations show that generally the Rayleigh distribution is better at representing the sea surface. In this case it can be shown that:

The most frequent wave amplitude $= 0.707\,(2m_o)^{0.5} = (m_o)^{0.5}$
Average wave amplitude $= 1.25\,(m_o)^{0.5}$
Average amplitude of $\frac{1}{3}$ highest waves $= 2\,(m_o)^{0.5}$
Average amplitude of $\frac{1}{10}$ highest waves $= 2.55\,(m_o)^{0.5}$

Shapes of wave spectra

Even in deep water, a wave system will only become fully developed if the duration and fetch are long enough. The wave components produced first are those of shorter length, higher frequency. With time the longer length components appear so that the shape of the spectrum develops as in Figure 5.7. A similar progression would be found for increasing wind speed. As the wind abates and the waves die down, the spectrum reduces, the longer waves disappearing first because they travel faster, leaving the storm area.

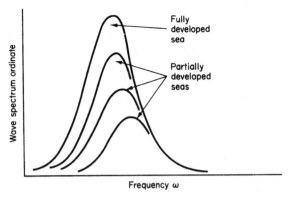

Figure 5.7 Developing spectra

The problem remains as to the shape a fully developed spectrum can be expected to take for a given wind speed. Early formulae attempted to define the spectrum purely in terms of wind speed and Pierson and Moskowitz's formula is:

$$S(\omega) = \frac{8.1 \times 10^{-3} g^2}{\omega^5} \exp\left[-0.74\left(\frac{g}{V\omega}\right)^4\right] \text{ m}^2\text{s}$$

where g and V are in ms^{-2} and ms^{-1} units respectively, V being the wind speed.

The spectrum now most widely adopted is the *Bretschneider spectrum*. This takes the form:

$$S(\omega) = \frac{A}{\omega^5} \exp \frac{-B}{\omega^4}$$

where A and B are constants.

When both the significant wave height $\zeta_{\frac{1}{3}}$ and the characteristic period T_1 are known:

$$A = \frac{173\zeta_{\frac{1}{3}}^2}{T_1^4}, \quad B = \frac{691}{T_1^4}, \quad T_1 = \frac{2\pi m_o}{m_1}$$

m_1 is the first moment of area of the energy spectrum about the axis $\omega = 0$. When only the significant wave height is known, $S(\omega)$ can be represented approximately by:

$$A = 8.10 \times 10^{-3} g^2 \quad \text{and} \quad B = 3.11/\zeta_{\frac{1}{3}}^2$$

WAVE STATISTICS

It has been seen how the wave surface can be characterized by a wave spectrum. The designer still needs to know the severity of waves any new design is likely to meet in service. For this, recourse is had to *ocean wave statistics*. Over the years wave data have been obtained from observations and measurements. Although they must be somewhat subjective, visual observations are available for large ocean areas, particularly the main shipping routes, and they have been successfully integrated with measured data. Measurements can be at fixed points in the ocean using buoys, taken by shipboard recorders or taken by satellite. On board recorders need careful calibration to remove the influence of the ship on the wave system being recorded. They tend to be used only for special trials. Even then buoys deployed locally by the trials ship are generally preferred. For one thing a suitably arranged group of buoys can give information on the dominant wave direction as well as on height and period.

The concept of using a satellite radar altimeter[5] was established by *Skylab* in 1973. The satellite *Seasat* was operational for a few months in 1978 and was the first to give global coverage. The prospect now is for two satellites to be operational at any one time. The higher the waves in the footprint of the satellite radar, the more spread out is the time of arrival of the return pulse. Adjusting the height of the return pulse to a constant value, the slope of the leading edge gives a measure of the significant wave height. Wind speed is indicated by the back scatter of the signal. Early radars did not permit the wave period to be measured but later synthetic aperture radars should fill this gap.

Statistical data on the probability of occurrence of various sea conditions at different times of the year with the predominant wave direction are available.[6,7] They are also available in PC form with wind data added. The data, based on a million sets of observations are presented for 50 sea areas covering the regularly sailed sea routes. There are some 3000 tables arranged by area, season and wave direction. Tables show, for instance, the number of observations within selected wave height and wave period bands. They show a spread of period for a given height and of height for a given period. This 'scatter' is not due to inaccuracies of observation but to the fact that the sea states observed are at various stages of development and include swell as well as sea components.

The data can be combined in many ways. They can, for example, be averaged over the North Atlantic or world wide. Doing this confirms the popular impression that the Atlantic is one of the roughest areas: 21.4 per cent of waves there can be expected to exceed 4 m whereas the corresponding percentage worldwide is 16.8.

OTHER EXTREME ENVIRONMENTS

In addition to the conditions of wind and waves to which all ships are subject, there are other extreme conditions the ship and equipment may need to allow for. These include driving rain, dust and sand which can abrade exposed surfaces, chemical deposits (including salt from spray) and fungi which can harm surfaces and eat away certain materials. Sea-spray and snow can cause icing up in cold climates. Ice impedes the operation of moving items and can pose a serious stability problem. The conditions upon which designs of ship and equipment should be based are laid down in various specifications. These also define suitable tests and should be consulted by the designer.

INTERNAL ENVIRONMENT

Besides the external environment in which a ship may operate, the naval architect is concerned with the environment inside the vessel. The vibration levels, for instance, must be kept low for comfort and efficient functioning of machinery. Noise must also be kept below certain levels. Vibration and noise are discussed in Chapter 11. Vertical accelerations associated with ship motions must be minimized to reduce the likelihood of motion sickness.

Other features of the internal environment the naval architect will control include:

(1) The *air quality* in terms of temperature, humidity, purity and odours. Typically about $0.3 \, m^3$ of fresh air are introduced for each person per minute. A person generates about 45 watts of sensible heat and 150 watts latent heat, depending upon the level of activity. These and the heat from machines, must be catered for by the air-conditioning system. The aim is to

maintain the temperature and humidity at such levels as people find comfortable. The problems of atmosphere management are most severe in submarines where systems are fitted to remove carbon dioxide, add oxygen and remove a wide range of impurities.

(2) Levels of *illumination*. These will depend upon the activity within a compartment but typically, in terms of lux, will be about 75 in cabins, 100 to 150 in public rooms, 50 in passageways, and 150 to 200 in machinery spaces.

MARINE POLLUTION

As well as the effect of the environment on the ship, it is important to consider the effect of the ship on the environment. In 1990, after the serious pollution that followed the grounding of the *Exxon Valdez*, the USA required all tankers using their waters to be of double hull construction. The IMO, 1993, accepted that the double hull would reduce oil outflow in many cases but also recognized that alternative design configurations were possible, and could be even more effective in certain types of incident. One alternative is the mid-deck design. By venting the lower tanks their tops are kept at atmospheric pressure. Penetration of the bottom leads to the entry of sea water, displacing the oil into 'overflow' tanks provided. The differential pressure is augmented by the fact that sea water is denser than the oil. The discussion on the best ways of reducing pollution following an incident, continues. Spillages are only one aspect of marine pollution.

The governing regulations are those developed by the IMO, known as *MARPOL 73/78* and which became internationally accepted in 1983. They deal with the discharge of oily water, sewage, and other waste products arising from the day-to-day operation of a ship. They also control the deliberate dumping of chemicals and so on. The detailed provisions of the regulations should be consulted, but broadly the limitations imposed relating to sewage are that raw sewage may not be discharged at less than 12 nautical miles (NM) from land; macerated and disinfected sewage at not less than 4 NM; only discharge from approved sewage treatment plants is permitted at less than 4 NM. No dunnage may be dumped at less than 25 NM from land and no plastics at all. Levels of pollution from all effluents must be very low.

The rules can have a significant affect upon the layout of, and equipment fitted in, ships. Sources of waste are grouped in vertical blocks to facilitate collection and treatment. Crude oil washing of the heavy oil deposits in bulk carrier oil tanks and segregated water ballast tanks are becoming common. Steam cleaning of tanks is being discontinued. Sewage presents some special problems. It can be heat treated and then burnt. It can be treated by chemicals but the residues have still to be disposed of. The most common system is to use treatment plant in which bacteria are used to break the sewage down. Because the bacteria will die if they are not given enough 'food', action must be taken if the throughput of the system falls below about 25 per cent of capacity, as when, perhaps, in port. There is usually quite a wide fluctuation in loading over a typical 24 hour day. Some ships, typically ferries, prefer to use holding tanks to hold the sewage until it can be discharged in port.

In warships the average daily arisings from garbage amount to 0.9 kg per person food waste and 1.4 kg per person other garbage. It is dealt with by a combination of incinerators, pulpers, shredders and compactors.

SUMMARY

The interactions between the ship and the environment in which it operates have been outlined. The greatest impacts of the environment on the ship arise from the wind, waves and temperature. The apparently confused ocean surface can be represented by the summation of a large number of individually small amplitude regular waves. The energy spectrum concept is useful in representing the irregular sea surface. Formulations of such spectra have been given and sources of statistical wave data discussed. The ship motions and hull stresses induced by these waves are discussed in later chapters. The need for the ship to avoid polluting its environment is a matter of growing concern and is increasingly the subject of national and international regulation.

References

1. Froude, R. E. (1905) Model experiments on hollow versus straight lines in still water and among artificial waves. *TINA*.
2. Milne-Thomson, L. M. (1949) *Theoretical hydrodynamics*. Macmillan.
3. Lamb, H. (1965) *Hydrodynamics*, Cambridge University Press.
4. Hogben, N. (1995) Increases in wave heights over the North Atlantic: A review of the evidence and some implications for the naval architect. *TRINA*.
5. Seakeeping and Weather. RINA International Conference, London, 1995.
6. Hogben, N. and Lumb, F. E. (1967) *Ocean wave statistics*. HMSO.
7. Hogben, N., Dacunha, N. M. C. and Oliver, G. F. (1986) *Global wave statistics*. British Maritime Technology Ltd.

6 Seakeeping

In their broadest sense the terms *seakeeping* and *seaworthiness* cover all those features of a vessel which influence its ability to remain at sea in all conditions, for which it has been designed, and carry out its intended mission. They should, therefore, embrace stability, strength, manoeuvrability and endurance as well as the motions of the ship and related phenomena. In this chapter only those aspects of a ship's performance directly attributable to the action of the waves are considered. Other aspects are discussed in later chapters.

Considered as a rigid body, a ship has six degrees of freedom. They are the three rotations of *roll (or heel)*, *pitching (or trim)* and *yaw*, together with the three translations of *heave*, *surge* and *sway*. For a stable ship the motions of roll, pitch and heave are oscillatory and these are the three motions dealt with here. The other three degrees of freedom will be excited in a seaway but are of lesser importance. As the ship is flexible other degrees of freedom will be excited but these are dealt with under strength and vibration.

SEAKEEPING QUALITIES

Motions Excessive motions are to be avoided if possible. They make for discomfort of passengers and crew, make the crew less efficient and make some tasks difficult, perhaps impossible. Apart from their amplitudes the phasing of motions can have significance. Phasing generally creates an area of minimum motion about two-thirds of the length from the bow. This becomes a 'desirable' area and in a cruise liner would be used for the more important passenger spaces.

Speed and powering In waves a ship experiences a greater resistance and the propulsor is working under less favourable conditions. These combined, possibly, with increased air resistance due to wind, cause a reduction in speed for a given power. The severity of motions, slamming and wetness can usually be alleviated by decreasing speed and a master may reduce speed voluntarily for this reason on top of any enforced reduction. For many ships their schedule is of great importance. The concept of *ship routeing* can be used to avoid the worst sea conditions and so suffer less in delay, danger and discomfort and saving on fuel. Savings of the order of 10 to 15 hours have been made in this way on the Atlantic crossing. Computerized weather routeing systems are now fitted to a number of ships allowing the master greater control rather than having to rely upon instructions from shore.

Wetness The bow can dig into the waves throwing water over the forecastle. At lesser motions spray is driven over the forward part of the ship. The main factors affecting these phenomena are the relative motion of the bow and wave surface and the freeboard forward.

Slamming Sometimes the pressures exerted by the water on the ship's hull become very large and what is known as slamming occurs. Slamming is characterized by a sudden change in vertical acceleration followed by a vibration of the ship's girder in its natural frequencies. The region of the outer bottom between 10 and 25 per cent of the length from the bow is the most vulnerable area.

SHIP MOTIONS

Fundamental to an understanding of the response of a ship to the seaway are the natural periods of oscillation in the three degrees of freedom, chosen to be dealt with in this chapter. These are considered first.

Undamped motion in still water

Consider a ship floating freely in still water which is suddenly disturbed. The motion following removal of the disturbing force is that to be considered.

Rolling
If φ is the inclination to the vertical at any instant, and the ship is stable, there will be a moment acting on it tending to return it to the upright. The value of this moment will be:

$$\rho g \, \nabla \times GZ = \Delta GM_T \, \varphi \text{ for small angles.}$$

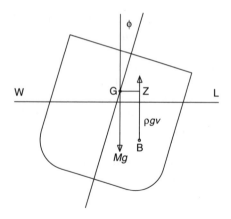

Figure 6.1 Rolling

By Newton's laws, this moment will impart an angular acceleration, such that:

$$\frac{\Delta k_x^2}{g} \frac{d^2\varphi}{dt^2} = -\Delta GM_T \, \varphi \text{ or } d^2\varphi/dt^2 + \frac{gGM_T}{k_x^2} \, \varphi = 0$$

This is the standard differential equation denoting simple harmonic motion with a period T_φ, defined by:

$$T_\varphi = 2\pi \left(\frac{k_x^2}{gGM_T}\right)^{0.5} = \frac{2\pi k_x}{(gGM_T)^{0.5}}$$

where k_x is the radius of gyration about a fore and aft axis.

This period is independent of φ and such rolling is said to be *isochronous*. The relationship holds for most ships up to angles of about 10° from the vertical. It will be noted that the greater GM_T the shorter the period. A ship with a short period of roll is said to be *stiff* and one with a long period of roll is termed *tender.* Most people find a slower motion, that is a tender ship, less unpleasant.

Pitching
This is controlled by a similar equation to that for roll. In this case:

$$T_\theta = \frac{2\pi k_y}{(gGM_L)^{0.5}} \text{ for small angles.}$$

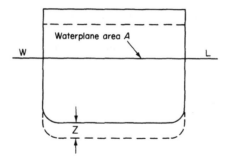

Figure 6.2 Heaving

Heaving
If z is the downward displacement at any instant there will be a net upward force on the ship, that is one tending to reduce z, which has a magnitude of $\rho g A_W z$ and the resulting motion is defined by:

$$\rho \nabla \frac{\mathrm{d}^2 z}{\mathrm{d} t^2} = -\rho g A_W z$$

where A_W is the waterplane area.

Again the motion is simple harmonic, this time of period:

$$T_z = 2\pi \left(\frac{\nabla}{g A_W} \right)^{0.5}$$

Added mass

In practice the motion of the ship disturbs the water around its hull and the overall effect is to appear to increase the mass and inertia of the ship[1]. 'Added mass' values vary with the frequency of motion but, to a first order, this variation can be ignored. Typically the effect for rolling is to increase the radius of gyration by about 5 per cent. In heaving its influence is greater and may amount to as much as an apparent doubling of the mass of the ship.

Damping

The other factor affecting the motion in still water is the damping[2]. In a viscous fluid the ship experiences a resistance to motion and damping represents the energy absorbed in overcoming this resistance. Damping is also felt because of the energy that goes into the wave system created by the ship. The simplest allowance for damping, taking rolling as a typical motion, is to assume that the damping moment varies linearly with the angular velocity. It always opposes the motion since energy is being absorbed.

Neglecting still the effects of added mass, the equation for rolling in still water becomes:

$$\frac{\Delta k_x^2}{g} \frac{d^2\varphi}{dt^2} + B \frac{d\varphi}{dt} + \Delta GM_T \varphi = 0$$

where B is a damping constant.

This has the form of the standard differential equation, $d^2\varphi/dt^2 + 2k\omega_0\, d\varphi/dt + \omega_0^2\varphi = 0$ where $\omega_0^2 = gGM_T/k_x^2$ and $k = Bg/2\,\omega_0\Delta k_x^2$ and the period of the motion is given by:

$$T_\varphi = \frac{2\pi}{\omega_0}\,(1 - k^2)^{-0.5} = 2\pi k_x \frac{(1 - k^2)^{-0.5}}{(gGM_T)^{0.5}}$$

The other modes of oscillation can be dealt with in a similar way. When damping is not proportional to the angular or linear velocity the differential equation is not capable of easy solution. For more background on these types of motion reference should be made to standard textbooks.

MOTIONS IN REGULAR WAVES

It was seen in Chapter 5 that the apparently random surface of the sea can be represented by the summation of a large number of regular sinusoidal waves, each with its own length, height, direction and phase. Further it was postulated that the response of the ship in such a sea could be taken as the summation of its responses to all the individual wave components. Hence the basic building block for the general study of motions in a seaway is the response to a regular sinusoidal wave.

For simplicity it is assumed that the pressure distribution within the wave is unaffected by the presence of the ship. This is a common assumption first made by R. E. Froude in his study of rolling and it is often referred to as *Froude's hypothesis*.

Rolling in a beam sea

The rolling a ship experiences is most severe in a beam sea. With Froude's hypothesis, the equation for motion will be that for still water with a forcing function added. This force arises from the changes in pressures acting on the hull due to the wave and could be found by integrating the pressures over the whole of the wetted surface.

The resultant force acting on a particle in the surface of a wave must act normal to the surface. If the wavelength is long compared to the beam of the ship, and it is these longer waves which will cause the more severe rolling, it is reasonable to assume that there is a resultant force acting on the ship normal to an 'effective surface', taking account of all the subsurfaces interacting with the ship. This is another useful concept proposed by Froude, who further assumed that the effective wave slope is that of the subsurface passing through the centre of buoyancy of the ship. With these assumptions and neglecting the added mass and damping, the equation of motion takes the form:

$$\frac{\Delta k_x^2}{g} \times \frac{\mathrm{d}^2\varphi}{\mathrm{d}t^2} + \Delta GM_T (\varphi - \varphi') = 0$$

where $\varphi' = \alpha \sin \omega t$, α being the maximum slope of the effective wave.

If the subscript 0 relates to unresisted rolling in still water it can be shown that the solution to the equation for resisted motion takes the form:

$$\varphi = \varphi_0 \sin (\omega_0 t + \beta) + \frac{\omega_0^2 \alpha}{\omega_0^2 - \omega^2} (\sin \omega t)$$

In this expression the first term is the free oscillation in still water and the second is a forced oscillation in the period of the wave.

When damping is present the free oscillation dies out in time, leaving the forced oscillation modified somewhat by the damping. In a truly regular wave train the ship would, after a while, roll only in the period of the wave. The highest forced roll amplitudes occur when the period of the wave is close to the natural period of roll when it is said to *resonate*. Thus heavy rolling of a ship at sea is mainly at frequencies close to its natural frequency.

Pitching and heaving in regular waves
For these motions attention is directed to head seas as these are the more severe case. It is not reasonable to assume the wave long in relation to the length of the ship and the wave surface can no longer be represented by a straight line. However the general approach of a forcing function still applies.

When a ship heads directly into a regular wave train it experiences hydrodynamic forces that can be resolved into a force at the centre of gravity and a moment about that point. As with rolling the resulting pitch and heave will be highest when the period of encounter with the waves is close to the natural period of motion in that mode. When the two periods are equal resonance occurs and it is only the action of the damping that prevents the amplitudes of motion becoming infinite. The amplitudes in practice may become quite large and in that case the master would normally change speed or course to change the period of encounter to avoid resonance. In the general study of oscillations the ratio of the periods of natural oscillation to that of the forcing function is known as the *tuning factor.* Damping, tuning factor and magnification are discussed in Chapter 11.

The amplitude of the pitching or heaving will also depend upon the height of the waves. It is usual to assume that the exciting forces are proportional to the wave height and, also, the resulting motion amplitude. This applies whilst the motions can be approximated to by a linear equation of motion.

Presentation of motion data

The presentation of motion data for a ship should be arranged so that it can be applied easily to geometrically similar ships in waves of varying amplitude. This is possible when the motions are linear, the basic assumptions being that:

(1) Translations are proportional to the ratio of linear dimensions in waves whose lengths vary in the same way. For geometric similarity the speed varies so that V^2/L is constant.

(2) Angular motions can be treated the same way bearing in mind that the maximum wave slope is proportional to wave height.

(3) All motion amplitudes vary linearly with wave height.

(4) Natural periods of motion vary as the square root of the linear dimension.

These assumptions permit the results of model experiments to be applied to the full scale ship. In watching model experiments the motion always seems rather 'rapid' because of the way period changes. Thus a $\frac{1}{25}$ scale model will pitch and heave in a period only a fifth of the full scale ship. A typical presentation of heave data is as in Figure 6.3.

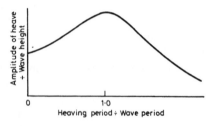

Figure 6.3 Response amplitude operators

Because wave period is related to wavelength the abscissa can equally be shown as the ratio of wave to ship length. The ordinates of the curve are known as *response amplitude operators* (RAOs) or *transfer functions.*

MOTIONS IN IRREGULAR SEAS

Usually a designer wishes to compare the seakeeping behaviour of two or more designs. If one design exhibited more acceptable response operators in all waves and at every speed of interest, the decision would be easy. Unfortunately usually one design will be superior under some conditions and another will be better under other conditions. The designer, then, needs some way of comparing designs in the generality of wave conditions.

It was seen that the energy spectrum was a very useful means of representing the nature of an irregular wave system. It is equally valuable in the study of a ship's motions in irregular seas. Before proceeding, the spectrum needs to be modified to reflect the fact that the ship is moving through the waves, whereas the wave spectra so far discussed are those recorded at a fixed point.

Period of encounter
As far as ship motions are concerned it is the period of encounter with the waves that is important rather than the absolute period of the wave. This is because the ship is moving relative to the waves and it will meet successive peaks and troughs in a shorter or longer time interval depending upon whether it is advancing into the waves or is travelling in their direction. The situation can be generalized by considering the ship at an angle to the wave crest line as shown in Figure 6.4.

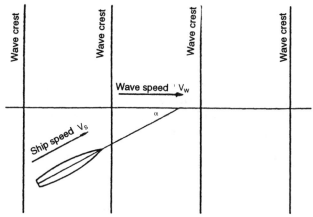

Figure 6.4 Period of encounter

Measured at a fixed point the wave period is $T_w = \lambda/V_w$. If the ship is travelling at V_s at α to the direction of wave advance, in a time T_E the ship will have travelled $T_E V_s \cos \alpha$ in the wave direction and the waves will have travelled $T_E V_w$. If T_E is the period of encounter the difference in the distances must be one wave length λ, and:

$$\lambda = T_E(V_w - V_s \cos \alpha)$$

and hence:

$$T_E = \frac{\lambda}{V_w - V_s \cos \alpha} = \frac{T_w}{1 - \dfrac{V_s}{V_w}\cos \alpha}$$

If the ship travels in the same direction as the waves the period of encounter is greater than the wave period. If it is running into the waves the period of encounter is less.

ENERGY SPECTRA

Modification of wave energy spectrum
From the expression for T_E it follows that:

$$\omega_E = \frac{2\pi}{T_E} = \omega\left(1 - \frac{V_s}{V_w}\cos \alpha\right) = \omega\left(1 - \frac{\omega V_s}{g}\cos \alpha\right)$$

If the abscissae of the 'absolute' wave spectra are multiplied by $[1 - (\omega V_s/g)\cos \alpha]$ the abscissae of what can be called an encounter spectrum are found. Ignoring any influence of the ship's presence on the waves, the area under the spectrum must remain the same, that is:

$$S(\omega_E)d\omega_E = S(\omega)d\omega \quad \text{and} \quad S(\omega_E) = S(\omega)d\omega/d\omega_E$$

$$= S(\omega)\left(1 - \frac{2\omega V_s}{g}\cos \alpha\right)^{-1}$$

So the ordinates of the spectrum must be multiplied by $[1 - (2\omega V_s/g)\cos \alpha]^{-1}$. In the case of a ship moving directly into the waves, that is $\alpha = 180°$, the multiplying factors become:

$$[1 + \omega V_s/g] \text{ for abscissae, } \quad \text{and} \quad [1 + 2\omega V_s/g]^{-1} \text{ for ordinates.}$$

Obtaining motion energy spectra
The energy spectrum for any given motion can be obtained by multiplying the ordinate of the wave encounter spectrum by the square

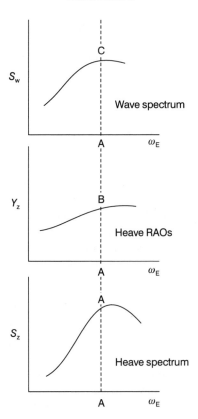

Figure 6.5 Motion energy spectrum

of the RAO for the motion concerned at the corresponding encounter frequency. Take heave as an example. If the response amplitude operator is $Y_z(\omega_E)$ for encounter frequency ω_E, then the energy spectrum for the heave motions is:

$$S_z(\omega_E) = [Y_z(\omega_E)]^2 S_w(\omega_E)$$

where $S_w(\omega_E)$ is the wave energy spectrum.

This is illustrated in Figure 6.5 where AA = (AB)^2(AC).

Having created the motion spectrum, its area can be found and various attributes of the motions deduced as they were for the wave system itself. Thus if m_{ho} is the area under the heave spectrum:

average heave amplitude   = 1.25 $(m_{ho})^{0.5}$
significant heave amplitude   = 2 $(m_{ho})^{0.5}$
average amplitude of $\frac{1}{10}$ highest heaves = 2.55 $(m_{ho})^{0.5}$

Such values as the significant motion amplitude in the given sea can be used to compare the performance of different designs in that sea. There remains the need to consider more than one sea, depending upon the areas of the world in which the design is to operate, and to take into account their probability of occurrence.

LIMITING FACTORS IN SEAKEEPING

A number of factors, apart from its general strength and stability, may limit a ship's ability to carry out its intended function[3]. Ideally these would be definable and quantifiable but generally this is not possible except in fairly subjective terms. The limits may be imposed by the ship itself, its equipment or the people on board. The seakeeping criteria most frequently used as potentially limiting a ship's abilities are speed in waves, slamming, wetness and human reactions.

Speed in waves
As the waves become more severe the power needed to propel the ship at a given speed increases. This is because of increased water and air resistance and the fact that the propulsors are working under adverse conditions. At some point the main machinery will not be able to provide the power needed and a speed reduction will be forced upon the master. The master may choose, additionally, to reduce speed to protect the ship against the harmful effects of slamming or wetness.

Slamming
Slamming is a high frequency transient vibration in response to the impact of waves on the hull, occurring at irregular intervals. The most vulnerable area is the ship's outer bottom between about 10 and 25 per cent of the length from the bow. The impact may cause physical damage and can accelerate fatigue failure in this area. For this reason this area of the outer bottom should be given special attention during survey. Slamming is relatively local and often in a big ship, those on a bridge well aft may not be aware of its severity. Because the duration of the slam is only of the order of $\frac{1}{30}$ of a second, it does not perceptibly modify the bodily motion of the ship but the ensuing vibration can last for 30 seconds. A prudent master will reduce speed when slamming badly. This speed reduction leads to less severe slamming or avoids it altogether. Often a change of direction helps. Lightly loaded cargo ships are particularly liable to slam with their relatively full form and shallow draught forward, and enforced speed reductions may be as high as 40 per cent. Slamming is less likely in high speed ships because of their finer form.

Slamming is likely when the relative velocity between the hull and water surface is large and when the bow is re-entering the water with a significant length of bottom roughly parallel to the sea surface. It is amplified if the bottom has a low rise of floor. The pressure acting in a slam can be shown to be proportional to the square of the velocity of impact and inversely proportional to the square of the tangent of the deadrise angle.

Wetness

By wetness is meant the shipping of heavy spray or green seas over the ship. The bow area is the region most likely to be affected and is assumed in what follows. It may limit a ship's speed and the designer needs some way of assessing the conditions under which it will occur and how severe it will be. To some degree wetness is subjective and it certainly depends upon the wind speed and direction as well as the wave system. In the past it was often studied by running models in waves but it is now usually assessed by calculating the relative motion of the bow and the local sea surface[3]. The assumption made is that the probability of deck wetness is the same as that of the relative motion exceeding the local freeboard. The greater the difference, the wetter the ship is likely to be.

Increased freeboard, say by increasing sheer forward is one means of reducing wetness. At sea the master can reduce wetness by reducing speed and, usually, changing the ship's heading relative to the predominant waves. Good round down on the deck will help clear water quickly. A bulwark can be used to increase the effective freeboard but in that case adequate freeing ports are needed to prevent water becoming trapped on the deck. The size of freeing ports to be fitted is laid down in international regulations. The designer would avoid siting other than very robust equipment in the area where green seas are likely. Any vents would face aft and water traps provided.

Propeller emergence

The probability of the propeller emerging from the water, as the result of ship motions, can be assessed in a similar way to wetness. That is, by calculating the motion of the ship aft relative to the local sea surface. If the propeller does emerge, even partially, it will be less effective in driving the ship. It will tend to race and cause more vibration.

Human performance

It is a common experience that ship motions can cause nausea and then sickness[4,5]. This discomfort can itself make people less efficient and make them less willing to work. Motions can make tasks physically more difficult to accomplish. Thus the movement of weights around the ship, say when replenishing a warship at sea, is made more difficult. Also tasks requiring careful alignment of two elements may become impossible without some mechanical aid. Over and above this the motions, and the drugs taken to alleviate the symptoms of motion sickness, may adversely affect a person's mental dexterity.

In broad terms the effects of motion on human behaviour depend upon the acceleration experienced and its period. The effect is most marked at frequencies between about 0.15 to 0.2 Hz. The designer can help by locating important activities in areas of lesser motion, by aligning the operator position with the ship's principal axes, providing an external visual frame of reference and providing good air quality free of odours.

OVERALL SEAKEEPING PERFORMANCE

An overall assessment of seakeeping performance is difficult because of the many different sea conditions a ship may meet and the different responses that may limit the ship's ability to carry out its function. A number of authorities have tried to obtain a single 'figure of merit' but this is difficult. The approach is to take the ship's typical operating pattern over a period long enough to cover all significant activities. From this is deduced:

(1) the probability of meeting various sea conditions, using statistics on wave conditions in various areas of the world[6];
(2) the ship speed and direction in these seas;
(3) the probability of the ship being in various conditions, deep or light load;
(4) the ship responses that are likely to be critical for the ship's operations.

From such considerations the probability of a ship being limited from any cause can be deduced for each set of sea conditions. These combined with the probability of each sea condition being encountered can lead to an overall probability of limitation.The relative merits of different designs can be 'scored' in a number of ways. Amongst those that have been suggested are:

(1) the percentage of its time a ship, in a given loading condition, can perform its intended function, in a given season at a specified speed;
(2) a generalization of (1) to cover all seasons and/or all speeds;
(3) the time a ship needs to make a given passage in calm water compared with that expected under typical weather conditions.

It is really a matter for the designer to establish what is important to an owner and then assess how this might be affected by wind and waves.

Acquiring seakeeping data

Computations of performance criteria require good data input, including that for waves, response operators and limitations experienced in ship operations.

Wave data

The sources of wave data were discussed in Chapter 5. The designer must select that data which is applicable to the design under review. The data can then be aggregated depending upon where in the world the ship is to operate and in which seasons of the year.

Response amplitude operators

The designer can call upon theory, model testing and full scale trials. Fortunately modern ship motion theories can give good values of responses for most motions. The most difficult are the prediction of large angle rolling, due to the important non-linear damping which acts, and motions in quartering seas. The equations of motion can be written down fairly easily but the problem is in evaluating the various coefficients in the equations. Most modern approaches are based on a method known as *strip theory* or *slender body theory*. The basic assumptions are those of a slender body, linear motion, a rigid and wall-sided hull, negligible viscous effects apart from roll damping and that the presence of the hull has no effect upon the waves. The hull is considered as composed of a number of thin transverse slices or strips. The flow about each element is assumed to be two-dimensional and the same as would apply if the body were an infinitely long oscillating cylinder of that cross section. In spite of what might appear fairly gross simplification, the theory gives good results in pitch and heave and with adjustment is giving improved predictions of roll. The same principles apply to calculating vibration frequencies as discussed in Chapter 11.

To validate new theories or where theory is judged to be not accurate enough, and for ships of unconventional form, *model tests* are still required.

For many years long narrow ship tanks were used to measure motions in head and following regular waves. Subsequently the wavemakers were modified to create long crested irregular waves. In the 1950s, as the analytical tools improved, a number of special seakeeping basins were built. In these free models could be manoeuvred in short and long crested wave systems. For motions, the response operators can be measured directly by tests in regular seas but this involves running a large number of tests at different speeds in various wavelengths. Using irregular waves the irregular motions can be analysed to give the regular components to be compared with the component waves.

Because the irregular surface does not repeat itself, or only over a very long period, a number of test runs are needed to give statistical accuracy. The number of runs, however, is less than for testing in regular waves. A third type of model test uses the *transient wave* approach. The wavemaker is programmed to generate a sequence of wave lengths which merge at a certain point along the length of the tank to provide the wave profile intended. The model is started so as to meet the wave train at the chosen point at the correct time. The model then experiences the correct wave spectrum and the resulting motion can be analysed to give the response operators. This method can be regarded as a special case of the testing in irregular waves. Whilst in theory one run would be adequate several runs are usually made to check repeatability.

The model can be viewed as an analogue computer in which the functions are determined by the physical characteristics of the model. To give an accurate reproduction of the ship's motion the model must be ballasted to give the correct displacement, draughts and moments of inertia. It must be run at the correct representative speed. To do all this in a relatively small model is difficult particularly when it has to be self-propelled and carry all the recording equipment. The model cannot be made too large otherwise a long enough run is not achievable in the confines of the tank. Telemetering of data ashore can help. Another approach has been to use a large model in the open sea in an area where reasonably representative conditions pertain.

Wetness and slamming depend upon the actual time history of wave height in relation to the ship. Direct model study of such phenomena can only be made by running the model in a representative wave train over a longish period. However, tests in regular waves can assist in slamming investigations by enabling two designs to be compared or by providing a check on theoretical analyses.

Then there are full scale ship trials. Some full scale data has been obtained for correlation with theory and model results. Direct correlation is difficult because of the need to find sea conditions approximating a long crested sea state during the trial period when the ship is rigged with all the measuring gear. A lot of useful statistical data, however, on the long term performance can be obtained from statistical recorders of motions and strains during the normal service routine. Such recorders are now fitted in many warships and merchant ships.

Deducing criteria

It is not always easy to establish exactly what are limiting criteria for various shipboard operations. They will depend to some extent upon the ability of the people involved. Thus an experienced helicopter pilot will be able to operate from a frigate in conditions which might prove dangerous for a lesser pilot. The criteria are usually obtained from careful questioning and observation of the crew. Large motion simulators can be used for scientific study of human performance under controlled conditions. These can throw light upon how people learn to cope with difficult situations. The nature of the usual criteria has already been discussed.

SHIP FORM AND SEAKEEPING PERFORMANCE

It is difficult to generalize on the effect of ship form changes on seakeeping because changing one parameter, for instance moving the centre of buoyancy, usually changes others. Methodical series data should be consulted where possible but in very general terms, for a given sea state:

(1) increasing size will reduce motions;
(2) increasing length will reduce the likelihood of meeting waves long enough to cause resonance;
(3) higher freeboard leads to a drier ship;
(4) flare forward can reduce wetness but may increase slamming;
(5) a high length/draught ratio will lead to less pitch and heave in long waves but increase the chances of slamming;
(6) a bulbous bow can reduce motions in short waves but increase them in long waves.

Because form changes can have opposite effects in different wave conditions, and a typical sea is made up of many waves, the net result is often little change. For conventional forms it has been found[7] that overall performance in waves is little affected by variations in the main hull parameters. Local changes can be beneficial. For instance fine form forward with good rise of floor can reduce slamming pressures.

STABILIZATION

A ship's rolling motions can be reduced by fitting a stabilization system. In principle pitch motions can be improved in the same way but in practice this is very difficult. An exception is the fitting of some form of pitch stabilizer between the two hulls of a catamaran which is relatively shorter than a conventional displacement ship. In this section attention is focused on roll stabilization. The systems may be *passive* or *active*.

Bilge keels

Of the passive systems, bilge keels are the most popular and are fitted to the great majority of ships. They are effectively plates projecting from the turn of bilge and extending over the middle half to two-thirds of the ship's length. To avoid damage they do not normally protrude beyond the ship's side or keel lines, but they need to penetrate the boundary layer around the hull. They cause a body of water to move with the ship and create turbulence thus dampening the motion and causing an increase in period and reduction in amplitude.

Although relatively small in dimension the bilge keels have large levers about the rolling axis and the forces on them produce a large moment opposing the rolling. They can produce a reduction in roll amplitude of more than a third. Their effect is generally enhanced by ahead speed. They are aligned with the flow of water past the hull in still water to reduce their drag in that state. When the ship is rolling the drag will increase and slow the ship a little.

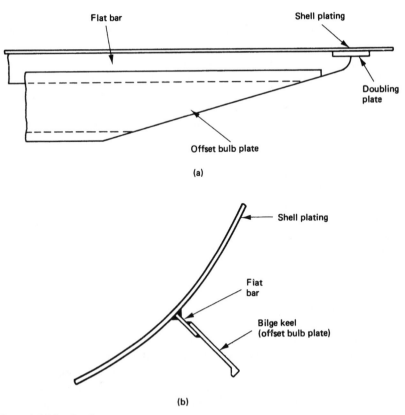

Figure 6.6 Bilge keel

Passive tanks

These use the movement of water in specially designed tanks to oppose the rolling motion. The tank is U-shaped and water moves from one side to the other and then back as the ship inclines first one way and then the other. Because of the throttling effect of the relatively narrow lower limb of the U joining the two sides of the tank, the movement of water can be made to lag behind the ship movements. By adjusting the throttling, that is by 'tuning' the tank, a lag approaching 90° can be achieved. Unfortunately the tank can only be tuned for one frequency of motion. This is chosen to be the ship's natural period of roll as this is the period at which really large motions can occur. The tank will stabilize the ship at zero speed but the effect of the tank's free surface on stability must be allowed for.

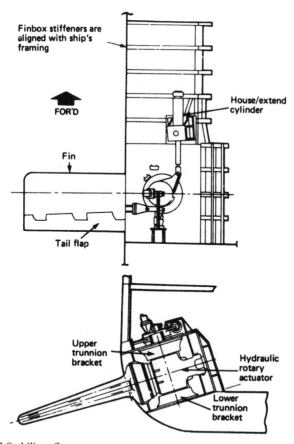

Figure 6.7 Stabilizer fin

Active fins

This is the most common of the active systems. One or more pairs of stabilizing fins are fitted. They are caused to move by an actuating system in response to signals based on a gyroscopic measurement of roll motions. They are relatively small although projecting out further than the bilge keels. The whole fin may move or one part may be fixed and the after section move. A flap on the trailing edge may be used to enhance the lift force generated. The fins may permanently protrude from the bilge or may, at the expense of some complication, be retractable, Figure 6.7.

The lift force on the fin is proportional to the square of the ship's speed. At low speed they will have little effect although the control system can adjust the amplitude of the fin movement to take account of speed, using larger fin angles at low speed.

Active tank

This is similar in principle to the passive tank system but the movement of water is controlled by pumps or by the air pressure above the water surface. The tanks either side of the ship may be connected by a lower limb or two separate tanks can be used. Figure 6.8 shows a system in which the air pressure above the water on the two sides is controlled to 'tune' the system. The air duct contains valves operated by a roll sensing device. The system can be tuned for more than one frequency. As with the passive system it can stabilize at zero ship speed. It does not require any projections outside the hull.

The capacity of the stabilization system is usually quoted in terms of the steady heel angle it can produce with the ship underway in still water. This is then checked during trials. It is possible to use modern theories to specify performance in waves but this would be difficult to check contractually.

SUMMARY

It has been shown that a ship's motions in irregular ocean waves can be synthesized from its motions in regular waves. Roll, pitch and heave responses in regular waves have been evaluated and the effects of added mass and damping discussed. The energy spectrum has been shown to be a powerful tool in the study of motions as it was in the study of waves. Factors limiting a ship's seakeeping capabilities, including the degradation of human performance, have been discussed and it has been seen how they can be combined to give an overall assessment of the probability that a ship will be able to undertake its intended

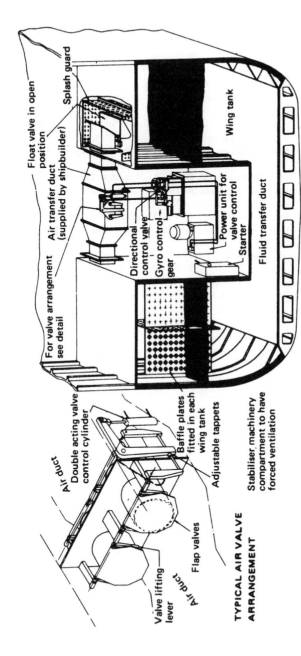

Figure 6.8 Tank stabilizer

mission. Means of limiting motions by stabilization have been outlined.

It has only been possible to deal with the subject in an elementary way. Rigorous treatments are available[8].

References

1. Lewis, F. M. (1929) The inertia of the water surrounding a vibrating ship. *TSNAME*.
2. Havelock, T. H. (1956) The damping of heave and pitch: a comparison of two-dimensional and three-dimensional calculations. *TINA*.
3. Lloyd, A. J. R. M. and Andrew, R. N. (1977) Criteria for ship speed in rough weather. *18th American Towing Tank Conference*.
4. O'Hanlon, J. F. and McCauley, M. E. (1973) Motion sickness incidence as a function of the frequency and acceleration of vertical sinusoidal motion. *Human Factors Research Inc, Technical Memorandum 1733–1*.
5. Bittner, A. C. and Guignard, J. C. (1985) Human factors engineering principles for minimising adverse ship motion effects: Theory and practice. *Naval Engineering Journal*, 97 No 4.
6. Hogben, N. and Lumb, F. E. (1967) *Ocean Wave Statistics*, HMSO.
7. Ewing, J. A., and Goodrich, G. J. (1967) The influence on ship motions of different wave spectra and of ship length. *TRINA*.
8. Lloyd, A. J. R. M. (1989) *Seakeeping. Ship behaviour in rough weather.* Ellis Horwood Series in Marine Technology.

7 Strength

Anyone who has been at sea in rough weather will be only too aware that a ship is heavily loaded and strained. It moves about quite violently and the structure groans as the parts move relative to each other. Looking at the waves causing the motion the impression is one of utter confusion. The individual will have become aware of two fundamental difficulties facing a naval architect, those of identifying the loading to which the structure is subjected and of calculating its response to that loading. The task of assessing the adequacy of a ship's structure is perhaps the most complex structural engineering problem there is. The stresses generated in the material of the ship and the resulting deformations must both be kept within acceptable limits by careful design and each element of the structure must play its part. There is generally no opportunity to build a prototype and the consequencies of getting things wrong can be catastrophic.

Many local strength problems in a ship can be solved by methods employed in general mechanical or civil engineering. This chapter concentrates on the peculiarly naval architectural problem of the strength of a hull in still water and in waves. From a consideration of the overall strength and loading of the hull it is possible to consider the adequacy of the strength of its constituent parts, the plating and grillages. The global calculations indicate stresses or strains acting in local areas to be taken into account in designing local details.

The complete structural problem is a dynamic one but, as with many other aspects of naval architecture, the situation in calm water is considered first. Even in this state the ship is subject to the forces of hydrostatic pressure and the weight of the ship and all it carries. Indeed, care is necessary when loading ships in port to ensure that the structure is not overloaded. Ships have been lost in harbour. In 1994 the OBO carrier *Trade Daring*, a ship of 145 000 dwt, broke in half while loading iron and manganese ore. Although this was a relatively old ship the lesson is there to be learnt.

A ship's ability to withstand very high occasional loading is ensured by designing to stress levels which are likely to be met perhaps only once in the life of the ship. Failures in ship structures are much more likely to be due to a combination of fatigue and corrosion. These cumulative failure mechanisms are increasingly determining the ship structure and its likely useful life span.

MODES OF FAILURE

To provide some logical progression through this difficult topic it is instructive to consider first the various ways in which a ship's structure may fail and the possible consequences. Although of rather complex make-up, the ship is essentially an elastic beam floating on the water surface and subject to a range of fluctuating and quasi-steady loads. Those loads will generate bending moments and shear forces which may act over the ship as a whole or be localized. The former will include the action of the sea. The latter will include the forces on heavy items composed of gravity forces and dynamic forces due to the accelerations imparted by the ship's motion. Then there is the thrust due to the main propulsion forces.

Failure can be said to occur when the structure can no longer carry out its intended function. If, in failing, one element merely sheds its load on to another which can withstand it there is usually no great safety problem although remedial action may be necessary. If, however, there is a 'domino' effect and the surrounding structural elements fail in their turn the result can be loss of the ship. Failure may be due to the structure:

(1) Becoming distorted due to being strained past the yield point. This will lead to permanent set and the distortion may lead to systems being unable to function. For instance, the shafts may be unable to turn.
(2) Cracking. This occurs when the material can no longer sustain the load applied and it parts. The loading may exceed the ultimate strength of the material or, more likely, failure is due to fatigue of the material.
(3) Instability. Very large deflections can occur under relatively light loads. In effect the structure behaves like a crippled strut.

The approach, then, to a study of a ship's structural strength is to assess the overall loading of the hull, determine the likely stresses and strains this engenders and the ability of the main hull girder to withstand them. Then local forces can be superimposed on the overall effects to ensure that individual elements of the structure are adequate and will continue to play their part in the total structure.

STRESSES

Whilst stress can be used as the yardstick by which to judge some aspects of failure it is not adequate for all. However it is appropriate to consider the stresses in a hull and how realistic calculations of them might be.

The first problem encountered is that due to the manufacturing process the ship has *built-in stresses*. In particular the rolling of the basic structural elements and their subsequent welding into the hull will induce strain and stress. The welding process can also introduce imperfections which act as discontinuities and cause stress concentrations, hence the importance of radiographic examination of welds to identify significant defects for remedial action. The resulting stresses can be high enough to cause local yielding of the material causing a redistribution of load locally. There will remain certain strains which are an unknown quantity but which will add to the probability of failure under extra applied loads, particularly in fatigue. Modern welding methods and greater accuracy of build geometry can reduce the levels of built-in strain but they do remain.

The next problem is the sheer complexity of the loading patterns and of the ship structure. Whilst modern research and computer methods provide an ability to deal with more and more complexity, some simplification of the load and structure is still needed. A simple example will illustrate this. Finite element analysis, which is discussed in outline later, is a very powerful tool but the finer the mesh used in way of a discontinuity, say the tip of a crack, the higher the stress obtained by calculation. In the limit it becomes infinite. Clearly some yielding will take place but the naval architect is left with the task of deciding what is acceptable. This can be determined by comparing theory with model or full scale experiments.

Traditionally the naval architect has treated the problem of overall hull strength as an equivalent static one, making fairly gross simplifications and then relying upon a comparison with the results of corresponding calculations for previously successful ships. This had the merit that although the stresses derived were nominal, and might bear no relation to the actual stresses, the new ship was likely to be satisfactory in service provided it did not differ significantly from the ships with which it was compared. The big drawback of the method was that it was a 'play safe' one. It could not tell the designer whether the new ship was grossly overdesigned or close to the limit of what was acceptable. The growing importance of ensuring structural weight is kept to a minimum has driven the naval architect to adopt more realistic design methods as they have become available. Even these, however, must be used with some caution because they cannot yet take account of every factor affecting the problem.

The study of ship strength is progressive in the sense that the designer first considers the situation in still water and then goes on to consider what happens in waves.

NATURE OF THE SHIP'S STRUCTURE

Some ships are made from glass reinforced plastics but the vast majority are of steel with possibly some aluminium in the superstructure areas. The following remarks relate to metal ships although GRP ships obey the same general principles[1]. The complete structure is composed of panels of plating, normally rectangular and supported on the four edges. They are subject to normal and in plane loads. Together with their supporting stiffeners in the two directions, a group of plating elements become a grillage which may be nominally in one plane or curved in one or two directions. Grillages are combined to create the hull, decks and bulkheads, all mutually supportive. Additional support is provided by pillars and strong frameworks, for instance hatch coamings.

Since, as will be seen, the major forces the hull must withstand are those due to longitudinal bending, the ship structure must be such that much of the material is disposed in the fore and aft direction. That is, the hull is primarily longitudinally structured, whilst taking account of transverse strength needs. The principal longitudinal elements are the decks, shell plating, inner bottom all of which are in the form of grillages, and additional longitudinal strengthening to these. The plating itself is relatively thin and the spacing of the stiffeners must be such as to prevent buckling. The transverse stiffening on decks, the *beams*, and on the side shell, the *side frames*, is usually by a variety of rolled sections. Transverse stiffening in the bottom consists of vertical plates, known as *floors*, extending from the outer to the inner bottom. Longitudinal stiffening of the bottom is by rolled section or plating called *longitudinal girders* or simply *longitudinals*. The central longitudinal keel girder is one of considerable importance. It is continuous fore and aft, extending from the flat keel to the tank top or inner bottom. Sided longitudinal girders are *intercostal.* That is, they are cut at each floor and welded to them. The resulting 'egg box' type construction of the double bottom is a very strong one and is capable of taking large loads such as those during docking and of resisting the loads caused by running aground.

Most ships now use a longitudinal system of stiffening. Most warships have used it for many years. It was adopted in some merchant ships quite early, for example in the *Great Eastern*, but then gave way to transversely framed structures. It was then adopted on a large scale in tankers and was known as the *Isherwood System*[2]. It consists of stiffening decks, side and bottom by longitudinal members the spacing being approximately equal to the spacing of beams and frames in transversely framed ships. In turn the longitudinals are supported by deep transverse members at a spacing of about 3 to 4 metres. These and the transverse bulkheads provide the necessary transverse strength.

The original Isherwood system was applied to tankers. The restriction in cargo space due to the deep transverses made it less popular for dry cargo ships. However, it is now most usual in these ships to find the decks and bottom longitudinally stiffened and the side structure transversely stiffened[3–6].

If decks, stiffened by transverse beams, were supported only at the sides of the ship, they would need to be very strong to carry the loads. Their dimensions, or *scantlings*, would become large. Introducing some support at intermediate positions reduces the span of the beams and hence their strength requirement and leads to a more efficient structure in terms of strength to weight ratio. This could be done by pillars but these restrict access in the holds. Usually heavy longitudinal members are used supported in turn by a few pillars and heavy transverse members at the hatches. The hatch end beams are themselves supported by longitudinal centreline bulkheads clear of the hatch opening. In areas which are predominantly longitudinally stiffened, deep transverse members are used for support.

Most structural elements contribute to the overall strength of the ship girder and have some local strength function as well. For instance the bottom and side shell must sustain water pressures normal to their surfaces, acting as struts with end and lateral loading. Side structure must withstand the loads due to coming alongside a jetty. Decks and bulkheads must withstand the weight of equipments mounted on them.

FORCES ON A SHIP IN STILL WATER

The buoyancy forces acting on a ship must equal in total the sum of the weight of the ship. However, over any given unit length of the hull the forces will not balance out. If the mass per unit length at some point is m and the immersed cross-sectional area is a, then at that point:

buoyancy per unit length = $\rho g a$ and
the weight per unit length = mg
Hence the net force per unit length = $\rho g a - mg$

If this net loading is integrated along the length there will be, for any point, a force tending to shear the structure such that:

Shear force, $S = \int (\rho g a - mg)\,dx$

the integration being from one end to the point concerned.

Integrating a second time gives the longitudinal bending moment. That is:

$$\textit{Longitudinal bending moment, } M = \int S\mathrm{d}x = \iint (\rho ga - mg)\,\mathrm{d}x\mathrm{d}x$$

Put the other way, load per unit length = $\mathrm{d}S/\mathrm{d}x = \mathrm{d}^2M/\mathrm{d}x^2$.

For any given loading of the ship the draughts at which it floats can be calculated. Knowing the weight distribution, and finding the buoyancy distribution from the Bonjean curves, gives the net load per unit length. Certain approximations are needed to deal with distributed loads such as shell plating. Also the point at which the net force acts may not be in the centre of the length increment used and typically the weight distribution at any point is assumed to have the same slope as the curve of buoyancy plotted against length. However, these approximations are not usually of great significance and certain checks can be placed upon the results. First the shear force and bending moment must be zero at the ends of the ship. If after integration there is a residual force or moment this is usually corrected arbitrarily by assuming the difference can be spread along the ship length. From the relationships deduced above when the net load is zero the shear force will have a maximum or minimum value and the moment curve will show a point of inflexion. Where net load is a maximum the shear force curve has a point of inflexion. Where shear force is zero, the bending moment is a maximum or minimum. Besides causing stresses in the structure the forces acting cause a deflection of the ship longitudinally. By simple beam theory it can be shown that the deflection y at any point is given by the equation:

$$EI \times \frac{\mathrm{d}^2y}{\mathrm{d}x^2} = \text{bending moment.}$$

When the ship is distorted so as to be concave up it is said to *sag* and the deck is in compression with the keel in tension. When the ship is convex up it is said to *hog*. The deck is then in tension and the keel in compression.

High still water forces and moments, besides being bad in their own right, are likely to mean high values in waves as the values at sea are the sum of the still water values and those due to a superimposed wave. The still water values can be used to determine which are likely to be stressful ship loading conditions.

The static forces of weight and buoyancy also act upon a transverse section of the ship as shown in Figure 7.1.

The result is a transverse distortion of the structure which the structure must be strong enough to resist. In addition these forces can

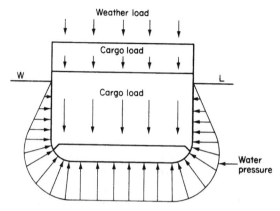

Figure 7.1 Loads on ship section

produce a local deformation of structure. The hydrostatic loads tend to dish plating between the supporting frames and longitudinals. The deck grillages must support the loads of equipment and cargo.

Thus there are three contributions made by items of structure, namely to the longitudinal, transverse and local strength. Longitudinal strength in a seaway is considered first.

FORCES ON A SHIP IN A SEAWAY

The mass distribution is the same in waves as in still water assuming the same loading condition. The differences in the forces acting are the buoyancy forces and the inertia forces on the masses arising from the motion accelerations, mainly those due to pitch and heave. For the present the latter are ignored and the problem is treated as a quasi-static one by considering the ship balanced on a wave. The buoyancy forces vary from those in still water by virtue of the different draughts at each point along the length due to the wave profile and the pressure changes with depth due to the orbital motion of the wave particles. This latter, the *Smith effect* referred to in Chapter 5, is usually ignored these days in the standard calculation to be described next. Ignoring the dynamic forces and the Smith effect does not matter as the results are used for comparison with figures from previous, successful, ships calculated in the same way.

The standard calculation is one that was used for many years. Nowadays the naval architect can extend the programs for predicting ship motion to give the forces acting on the ship. Such calculations have been compared with data from model experiments and full scale trials and found to correlate quite well.

THE STANDARD STATIC LONGITUDINAL STRENGTH APPROACH

The ship is assumed to be poised, in a state of equilibrium, on a trochoidal wave of length equal to that of the ship. Clearly this is a situation that can never occur in practice but the results can be used to indicate the maximum bending moments the ship is likely to experience in waves. The choice of wave height is important. To a first order it can be assumed that bending moments will be proportional to wave height. Two heights have been commonly used $L/20$ and $0.607(L)^{0.5}$ where L is in metres. In recent years the latter has been more generally used because it was felt to represent more closely the wave proportions likely to be met in deep oceans. Steeper waves have been used for smaller vessels operating in areas such as the North Sea. It is a matter for the naval architect to decide in the light of the intended service areas of the ship.

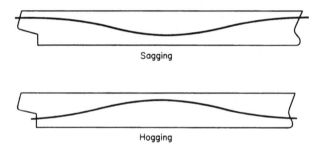

Sagging

Hogging

Figure 7.2 Ship on wave

Two conditions are considered, one with a wave crest amidships and the other with wave crests at the ends of the ship. In the former the ship will hog and in the latter it will sag. In some cases the hogging and sagging was exaggerated by modifying the mass distribution. There was little point as the calculation was a comparative one only and the resulting condition was an artificial one. It has not been done for some years. By moving the ship to various positions in relation to the wave crest the cycle of bending moment experienced by the ship can be computed.

The bending moments obtained include the still water moments. It is useful to separate the two as, whilst the still water bending moment depends upon the mass distribution besides the buoyancy distribution, the bending moment due to the waves themselves depends only on the geometry of the ship and wave.

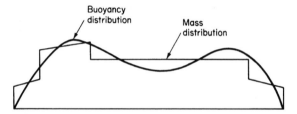

Figure 7.3 Bouyancy and mass distributions

First the ship must be balanced on the wave. This is not easy and can involve a number of successive approximations to the ship's attitude before the buoyancy force equals the weight and the centre of buoyancy is in line with the centre of gravity. One method of facilitating the process was proposed by Muckle[7]. Assume now that a balance has been obtained and the buoyancy and mass distribution curves are as shown in Figure 7.3.

If A is the cross-sectional area at any point, allowing for the wave profile, the net load per unit length at that point is $\rho g A - mg$, from which the shearing force and bending moment are:

$$F = \int (\rho g A - mg)\,dx$$

$$M = \int F\,dx = \iint (\rho g A - mg)\,dx\,dx$$

The integrals are evaluated by dividing the ship into a number of sections, say 40, calculating the mean buoyancy and weight per unit length in each section, and evaluating the shearing force and bending moment by approximate integration.

Shearing force and bending moment curves

Typical curves are shown in Figure 7.4. Both shearing force and bending moment must be zero at the ends of the ship. The shearing force rises to a maximum value at points about a quarter of the length from the ends and is zero near amidships. The bending moment curve rises to a maximum at the point where the shearing force is zero, and has points of inflexion where the shearing force has a maximum value.

The influence of the still water bending moment on the total moment is shown in Figure 7.5. For a ship with a given total mass and still water draughts, the wave sagging and hogging moments are effectively constant for a given wave. If the still water moment is changed by varying the mass distribution the total moment alters by the

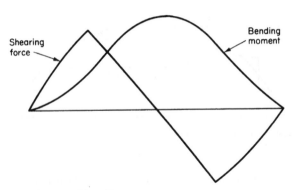

Figure 7.4 Shearing force and bending moment

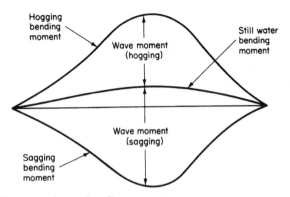

Figure 7.5 Still water and wave bending moments

same amount. Whether the greater bending moment occurs in sagging or hogging depends on the type of ship depending, inter alia, upon the block coefficient. At low block coefficients the sagging bending moment is likely to be greater, the difference reducing as block coefficient increases.

Example 7.1

Consider a vessel of constant rectangular cross section, 140 m long, 20 m beam and 13 m deep, with total mass 25 830 tonnes, 20 830 of which is uniformly spread over the length and the rest distributed uniformly over the central 10 m. Calculate the bending moments and shearing forces.

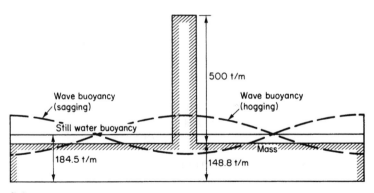

Figure 7.6

Solution

The mass distribution curve will be as in Figure 7.6 and the maximum bending moment will be at amidships.

The still water buoyancy distribution will be constant at $\dfrac{25\,830}{140} = 184.5$ t/m

The *BM* due to buoyancy $= \dfrac{25\,830}{2} \times \dfrac{140}{4} \times \dfrac{9.81}{1000}$

$$= 4434 \text{ MNm}$$

The *BM* due to weight $= \left(\dfrac{20\,830}{2} \times \dfrac{140}{4} + \dfrac{5000}{2} \times \dfrac{5}{2} \right) \times \dfrac{9.81}{1000}$

$$= 3637 \text{ MNm}$$

The net *BM* = 797 MNm sagging moment.

Suppose now that the vessel is poised on a sinusoidal wave equal to its own length and of height $0.607(L)^{0.5}$, that is a wave 140 m long and 7.2 m high. The wave height at any point above the still water level, when the wave crests are at the ends, is:

$$h = \frac{7.2}{2} \cos \frac{2\pi x}{140}$$

and:

$$\text{Buoyancy per metre} = 1.025 \times 20 \times 3.6 \times 9.81$$
$$\times 10^{-3} \cos \frac{2\pi x}{140}$$

$$= 0.724 \cos \frac{2\pi x}{140} \, \text{MN/m}$$

By integration, the wave shearing force is:

$$F = \int 0.724 \cos \frac{2\pi x}{140} \, dx$$

$$= 0.724 \times \frac{140}{2\pi} \sin \frac{2\pi x}{140} + \text{a constant.}$$

Since F is zero at $x = 0$, the constant is zero.
Integrating again the bending moment is:

$$M = \int 0.724 \times \frac{140}{2\pi} \sin \frac{2\pi x}{140} \, dx$$

$$= -0.724 \times \frac{140^2}{4\pi^2} \cos \frac{2\pi x}{140} + \text{a constant.}$$

Since $M = 0$ at $x = 0$, the constant $= 0.724 \times 140^2/4\pi^2 = 359$
and:

$$M = 359 \left(1 - \cos \frac{2\pi x}{140}\right)$$

Putting $x = 70$ the wave bending moment at amidships is found to be 718 MNm sagging. With the wave crest amidships the wave moment would be of the same magnitude but hogging. The total moments are obtained by adding the still water and wave moments, giving:

Sagging $= 797 + 718 = 1515 \, \text{MNm}$
Hogging $= 797 - 718 = 79 \, \text{MNm}$

Had the mass of 5000 tonnes been distributed uniformly over the whole ship length the still water bending moment would have been zero, giving equal sagging and hogging bending moments of 718 MNm.

The influence of small weight changes can be demonstrated by *influence lines*.

Influence lines

The ship will not often be in the condition assumed in the standard calculation. It is useful for an operator to be able to assess readily the effects on longitudinal strength of additions or removals of weight relative to the standard distribution. For small weight changes, influence lines can be used to show the effect on the maximum bending moment due to a unit weight added at any point along the length. Lines are drawn for the hogging and sagging conditions. The lines are found by taking a unit weight at some point along the length and calculating the parallel sinkage and trim this causes to the ship balanced on the wave. It can be shown that if the maximum bending moment occurs at k and the centre of flotation is at f aft of amidships respectively, the increase in maximum bending moment per unit weight can be represented by two straight lines as in Figure 7.7 in which $E = I_a/I$ and $F = M_a/A$, and M_a and I_a are the first and second moments of the area of the waterplane about an axis at the point of maximum bending moment. A and I are the area and least second moment of area of the complete waterplane.

In this approximation the centre of flotation and the point of maximum bending moment are assumed to be close, and k and f are positive if aft of amidships. The ordinate at any point in Figure 7.7 represents the increase in the maximum bending moment if small unit weight is added at that point.

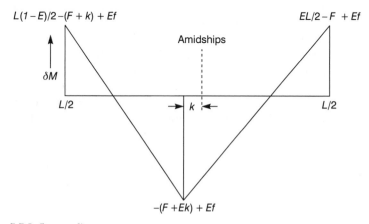

Figure 7.7 Influence lines

RESPONSE OF THE STRUCTURE

Having determined the shear forces and bending moments it is necessary to find the stresses in the structure and the overall deflection. For a beam in which the bending moment at some point x from one end is M, the stress f at z from the neutral axis of the section is given by:

$$f = \frac{Mz}{I} = \frac{M}{Z}$$

where I is the second moment of area about the neutral axis of the section at x and $Z = I/z$ is called the *section modulus*.

The maximum stresses will occur when z is a maximum, that is at the top and bottom of the section. They will be equal if the neutral axis is at mid-depth of the section.

This relationship was derived for beams subject to pure bending and in which plane sections remained plane. Although a ship's structure is much more complex, applying the simple formula has been found to give reasonable results.

Calculation of section modulus

The first section modulus to be considered is that for amidships as it is in that area that the maximum bending moments are likely. Two cases have to be considered. The first is when all the material is the same. The second is when different materials are present in the section.

To contribute effectively to the section modulus, material in the cross-section must be continuous for a reasonable length fore and aft. Typically the members concerned are the side and bottom plating, deck plating, longitudinal deck and shell stiffeners and any longitudinal bulkheads. The structure must not be such that it is likely to buckle under load and fail to take its fair share of the load. Because wide panels of thin plating are liable to shirk their load it is usual to limit the plating contribution to 70 times its thickness if the stiffener spacing is greater than this. Having decided which structural elements will contribute, the section modulus is calculated in a tabular form.

An *assumed neutral axis* (ANA) is chosen at a convenient height above the keel. The area of each element above and below the ANA, the first and second moments about the ANA and the second moments about each element's own centroid are calculated. The differences of the first moments divided by the total area gives the distance of the true NA

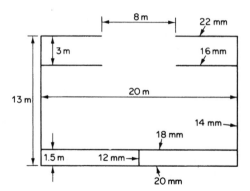

Figure 7.8

from the ANA. The second moments of area give the moment of inertia about the ANA and this can be corrected for the position of the true NA. This is illustrated for the diagrammatic cross section shown in Figure 7.8, noting that the second moments of thin horizontal members about their own centroids will be negligible.

It will be noted that material in the centre of the top two decks is not included. This is to compensate for the large hatch openings in these decks. Because of the ship's symmetry about its middle line, it is adequate to carry out the calculation for one side of the ship and then double the resulting answer. In this example the ANA has been taken at the keel.

From Table 7.1, the height of the NA
above the keel
$$= \frac{4.136}{0.799} = 5.18 \, \text{m}$$

Second moment of area of half
section about keel $= 40.008 + 2.565$ $= 42.573 \, \text{m}^4$

and about the actual
$\text{NA} = 42.573 - 0.799 \, (5.18)^2$ $= 21.163 \, \text{m}^4$

For the whole section the Z values are:

$$Z_{\text{deck}} = \frac{42.326}{7.82} = 5.41 \, \text{m}^3$$

$$Z_{\text{keel}} = \frac{42.326}{5.18} = 8.17 \, \text{m}^3$$

Table 7.1 Calculation of properties of simplified section in Figure 7.8

Item	Scantlings	Area (m²)	Lever about keel (m)	Moment about keel (m³)	Second moment (m⁴)	Second moment about own centroid (m⁴)
Upper deck	6 × 0.022	0.132	13	1.716	22.308	0
Second deck	6 × 0.016	0.096	10	0.960	9.600	0
Side shell	13 × 0.014	0.182	6.5	1.183	7.690	2.563
Tank top	10 × 0.018	0.180	1.5	0.270	0.405	0
Bottom shell	10 × 0.020	0.200	0	0	0	0
Centre girder	1.5 × 0.006	0.009	0.75	0.007	0.005	0.002
Summations		0.799		4.136	40.008	2.565

If the bending moments for this structure are those calculated in Example 7.1, the stresses can be found. The still water stresses are:

$$\text{In the deck} = \frac{797}{5.41} = 147.3 \, \text{MN/m}^2$$

$$\text{In the keel} = \frac{797}{8.17} = 97.6 \, \text{MN/m}^2$$

The wave bending stresses are:

$$\text{In the deck} = \frac{718}{5.41} = 132.7 \, \text{MN/m}^2$$

$$\text{In the keel} = \frac{718}{8.17} = 87.9 \, \text{MN/m}^2$$

This gives total stresses in the deck of 280.0 or 14.6 MN/m² compression, and in the keel stresses of 185.5 or 9.7 MN/m² tension, depending upon whether the ship is sagging or hogging.

The sagging stresses would be too high for a mild steel ship and some action would be needed. One way would be to spread the central 5000 tonne load uniformly over the whole ship length. This would reduce the stresses to 132.7 MN/m² in the deck and 87.9 MN/m² in the keel. If it was desired to increase the section modulus to reduce the stresses, the best place to add material would be in the keel or upper deck, whichever had the higher stress. That is, to add material as far from the

NA as possible. However, the change in the lower of the two original stresses must be watched. The general problem of adding material to a cross section is discussed later.

Sections with two materials

Some ships' strength cross section is composed of two different materials. Typically the hull may be steel and the superstructure aluminium. Other materials used may be wood or reinforced plastic. In such a case it is convenient to think in terms of an effective modulus in one of the materials. Usually this would be in terms of steel.

The stress, σ, in a beam at a point z from the NA is Ez/R, where R is the radius of curvature. Provided transverse sections of the beam or ship remain plane, this relationship will hold as the extension or strain at any given z will be the same. For equilibrium of the section, the net force across it must be zero. Hence using subscripts s and a for steel and aluminium:

$$\Sigma(\sigma_s A_s + \sigma_a A_a) = 0 \quad \text{and} \quad \Sigma\left(\frac{E_s A_s z_s}{R}\right) + \left(\frac{E_a A_a z_a}{R}\right) = 0$$

that is:

$$\Sigma\left(A_s z_s + \frac{E_a}{E_s}\right) A_a z_a = 0$$

The corresponding bending moment is:

$$M = \Sigma(\sigma_s A_s z_s + \sigma_a A_a z_a)$$

$$= \frac{E_s}{R} \Sigma\left(A_s z_s^2 + \frac{E_a}{E_s} A_a z_a^2\right)$$

$$= \frac{E_s I_E}{R}$$

where I_E is the effective second moment of area.

The composite cross-section can therefore be considered made up of material s, usually steel, if an effective area of material a is used in place of the actual area. The effective area is the actual multiplied by the ratio E_a/E_s. For different steels the ratio is effectively unity, for aluminium alloy/steel it is about $\frac{1}{3}$ and for grp/steel it is about $\frac{1}{10}$.

Changes to section modulus

It is often desirable to change the section modulus in the early design
stages. The effect of changes is not always immediately obvious.
Consider the addition of an element of structure above the neutral axis,
but below the upper deck, as in Figure 7.9. Assume the element is of
area a and that the original section had area A, and radius of gyration
k. With the addition of a the NA is raised by $az/(A + a) = \delta z$.

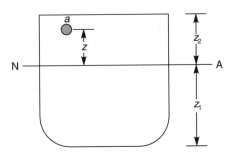

Figure 7.9 Changing section modulus

The new second moment of inertia is:

$$I + \delta I = I + az^2 - (A + a)\left(\frac{az}{A + a}\right)^2 \quad \text{and} \quad \delta I = \frac{Aaz^2}{A + a}$$

For a given bending moment, the stesses will not increase if the section
modulus is not reduced. This condition is that:

$$\frac{I + \delta I}{z + \delta z} - \frac{I}{z} \text{ is greater than zero, that is } \frac{\delta I}{I} \text{ is greater than } \frac{\delta z}{z}$$

As depicted δI is positive and $\delta z/z_2$ is negative so $\delta I/I$ is always greater
than $\delta z/z$ at the deck provided the material is added within the section.
At the keel the condition becomes:

$$\frac{Aaz^2}{Ak^2 (A + a)} \text{ must be greater than } az/z_1 (A + a) \text{ or } z \text{ must be greater}$$
than k^2/z_1

Thus to achieve a reduction in keel stress the material must be added
at a height greater than k^2/z_1 from the neutral axis.

Corresponding relationships can be worked out for material added below the neutral axis. If the new material is added above the upper deck then the maximum stress will occur in it rather than in the main deck. It can be shown that in this case there is a minimum area that must be added at any given height in order to reduce the stress in the deck.

STRESS CONCENTRATIONS

So far only the general stresses in a structure have been considered. There are several reasons why local stresses may exceed considerably those in the vicinity. The design may introduce points at which the loads in a large structural element are led into a relatively small member. It is useful in looking at a structure to consider where the load in a member can go next. If there is no natural, and even, 'flow' then a concentration of stress can occur. Some such details are bound to arise at times, in way of large deck openings for instance, or where the superstructure ends. In such cases the designer must take care to minimize the stress concentration. Well rounded corners to hatch openings are essential and added thickness of plating abreast the hatches reduces the stress for a given load. The magnitude of this effect can be illustrated by the case of an elliptical hole in an infinitely wide plate subject to uniform tensile stress across the width. If the long axis of the ellipse is $2a$ and the minor axis is $2b$, then with the long axis across the plate the stresses at the ends of the long axis will be augmented by a factor $[1 + (2a/b)]$. If the hole is circular this concentration factor becomes 3. There will be a compressive stress at the ends of the minor axis equal in magnitude to the tensile stress in the plate. In practice there is little advantage in giving a hatch corner a radius of more than about 15 per cent of the the hatch width. The side of the hatch should be aligned with the direction of stress otherwise there could be a further stress penalty of about 25 per cent.

Apart from design features built into the ship, stress concentrations can be introduced as the ship is built. Structural members may not be accurately aligned either side of a bulkhead or floor. This is why important members are made continuous and less important members are made intercostal, that is they are cut and secured either side of the continuous member. Other concentrations are occasioned by defects in the welding and other forming processes. Provided the size of these defects is not large, local redistribution of stresses can occur due to yielding of the material. However large defects, found perhaps as a result of radiographic inspection, should be repaired.

Built-in stresses

Taking mild steel as the usual material from which ships are built, the plates and sections used will already have been subject to strain before construction starts. They may have been rolled and unevenly cooled. Then in the shipyard they will be shaped and then welded. As a result they will already have *residual stresses and strains* before the ship itself is subject to any load. These built-in stresses can be quite large and even exceed the yield stress locally. Built-in stresses are difficult to estimate but in frigates[8] it was found that welding the longitudinals introduced a compressive stress of 50 MPa in the hull plating, balanced by regions local to the weld where the tensile stresses reached yield.

Cracking and brittle fracture

In any practical structure cracks are bound to occur. Indeed the build process makes it almost inevitable that there will be a range of crack-like defects present before the ship goes to sea for the first time. This is not in itself serious but cracks must be looked for and corrected before they can cause a failure. They can extend due to fatigue or brittle fracture mechanisms. Even in rough weather fatigue cracks grow only slowly, at a rate measured in mm/s. On the other hand, under certain conditions, a brittle fracture can propagate at about 500 m/s. The *MV Kurdistan* broke in two in 1979[9] due to brittle fracture. The MV *Tyne Bridge* suffered a four metre crack[10]. At one time it was thought that thin plating did not suffer brittle fracture but this was disproved by the experience of RN frigates off Iceland in the 1970s. It is therefore vital to avoid the possiblity of brittle fracture. The only way of ensuring this is to use steels which are not subject to this type of failure under service conditions encountered[11].

The factors governing brittle fracture are the stress level, crack length and material *toughness*. Toughness depends upon the material composition, temperature and strain rate. In structural steels failure at low temperature is by cleavage. Once a crack is initiated the energy required to cause it to propagate is so low that it can be supplied from the release of elastic energy stored in the structure. Failure is then very rapid. At higher temperatures fracture initiation is by growth and coalescence of voids and subsequent extension occurs only by increased load or displacement[12]. The temperature for transition from one fracture mode to the other is called the *transition temperature*. It is a function of loading rate, structural thickness, notch acuity and material microstructure.

Unfortunately there is no simple physical test to which a material can be subjected that will determine whether it is likely to be satisfactory in terms of brittle fracture. This is because the behaviour of the structure depends upon its geometry and method of loading. The choice is between a simple test like the *Charpy test* and a more elaborate and expensive test under more representative conditions such as the *Robertson crack arrest test.* The Charpy test is still widely used for quality control.

Since cracks will occur, it is necessary to use steels which have good crack arrest properties. It is recommended[11] that one with a crack arrest toughness of 150 to $200\,\text{MPa(m)}^{0.5}$ is used. To provide a high level of assurance that brittle fracture will not occur, a Charpy crystallinity of less than 70 per cent at $0°C$ should be chosen. For good crack arrest capability and virtually guaranteed fracture initiation avoidance, the Charpy crystallinity at $0°C$ should be less than 50 per cent. Special crack arrest strakes are provided in some designs. The steel for these should show a completely fibrous Charpy fracture at $0°C$.

Fatigue

Fatigue is by far and away the most common cause of failure[13] in general engineering structures. It is of considerable importance in ships which are usually expected to remain in service for 20 years or more. Even when there is no initial defect present, repeated stressing of a member causes a crack to form on the surface after a certain number of cycles. This crack will propagate with continued stress repetitions. Any initial crack-like defect will propagate with stress cycling. *Crack initiation* and *crack propagation* are different in nature and need to be considered separately.

Characteristically a fatigue failure, which can occur at stress levels lower than yield, is smooth and usually stepped. If the applied stressing is of constant amplitude the fracture can be expected to occur after a defined number of cycles. Plotting the stress amplitude against the number of reversals to failure gives the traditional *S–N curve* for the material under test. The number of reversals is larger the lower the applied stress until, for some materials including carbon steels, failure does not occur no matter how many reversals are applied. There is some evidence, however, that for steels under corrosive conditions there is no lower limit. The lower level of stress is known as the *fatigue limit.*

For steel it is found that a log–log plot of the S–N data yields two straight lines as in Figure 7.10. Further, laboratory tests[14] of a range of

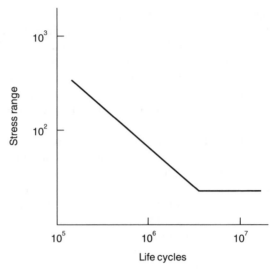

Figure 7.10 S–N curve

typical welded joints have yielded a series of log–log S–N lines of equal slope.

The standard data refers to constant amplitude of stressing. Under these conditions the results are not too sensitive to the mean stress level provided it is less than the elastic limit. At sea, however, a ship is subject to varying conditions. This can be treated as a spectrum for loading in the same way as motions are treated. A transfer function can be used to relate the stress range under spectrum loading to that under constant amplitude loading. Based on the welded joint tests referred to above[14], it has been suggested that the permissible stress levels, assuming twenty million cycles as typical for a merchant ship's life, can be taken as four times that from the constant amplitude tests. This should be associated with a safety factor of four thirds.

SUPERSTRUCTURES

Superstructures and deckhouses are major discontinuities in the ship girder. They contribute to the longitudinal strength but will not be fully efficient in so doing. They should not be ignored as, although this would 'play safe' in calculating the main hull strength, it would run the risk that the superstructure itself would not be strong enough to take the loads imposed on it at sea. Also they are potential sources of stress concentrations, particularly at their ends. For this reason they should not be ended close to highly stressed areas such as amidships.

A superstructure is joined to the main hull at its lower boundary. As the ship sags or hogs this boundary becomes compressed and extended respectively. Thus the superstructure tends to be arched in the opposite sense to the main hull. If the two structures are not to separate, there will be shear forces due to the stretch or compression and normal forces trying to keep the two in contact.

The ability of the superstructure to accept these forces, and contribute to the section modulus for longitudinal bending, is regarded as an efficiency. It is expressed as:

$$Superstructure\ efficiency\ =\ \frac{\sigma_0 - \sigma_a}{\sigma_0 - \sigma}$$

where σ_0, σ_a and σ are the upper deck stresses if no superstructure were present, the stress calculated and that for a fully effective superstructure.

The efficiency of superstructures can be increased by making them long, extending them the full width of the hull, keeping their section reasonably constant and paying careful attention to the securings to the main hull. Using a low modulus material for the superstructure, for instance GRP[15], can ease the interaction problems. With a Young's modulus of the order of $\frac{1}{10}$ of that of steel, the superstructure makes little contribution to the longitudinal strength. In the past some

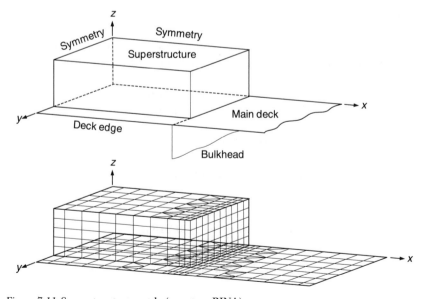

Figure 7.11 Superstructure mesh (courtesy RINA)

designers have used expansion joints at points along the length of the superstructure. The idea was to stop the superstructure taking load. Unfortunately they also introduce a source of potential stress concentration and are now avoided.

Nowadays a finite element analysis would be carried out to ensure the stresses were acceptable where the ends joined the main hull. A typical mesh is shown in Figure 7.11.

Example 7.2

The midship section of a steel ship has the following particulars:

Cross-sectional area of longitudinal material	$= 2.3\,m^2$
Distance from neutral axis to upper deck	$= 7.6\,m$
Second moment of area about the neutral axis	$= 58\,m^4$

A superstructure deck is to be added 2.6 m above the upper deck. This deck is 13 m wide, 12 mm thick and is constructed of aluminium alloy. If the ship must withstand a sagging bending moment of 450 MNm. Calculate the superstructure efficiency if, with the superstructure deck fitted, the stress in the upper deck is measured as 55 MN/m².

Solution

Since this is a composite structure, the second moment of an equivalent steel section must be found first. The stress in the steel sections can then be found and, after the use of the modular ratio, the stress in the aluminium.

Taking the Young's modulus of aluminium as 0.322 that of steel, the effective steel area of the new section is:

$$2.3 + (13 \times 0.012)0.322 = 2.35\,m^2$$

The movement upwards of the neutral axis due to adding the deck:

$$(13 \times 0.012)(7.6 + 2.6)\frac{0.322}{2.35} = 0.218\,m$$

The second moment of the new section about the old NA is:

$$58 + 0.322(13 \times 0.012)(7.6 + 2.6)^2 = 63.23\,m^4$$

The second moment about the new NA is:

$$63.23 - 2.35(0.218)^2 = 63.12\,\mathrm{m}^4$$

The distance to the new
deck from the new NA $= 7.6 + 2.6 - 0.218 = 9.98\,\mathrm{m}$

Stress in new deck
(as effective steel) $= \dfrac{450 \times 9.98}{63.12} = 71.15\,\mathrm{MN/m}^2$

Stress in deck as aluminium $= 0.322 \times 71.15 = 22.91\,\mathrm{MN/m}^2$

The superstructure efficiency relates to the effect of the super-structure on the stress in the upper deck of the main hull. The new stress in that deck, with the superstructure in place, is given as $55\,\mathrm{MN/m}^2$. If the superstructure had been fully effective it would have been:

$$\frac{450(7.6 - 0.218)}{63.12} = 52.63\,\mathrm{MN/m}^2$$

With no superstructure
the stress was $\dfrac{450 \times 7.6}{58} = 58.97\,\mathrm{Mn/m}^2$

Hence the superstructure
efficiency $= \dfrac{58.97 - 55}{58.97 - 52.63} = 62.6\%.$

Stresses associated with the standard calculation

The arbitrary nature of the standard strength calculation has already been discussed. Any stresses derived from it can have no meaning in absolute terms. That is they are not the stresses one would expect to measure on a ship at sea. Over the years, by comparison with previously successful designs, certain values of the derived stresses have been established as acceptable. Because the comparison is made with other ships, the stress levels are often expressed in terms of the ship's principal dimensions. Two formulae which although superficially quite different yield similar stresses are:

$$\text{Acceptable stress} = 77.2\left(\frac{L}{304.8} + 1\right) \text{ MN/m}^2 \text{ with } L \text{ in metres.}$$

$$= 5\left(\frac{L}{1000} + 1\right) \text{ tonf/in}^2 \text{ with } L \text{ in feet.}$$

$$\text{Acceptable stress} = 23(L)^{\frac{1}{3}} \text{MN/m}^2$$

$$= (L)^{\frac{1}{3}} \text{tonf/in}^2$$

Until 1960 the classification societies used tables of dimensions to define the structure of merchant ships, so controlling indirectly their longitudinal strength. Vessels falling outside the rules could use formulae such as the above in conjunction with the standard calculation but would need approval for this. The societies then changed to defining the applied load and structural resistance by formulae. Although stress levels as such are not defined they are implied. In the 1990s the major societies agreed, under the *International Association of Classification Societies* (IACS), a common standard for longitudinal strength. This is based on the principle that there is a very remote probability that the load will exceed the strength over the ship's lifetime.

The still water loading, shear force and bending moment are calculated by the simple methods already described. To these are added the wave induced shear force and bending moments represented by the formulae:

Hogging BM $= 0.19MCL^2BC_b$ kN m
Sagging BM $= -0.11MCL^2B(C_b + 0.7)$ kN m

where dimensions are in metres and:

$$C_b \geqslant 0.6$$

$$\text{and } C = 10.75 - \left(\frac{300 - L)}{100}\right)^{1.5} \text{ for } 90 \leqslant L \leqslant 300 \text{ m}$$

$$= 10.75 \text{ for } 300 < L < 350 \text{ m}$$

$$= 10.75 - \left(\frac{L - 350}{150}\right)^{1.5} \text{ for } 350 \leqslant L$$

M is a distribution factor along the length. It is taken as unity between $0.4L$ and $0.65L$ from the stern; as $2.5x/L$ at x metres from the stern to $0.4L$ and as $1.0 - (x - 0.65L)/0.35L$ at x metres from the stern between $0.65L$ and L.

The IACS propose taking the wave induced shear force as:

Hogging SF $= 0.3F_1 CLB(C_b + 0.7)$ kN
Sagging SF $= -0.3F_2 CLB(C_b + 0.7)$ kN

F_1 and F_2 vary along the length of the ship. If $F = 190C_b/[110(C_b + 0.7)]$, then moving from the stern forward in accordance with:

Distance from stern Length	0	0.2–0.3	0.4–0.6	0.7–0.85	1
F_1	0	0.92F	0.7	1.0	0
F_2	0	0.92	0.7	F	0

Between the values quoted the variation is linear.

The formulae apply to a wide range of ships but special steps are needed when a new vessel falls outside this range or has unusual design features that might affect longitudinal strength.

The situation is kept under constant review and as more advanced computer analyses become available, as outlined later, they are adopted by the classification societies. Because they co-operate through IACS the classification societies' rules and their application are similar although they do vary in detail and should be consulted for the latest requirements when a design is being produced. The general result of the progress made in the study of ship strength has been more efficient and safer structures.

SHEAR STRESSES

So far attention has been focused on the longitudinal bending stress. It is also important to consider the shear stresses generated in the hull. The simple formula for shear stress in a beam at a point distant y from the neutral axis is:

Shear stress $= FA\bar{y}/It$

where:

F = shear force
A = cross sectional area above y from the NA of bending

$\bar{y}$ = distance of centroid of A from the NA
I = second moment of complete section about the NA
t = thickness of section at y

The distribution of shear stress over the depth of an I-beam section is illustrated in Figure 7.12. The stress is greatest at the neutral axis and zero at the top and bottom of the section. The vertical web takes by far the greatest load, typically in this type of section over 90 per cent. The flanges, which take most of the bending load, carry very little shear stress.

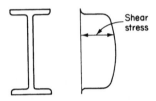

Figure 7.12 Shear stress

In a ship in waves the maximum shear forces occur at about a quarter of the length from the two ends. In still water large shear forces can occur at other positions depending upon the way the ship is loaded. As with the I-beam it will be the vertical elements of the ship's structure that will take the majority of the shear load. The distribution between the various elements, the shell and longitudinal bulkheads say, is not so easy to assess. The overall effects of the shear loading are to:

(1) distort the sections so that plane sections no longer remain plane. This will affect the distribution of bending stresses across the section. Generally the effect is to increase the bending stress at the corners of the deck and at the turn of bilge with reductions at the centre of the deck and bottom structures. The effect is greatest when the hull length is relatively small compared to hull depth.

(2) increase the deflection of the structure above that which would be experienced under bending alone. This effect can be significant in vibration and is discussed more in a later chapter.

Hull deflection

Consider first the deflection caused by the bending of the hull. From beam theory:

$$\frac{M}{I} = \frac{E}{R}$$

where R is the radius of curvature.

If y is the deflection of the ship at any point x along the length, measured from a line joining the two ends of the hull, it can be shown that:

$$R = \frac{-\left[1 + \left(\dfrac{dy}{dx}\right)^2\right]^{1.5}}{d^2y/dx^2}$$

For the ship only relatively small deflections are involved and $(dy/dx)^2$ will be small and can be ignored in this expression. Thus:

$$\frac{-d^2y}{dx^2} = \frac{1}{R} \quad \text{and} \quad M = -EI\frac{d^2y}{dx^2}$$

The deflection can be written as:

$$y = -\iint \frac{M}{EI}\,dxdx + Ax + B \quad \text{where A and B are constants.}$$

In practice the designer calculates the value of I at various positions along the length and evaluates the double integral by approximate integration methods.

Since the deflection is, by definition, zero at both ends B must be zero. Then:

$$A = \frac{1}{L}\iint_L \frac{M}{EI}\,dxdx \quad \text{and} \quad y = -\iint \frac{M}{EI}\,dxdx + \frac{x}{L}\iint_L \frac{M}{EI}\,dxdx$$

The shear deflection is more difficult to calculate. An approximation can be obtained by assuming the shear stress uniformly distributed over the 'web' of the section. If, then, the area of the web is A_w, then:

$$\text{shear stress} = \frac{F}{A_w}$$

If the shear deflection over a short length, dx, is:

$$dy = \frac{F}{A_w C} dx$$

where C is the shear modulus.

The shear deflection can be obtained by integration.

If the ratio of the shear to bending deflections is r, r varies as the square of the ship's depth to length ratio and would be typically between 0.1 and 0.2.

DYNAMICS OF LONGITUDINAL STRENGTH

The concept of considering a ship balanced on the crest, or in the trough, of a wave is clearly an artificial approach although one which has served the naval architect well over many years. In reality the ship in waves will be subject to constantly changing forces. Also the accelerations of the motions will cause dynamic forces on the masses comprising the ship and its contents. These factors must be taken into account in a dynamic analysis of longitudinal strength.

In Chapter 6 the *strip theory* for calculating ship motions was outlined briefly. The ship is divided into a number of transverse sections, or strips, and the wave, buoyancy and inertia forces acting on each section are assessed allowing for added mass and damping. From the equations so derived the motions of the ship, as a rigid body, can be determined. The same process can be extended to deduce the bending moments and shear forces acting on the ship at any point along its length. This provides the basis for modern treatments of longitudinal strength.

As with the motions, the bending moments and shear forces in an irregular sea can be regarded as the sum of the bending moments and shear forces due to each of the regular components making up that irregular sea. The bending moments and shear forces can be represented by *response amplitude operators* and energy spectra derived in ways analogous to those used for the motion responses. From these the root mean square, and other statistical properties, of the bending moments and shear forces can be obtained. By assessing the various sea conditions the ship is likely to meet on a voyage, or over its lifetime, the history of its loading can be deduced.

The response amplitude operators (RAOs) can be obtained from experiment as well as by theory. Usually in model tests a segmented model is run in waves and the bending moments and shear forces are derived from measurements taken on balances joining the sections. Except in extreme conditions the forces acting on the model in regular

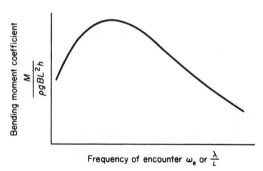

Figure 7.13 Bending moment plot

waves are found to be proportional to wave height. This confirms the validity of the linear superposition approach to forces in irregular seas. A typical plot of non-dimensional bending moment against frequency of encounter is presented in Figure 7.13. In this plot h is the wave height.

Similar plots can be obtained for a range of ship speeds, the tests being done in regular waves of various lengths or in irregular waves. The merits of different testing methods were discussed in Chapter 6 on seakeeping. That chapter also described how the encounter spectrum for the seaway was obtained from the spectrum measured at a fixed point.

The process by which the pattern of bending moments the ship is likely to experience, is illustrated in Example 7.3. The RAOs may have been calculated or derived from experiment.

Example 7.3

Bending moment response operators (M/h) for a range of encounter frequencies are:

RAO (M/h) MN	0	103	120	106	95	77	64
ω_e rad/s	0	0.4	0.8	1.2	1.6	2.0	2.4

A sea spectrum, adjusted to represent the average conditions over the ship life, is defined by:

ω_e	0	0.4	0.8	1.2	1.6	2.0	2.4
Spectrum ord, m^2/s	0	0.106	0.325	0.300	0.145	0.060	0

The bending moments are the sum of the hogging and sagging moments, the hogging moment represented by 60 per cent of the total. The ship spends 300 days at sea each year and has a life of 25 years. The average period of encounter during its life is six seconds. Calculate the value of the bending moment that is only likely to be exceeded once in the life of the ship.

Solution
The bending moment spectrum can be found by multiplying the wave spectrum ordinate by the square of the appropriate RAO. For the overall response the area under the spectrum is needed. This is best done in tabular form using Simpson's First Rule.

Table 7.2

ω_e	$S(\omega_e)$	RAO	$(RAO)^2$	$E(\omega_e)$	*Simpson's multiplier*	*Product*
0	0	0	0	0	1	0
0.4	0.106	103	10609	1124.6	4	4498.4
0.8	0.325	120	14400	4680.0	2	9360.0
1.2	0.300	106	11236	3370.8	4	13483.2
1.6	0.145	95	9025	1308.6	2	2617.2
2.0	0.060	77	5929	355.7	4	1422.8
2.4	0	64	4096	0	1	0
					Summation	31381.6

In the Table 7.2, $E(\omega_e)$ is the ordinate of the bending moment spectrum. The total area under the spectrum is given by:

$$\text{Area} = \frac{0.4}{3}\, 31381.6 = 4184.2 \, \text{MN}^2\text{m}^2/\text{s}^2$$

The total number of stress cycles during the ship's life:

$$= \frac{3600 \times 24 \times 300 \times 25}{6} = 1.08 \times 10^8$$

Assuming the bending moment follows a Rayleigh distribution, the probability that it will exceed some value M_e is given by:

$$\exp -\frac{M_e^2}{2a}$$

where $2a$ is the area under the spectrum.

In this case it is desired to find the value of bending moment that is only likely to be exceeded once in 1.08×10^8 cycles, that is its probability is $(1/1.08) \times 10^{-8} = 0.926 \times 10^{-8}$.

Thus M_e is given by:

$$0.926 \times 10^{-8} = \exp \frac{- M_e^2}{4184.2}$$

Taking natural logarithms both sides of the equation:

$$-18.5 = \frac{- M_e^2}{4184.2} \text{ giving } M_e = 278 \, \text{MNm}$$

The hogging moment will be the greater component at 60 per cent. Hence the hogging moment that is only likely to be exceeded once in the ship's life is 167 MNm.

Statistical recording at sea

For many years a number of ships have been fitted with *statistical strain gauges*. These have been of various types but most use electrical resistance gauges to record the strain. They usually record the number of times the strain lies in a certain range during recording periods of 20 or 30 minutes. From these data histograms can be produced and curves can be fitted to them. Cumulative probability curves can then be produced to show the likelihood that certain strain levels will be exceeded.

The strain levels are usually converted to stress values based on a knowledge of the scantlings of the structure. These are an approximation, involving assumptions as to the structure that can be included in the section modulus. However, if the same guidelines are followed as those used in designing the structure the data are valid for comparisons with predictions. Direct comparison is not possible, only ones based on statistical probabilities. Again to be of use it is necessary to record the sea conditions applying during the recording period. With short periods the conditions are likely to be sensibly constant. The sea conditions are recorded on a basis of visual observation related to the Beaufort scale. This was defined in the chapter on the environment but for this purpose it is usual to take the Beaufort numbers in five groups as in Table 7.3.

For a general picture of a ship's structural loading during its life the recording periods should be decided in a completely random manner. Otherwise there is the danger that results will be biased. If, for instance, the records are taken when the master feels the conditions are leading to significant strain the results will not adequately reflect the many

Table 7.3

Weather group	Beaufort number	Sea conditions
I	0 to 3	Calm or slight
II	4 to 5	Moderate
III	6 to 7	Rough
IV	8 to 9	Very rough
V	10 to 12	Extremely rough

periods of relative calm a ship experiences. If they are taken at fixed time intervals during a voyage they will reflect the conditions in certain geographic areas if the ship follows the same route each time.

The data from a ship fitted with statistical strain recorders will give:

(1) the ship's behaviour during each recording period. The values of strain, or the derived stress, are likely to follow a Rayleigh probability distribution.
(2) the frequency with which the ship encounters different weather conditions.
(3) the variation of responses in different recording periods within the same weather group.

The last two are likely to follow a Gaussian, or normal, probability distribution.

The data recorded in a ship are factual. To use them to project ahead for the same ship the data need to be interpreted in the light of the weather conditions the ship is likely to meet. These can be obtained from sources such as *Ocean Wave Statistics*[16]. For a new ship the different responses of that ship to the waves in the various weather groups are also needed. These could be derived from theory or model experiment as discussed above.

In fact a ship spends the majority of its time in relatively calm conditions. This is illustrated by Table 7.4 which gives typical percentages of time at sea spent in each weather group for two ship types. When the probabilities of meeting various weather conditions and of exceeding certain bending moments or shear forces in those various conditions are combined the results can be presented in a curve such as Figure 7.14. This shows the probability that the variable x will exceed some value x_j in a given number of stress cycles. The variable x may be a stress, shear force or bending moment.

The problem faced by a designer is to decide upon the level of

Table 7.4 Percentage of time spent at sea in each weather group.

	Weather group				
	I	II	III	IV	V
General routes	51	31	14	3.5	0.5
Tanker routes	71	23	5.5	0.4	0.1

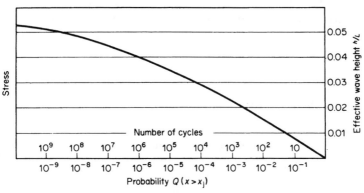

Figure 7.14 Probability curve

bending moment or stress any new ship should be able to withstand. If the structure is overly strong it will be heavier than it need be and the ship will carry less payload. If the structure is too weak the ship is likely to suffer damage. Repairs cost money and lose the ship time at sea. Ultimately the ship may be lost.

If a ship life of 25 years is assumed, and the ship is expected to spend on average 300 days at sea per year, it will spend 180 000 hours at sea during its life. If its stress cycle time is t seconds it will experience:

$$180\,000 \times 3600/t \text{ stress cycles.}$$

Taking a typical stress cycle time of six seconds leads to just over 10^8 cycles. If, in Figure 7.14 an ordinate is erected at this number of cycles, a stress is obtained which is likely to be exceeded once during the life of the ship. That is there is a probability of 10^{-8} that the stress will be exceeded. This probability is now commonly accepted as a reasonable design probability. The designer designs the structure so that the stress considered acceptable has this probability of occurrence.

Effective wave height

This probabilistic approach to strength is more realistic than the standard calculation in which the ship is assumed balanced on a wave. It would be interesting though, to see how the two might roughly compare. This could be done by balancing the ship, represented by the data in Figure 7.14, on waves of varying height to length ratio, the length being equal to the ship length. The stresses so obtained can be compared with those on the curve and an ordinate scale produced of the *effective wave height*. That is, the wave height that would have to be used in the standard calculation to produce that stress. Whilst it is dangerous to generalize, the stress level corresponding to the standard $L/20$ wave is usually high enough to give a very low probability that it would be exceeded. This suggests that the standard calculation is conservative.

Horizontal flexure and torsion

So far, attention has been focused on longitudinal bending of the ship's girder in the vertical plane. Generally the forces which cause this bending will also produce forces and moments causing the ship to bend in the horizontal plane and to twist about a fore and aft axis. The motions of rolling, yawing and swaying will introduce horizontal accelerations but the last two are modes in which the ship is neutrally stable. It is necessary therefore to carry out a detailed analysis of the motions and derive the bending moments and torques acting on the hull. Since these flexures will be occurring at the same time as the ship experiences vertical bending, the stresses produced can be additive. For instance the maximum vertical and horizontal stresses will be felt at the upper deck edges. However, the two loadings are not necessarily in phase and this must be taken into account in deriving the composite stresses.

Fortunately the horizontal bending moment maxima are typically only some 40 per cent of the vertical ones. Due to the different section moduli for the two types of bending the horizontal stresses are only about 35 per cent of the vertical values for typical ship forms. The differing phase relationships means that superimposing the two only increases the deck edge stresses by about 20 per cent over the vertical bending stresses. These figures are quoted to give some idea of the magnitude of the problem but should be regarded as very approximate.

Horizontal flexure and torsion are assuming greater significance for ships with large hatch openings such as in container ships. They are also more significant in modern aircraft carriers. It is not possible to deal with them in any simple way although their effects will be included in statistical data recorded at sea if the recorders are sited carefully.

STRENGTH OF STRUCTURAL ELEMENTS

Up to this point it is the overall loading and strength of the hull that has been considered. It was pointed out that in deciding which structure to include in the section modulus care was necessary to ensure that the elements chosen could in fact contribute and would not 'shirk' their load. In this section the loading on, and strength of, individual elements will be considered.

The basic structural element is a plate with some form of edge support. Combining the plates and their supporting members leads to grillages. Bulkheads, decks and shell are built up from grillages. Most of the key elements are subject to varying loading so that at times they will be in tension and at others in compression. Whilst a structure may be more than adequate to take the direct stresses involved, premature failure can occur through buckling in compression. This may be aggravated by lateral pressure on the plating as occurs in the shell and boundaries of tanks containing liquids.

Buckling
A structure subject to axial compression will be able to withstand loading up to a *critical load* below which buckling will not occur. Above this load a lateral deflection occurs and collapse will eventually follow. Euler showed that for an ideally straight column the critical load is:

$$P_{cr} = \frac{\pi^2 EI}{l^2}$$

where:

l = column length.
I = second moment of area of the cross section.

This formula assumes the ends of the column are pin jointed. The critical stress follows as:

$$p_{cr} = \frac{\pi^2 EI}{Al^2} = \frac{\pi^2 E}{(l/k)^2}$$

where k is the radius of gyration.

If the ends of the strut were not pin jointed but prevented from rotating, the critical load and stress are increased fourfold. The ratio l/k is sometimes called the *slenderness ratio*. For a strip of plating between supporting members, k will be proportional to the plate thickness. Thus the slenderness ratio can be expressed as the ratio of the plate span to thickness.

When a panel of plating is supported on its four edges, the support along the edges parallel to the load application has a marked influence on the buckling stress. For a long, longitudinally stiffened panel, breadth b and thickness t, the buckling stress is approximately:

$$\frac{\pi^2 E t^2}{3(1 - \nu^2) b^2}$$

where ν is the Poisson's ratio for the material.

For a broad panel, length S, with transverse stiffening, the buckling stress is:

$$\frac{\pi^2 E t^2 \left[1 + \left(\frac{S}{b}\right)^2 \right]^2}{12(1 - \nu^2) S^2}$$

The ratio of the buckling stresses in the two cases, for plates of equal thickness and the same stiffener spacing is: $4[1 + (S/b)^2]^{-2}$

Assuming the transversely stiffened panel has a breadth five times its length, this ratio becomes 3.69. Thus the critical buckling stress in a longitudinally stiffened panel is almost four times that of the transversely stiffened panel, demonstrating the advantage of longitudinal stiffening.

The above formulae assume initially straight members, axially loaded. In practice there is likely to be some initial curvature. Whilst not affecting the elastic buckling stress this increases the stress in the member due to the bending moment imposed. The total stress on the concave side may reach yield before instability occurs. On unloading there will be a permanent set. Practical formulae attempt to allow for this and one is the Rankine-Gordon formula. This gives the buckling load on a column as:

$$\frac{f_c A}{1 + C(l/k)^2}$$

where
  f_c and C are constants depending on the material
  C depends upon the fixing conditions
  A is the cross-sectional area
  l/k is the slenderness ratio.

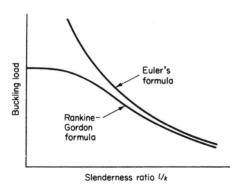

Figure 7.15 Comparison of strut formulae

The Euler and Rankine-Gordon formulae are compared in Figure 7.15. At high slenderness ratio the two give similar results. At low slenderness ratios failure due to yielding in compression occurs first.

In considering the buckling strength of grillages the strength of the stiffening members must be taken into account besides that of the plating. The stiffening members must also be designed so that they do not *trip*. Tripping is the torsional collapse of the member when under lateral load. Tripping is most likely in asymmetrical sections where the free flange is in compression. Small *tripping brackets* can be fitted to support the free flange and so reduce the risk.

Example 7.4

In Example 7.2 on the aluminium superstructure determine whether a transverse beam spacing of 730 mm would be adequate to resist buckling.

Solution
Treating the new transversely stiffened deck as a broad panel and applying Euler's equation for a strut, its buckling stress is given by the formula:

$$\frac{\pi^2 E t^2 [1 + (S/b)^2]^2}{[12(1 - \nu^2)] S^2}$$

Taking Poisson's ratio, ν, as 0.33 the critical stress is:

$$\pi^2 \times 67\,000 \times (0.012)^2 \frac{[1 + (0.73^2/13)]^2}{12[1 - (0.33)^2](0.73)^2} = 16.82\,\text{MN/m}^2$$

Since the stress in the aluminium deck is $22.91 \, \text{MN/m}^2$ this deck would fail by buckling. The transverse beam spacing would have to be reduced to about $620 \, \text{mm}$ to prevent this.

These relationships indicate the key physical parameters involved in buckling but do not go very far in providing solutions to ship type problems.

Load-shortening curves

Theoretical and experimental studies[17] show that the stiffness and strength of rectangular plate elements of an orthogonally stiffened shell are strongly influenced by imperfections including residual stresses in the structure arising from the fabrication process and initial deformations of plate and stiffener. These studies were the culmination of a large research programme involving longitudinally loaded plates with stringers b apart, between transverse frames a apart. The plate thickness was t, the radius of gyration of a stringer with a width b of plating was r and the stringer area was A_s. The stress was σ and strain ε with subscript o denoting yield. Stringers used were tee bars and flat plate. The following parameters were used:

$$\text{Plate slenderness, } \beta = \frac{b}{t} \times \left(\frac{\sigma_o}{E}\right)^{0.5}$$

$$\text{Stringer slenderness, } \lambda = \frac{a}{r\pi} \left(\frac{\sigma_o}{E}\right)^{0.5}$$

$$\text{Stiffener area ratio} = \frac{A_s}{A} \text{ where } A = A_s + bt$$

The outcome of the research was a series of *load-shortening curves* as shown in Figure 7.16. These are for a range of stringer and plate slenderness with average imperfections. Average imperfections were defined as a residual stress 15 per cent of yield and a maximum initial plate deflection of $0.1\beta^2$.

The results are sensitive to stiffener area ratio, particularly for low λ and high β, Figure 7.17, in which σ'_u is the ratio of the average compressive stress at failure over the plate and stiffener cross section to the yield stress. Peak stresses in Figure 7.16 correspond to the strengths indicated in Figure 7.17(b). Figure 7.18 shows the influence of lateral pressure on compressive strength for the conditions of Figure 7.16. The effect is most marked for high λ and increases with β. Q is the corresponding head of seawater.

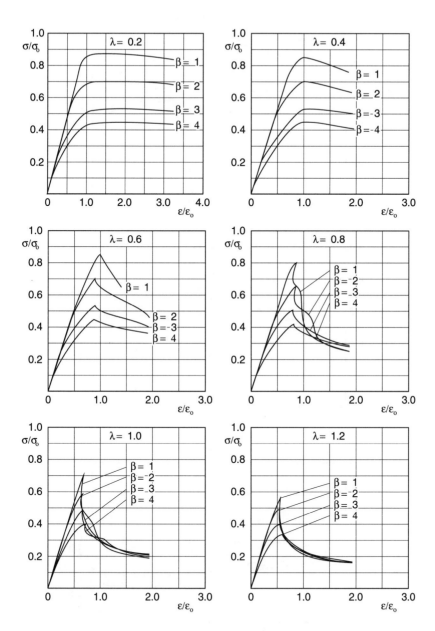

Figure 7.16 Load shortening curves (courtesy RINA[14])

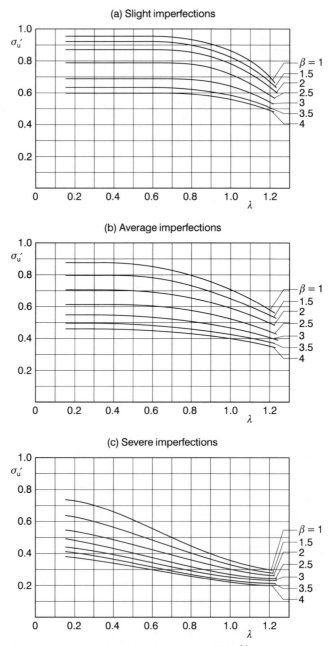

Figure 7.17 Compressive strength of panels (courtesy RINA[14])

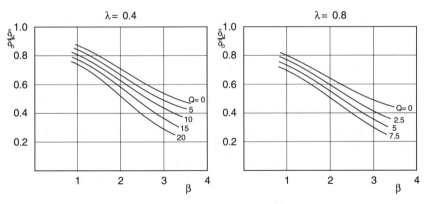

Figure 7.18 Influence of lateral pressure (courtesy RINA[14])

The importance of the load-shortening curves is that they allow a designer to establish how elements of the structure will behave both before and after collapse and hence the behaviour of the ship section as a whole. Even after collapse elements can still take some stress. However, from Figure 7.16 for λ equal to or greater than 0.6 the curves show a drastic reduction in strength post collapse. For that reason it is recommended that designs be based on λ values of 0.4 or less and β values of 1.5 or less.

Using such approaches leads to a much more efficient structure than would be the case if the designer did not allow the yield stress to be exceeded.

TRANSVERSE STRENGTH

The loads on a transverse section of the ship in waves are those calculated from the motions of the ship including the inertia and gravity forces. Additionally there may be forces generated by the movement of liquids within tanks, *sloshing* as it is termed. However, this dynamic loading in a seaway is not the complete story. The scantlings of the section must be able to withstand the loads at the waterline due to berthing and the racking strains imposed during docking.

The most satisfying approach would be to analyse the three dimensional section of the ship between main transverse bulkheads as a whole, having ascertained the boundary conditions from a global finite element analysis of the complete hull. This would be the approach adopted by those with access to the necessary computers and software. In many cases a simpler approach is needed.

For berthing loads it may be adequate to isolate a grillage in way of the waterline and assess the stresses in it due to the loads on fenders in coming alongside. In general, however, it is not reasonable to deal with side frames, decks and double bottom separately because of the difficulty of assessing the end fixities of the various members due to the presence of the others, and the influence of longitudinal stiffening. These are likely to be critical. For instance, a uniformly loaded beam, simply supported at its ends, has a maximum bending moment at its centre with zero moments at its ends. If the ends are fixed the maximum bending moment reduces by a third and is at the ends.

The usual approximation is to take a slice through the ship comprising deck beam, side frame and elements of plating and double bottom structure. This section is then loaded and analysed as a framework. The transverse strength of a superstructure is usually analysed separately but by the same technique. The frameworks the naval architect is concerned with are portals, in the superstructure, say, ship-shape rings in the main hull and circular rings in the case of submarine hulls. Transverse bulkheads provide great strength against racking of the framework. Some of this support will be transmitted to frames remote from the bulkhead by longitudinal members although these will themselves deflect under the loading as illustrated in Figure 7.19. Ignoring this support means results are likely to be conservative and should really be used as a guide to distributing structure and for

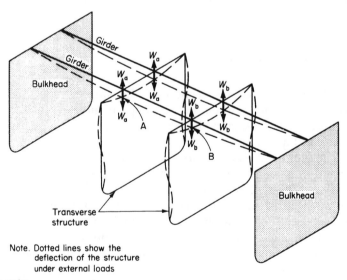

Note. Dotted lines show the
deflection of the structure
under external loads

Figure 7.19 Transverse strains

comparison with similar successful designs, rather than to obtain absolute values of stress or deflection.

It is not appropriate in this book to deal with the analysis of frameworks in detail. There are many textbooks available to which reference should be made for detailed explanations and for an understanding of all the underlying assumptions. Very briefly, however, the methods of analysis available are:

(1) *Energy methods.* These are based on the theorem of Castigliano which postulates that the partial derivative of the total strain energy with respect to each applied load is equal to the displacement of the structure at the point of application in the direction of the load.

(2) *Moment distribution methods.* This is an iterative process. All members of the framework are initially considered fixed rigidly and the bending moments at the joints calculated. Then one joint is relaxed by allowing it to rotate. The bending moment acting is distributed between the members forming the joint according to their inertias and lengths. Half the distributed moment is transmitted to a member's far end which is still held rigid. Joints are relaxed in turn and the process repeated until the moments are in balance.

(3) *Slope-deflection methods.* If M is the bending moment at some point along a beam the area under the curve of M/EI between two points on the beam gives the change in slope between those points. Further, if the moment of the curve between the points is taken about the first point, the moment gives the perpendicular distance of the first point from the tangent at the second point. By expressing the changes in deflection at the ends of portal members in terms of the applied loads and the (unknown) moments at their ends, a series of equations are produced which can be solved to give the unknown moments.

FINITE ELEMENT ANALYSIS

Mention has been made several times of finite element analysis techniques which are the basis of modern computer based analysis methods in structures and hydrodynamics. These are very powerful techniques using the mathematics of matrix algebra. In this book it is only possible to give the reader a simplified explanation of the principles involved in the method. The structure is imagined to be split up into a series of elements, usually rectangular or triangular. The corners where the elements meet are called *nodes*. For each element an

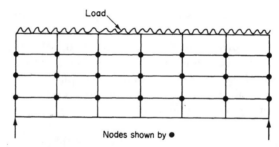

Figure 7.20 Beam finite elements

expression is derived for the displacement at its nodes. This gives strains and stresses. The displacements of adjoining elements are made compatible at each node and the forces related to the boundary forces. The applied loads and internal forces are arranged to be in equilibrium.

As an illustration, Figure 7.20 shows a plate girder supported at its ends and carrying a load. Simple beam formulae would not give accurate results if the beam is deep compared with its length. To apply finite element analysis the beam is imagined to be split into small elements as shown. These are connected only at their corners, the nodes. Distortion of the beam under load leads to forces at the nodes. The displacements at any node must be the same for each element

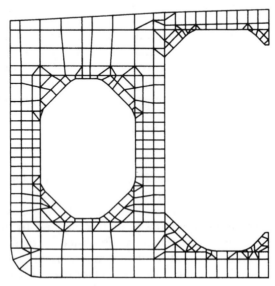

Figure 7.21 Transverse section elements

connected at that node. This condition and the boundary conditions enable the nodal forces to be calculated. The strains involved in the displacements lead to a pattern of stress distribution in the beam. The finer the mesh the more accurately the stress pattern will be represented. In a more complex structure such as that shown in Figure 7.21, elements of different shape and size can be used. Smaller elements would be used where it was suspected that the stresses would be highest and more variable.

The starting point in a comprehensive structural design approach would be a finite element analysis of the complete hull using a relatively coarse mesh. The data from this global analysis would then be used to define the boundary conditions for more limited areas which would be studied using a finer mesh.

Corrosion protection

The surface of all metalwork, inside and outside the ship, needs to be protected against the corrosive effects of the sea environment and of some of the cargoes carried. Most failures of marine structures are due to a combination of corrosion and fatigue. Both can be described as cumulative damage mechanisms. High tensile steels are as liable to corrosion as mild steel. Hence when they are used to produce a lighter weight structure, corrosion can assume even greater significance.

Types of corrosion
These can be classified as:

(1) **General corrosion.** This occurs relatively uniformly over the surface and takes place at a predictable rate.
(2) **Pitting.** Localized corrosion can occur under surface deposits and in crevices. Pits can act as stress raisers and initiate fatigue cracks, but the main concern with modern shipbuilding steels is penetration and subsequent pollution.
(3) **Differential aeration.** Debris and fouling on a surface can lead to different concentrations of oxygen which trigger local corrosion.
(4) **Galvanic action.** Sea water acts as an electrolyte so that electro-chemical corrosion can occur. This may be between different steels or even between the same steel when subject to different amounts of working or when a partial oxide film is present. In the 'cell' that is created it is the anodic area that is eaten away. A few average values of electrical potential for different metals in sea water of 3.5 per cent salinity and 25°C are listed in Table 7.5.

Table 7.5

Material	Potential (volts)
Magnesium alloy sheet	−1.58
Galvanised iron	−1.06
Aluminium alloy (5% Mg)	−0.82
Aluminium alloy extrusion	−0.72
Mild steel	−0.70
Brass	−0.30
Austenitic stainless steel	−0.25
Copper	−0.25
Phosphor bronze	−0.22

If the difference exceeds about 0.25 volts, significant corrosion of the metal with the higher potential can be expected.

(5) *Stress corrosion.* The combined action of corrosion and stress can cause accelerated deterioration of the steel and cracking. The cracks grow at a negligible rate below a certain stress intensity depending upon the metal composition and structure, the environment, temperature and strain rate. Above this threshold level the rate of crack propagation increases rapidly with stress intensity. Environment is important. The rate of crack propagation in normal wet air can be an order of magnitude higher than in a vacuum.

Protection against corrosion

Protective coatings
Painting can provide protection all the while the paint film is intact. If it becomes removed in a local area that area can become seriously pitted. Classification societies specify a comprehensive range of protective coatings for a ship's structure depending upon the spaces concerned. Typical corrosion rates[18] for different ship types against age of ship are presented in Figure 7.22.

Cathodic protection
Two methods of protecting a ship's hull are commonly used under the term *cathodic protection.* The first, a passive system, uses a sacrificial anode placed near the area to be protected. Typically this might be a piece of zinc or magnesium. The corrosion is concentrated on the anode. A more effective system, an active one, is to impress a current upon the area concerned, depressing the potential to a value below any

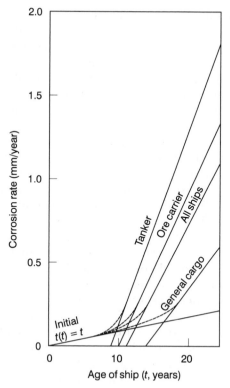

Figure 7.22 Corrosion rates (courtesy RINA)

naturally anodic area. The potential is measured against a standard reference electrode in the water. Typical current densities required to be effective are $32\,mA/m^2$ for painted steel and $110\,mA/m^2$ for bare steel, but they vary with water salinity and temperature as well as the ship's speed and condition of the hull. The system can be used to protect the inner surfaces of large liquid cargo tanks.

Monitoring off-line loads on the main hull at sea is now fairly routine with stress monitoring systems fitted to a number of bulk carriers. These systems are being developed to give the Master warning of impending structural problems and to include on-line corrosion monitoring.

STRUCTURAL SAFETY

Various modes of failure were outlined early on. A designer must evaluate the probability of failure and reduce its likelihood. First a suitable material must be chosen. For a steel ship this means a steel with adequate notch toughness in the temperatures and at the strain rates expected during service. Allowance must be made for residual stresses arising from the fabrication methods. Welding processes must be defined and controlled to give acceptable weld quality, to avoid undue plate distortion and defects in the weld. Openings must be arranged to reduce stress concentrations to a minimum. Allowance must be made for corrosion.

Even with these safeguards there will be many reasons why actual stresses might differ from those calculated. There remain a number of simplifying assumptions regarding structural geometry made in the calculations although with the modern analytical tools available these are much less significant than formerly. The plating will not be exactly the thickness specified because of rolling tolerances. Material properties will not be exactly those specified. Fabrication will lead to departures from the intended geometry. Intercostal structure will not be exactly in line either side of a bulkhead, say. Structure will become dented and damaged during service. All these introduce some uncertainty in the calculated stress values.

Then the loading experienced may differ from that assumed in the design. The ship may go into areas not originally planned. Weather conditions may not be as anticipated. Whilst many of these variations will average out over a ship's life it is always possible that a ship will experience some unusually severe combination of environmental conditions.

Using the concept of load-shortening curves for the hull elements it is possible to determine a realistic value of the ultimate bending moment a hull can develop before it fails. The designer can combine information on the likelihood of meeting different weather conditions with its responses to those conditions, to find the loading that is likely to be exceeded only once in a ship's life. However, one would be unwise to regard these values as fixed because of the uncertainties discussed above. Instead it is prudent to regard both loading and strength as probability distributions as in Figure 7.23. In this figure load and strength must be expressed in the same way and this would usually be in terms of bending moment.

In Figure 7.23 the area under the loading curve to the right of point A represents the probability that the applied load will exceed the strength at A. The area under the strength curve to the left of A represents the probability that the strength will be less than required to withstand the load at A. The tails of the actual probability distributions of load and strength are difficult to define from recorded data unless assumptions are made as to their mathematical form. Many authorities assume that the distributions are Rayleigh or Gaussian so that the tails

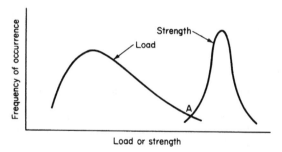

Figure 7.23 Load and strength distributions

are defined by the mean and variance of the distributions. They can then express the safety in terms of a load factor based on the average load and strength. This may be modified by another factor representing a judgement of the consequences of failure.

Having ascertained that the structure is adequate in terms of ultimate strength, the designer must look at the fatigue strength. Again use is made of the stressing under the various weather conditions the ship is expected to meet. This will yield the number of occasions the stress can be expected to exceed certain values. Most fatigue data for steels relate to constant amplitude tests so the designer needs to be able to relate the varying loads to this standard data as was discussed earlier.

SUMMARY

It has been shown how the vertical bending moments and shearing forces a ship experiences in still water and in waves can be assessed together with a limited discussion on horizontal bending and torsion of the main hull. This vertical loading was used, with estimates of the hull modulus, to deduce the stresses and deflections of the hull. The ability of the various structural elements to carry load before and after buckling was looked at leading to an ultimate load carrying capability. It has been suggested that the structure should be so designed that the maximum bending moment it can withstand is likely to be experienced only once in the life of the ship. Thus the chances of the hull failing from direct overloading are minimized. Failure, if it occurs, is much more likely to be due to a combination of fatigue and corrosion. These two cumulative failure mechanisms have been outlined. Associated with fatigue is the behaviour of steels in the presence of crack-like defects which act as stress concentrations and may cause brittle fracture below certain temperatures and at high strain rates. This highlighted the need to use notch ductile steels. The possible failure modes have been outlined and overall structural safety discussed.

References

1. Harrhy, J. (1972) Structural design of single skin glass reinforced plastic ships. *RINA Symposium on GRP Ship Construction.*
2. Isherwood, J. W. (1908) A new system of ship construction. *TINA.*
3. Murray, J. M. (1965) Notes on the longitudinal strength of tankers. *TNEC.*
4. Meek, M., Adams, R., Chapman, J. C., Reibel, H. and Wieske, P.. (1972) The structural design of the OCL container ships. *TRINA.*
5. McCallum, J. (1974) The strength of fast cargo ships. *TRINA.*
6. Yuille, I. M. and Wilson, L. B. (1960) Transverse strength of single hulled ships. *TRINA.*
7. Muckle, W. (1954) The buoyancy curve in longitudinal strength calculations. *Shipbuilder and Marine Engine Builder,* Feb.
8. Somerville, W. L., Swan, J. W. and Clarke, J. D. (1977) Measurements of Residual Stresses and Distortions in Stiffened Panels. *Journal of Strain Analysis,* Vol. 12, No 2.
9. Corlett, E. C. B., Colman, J. C. and Hendy, N. R. (1988) *KURDISTAN* – The Anatomy of a Marine Disaster. *TRINA.*
10. Department of Transport (1986). A Report into the Circumstances Attending the Loss of *MV DERBYSHIRE.* Appendix 7 Examination of Fractured Deck Plate of *MV TYNE BRIDGE.* March.
11. Sumpter, J. D. G., Bird, J., Clarke, J. D. and Caudrey, A. J. (1989) Fracture Toughness of Ship Steels. *TRINA.*
12. Sumpter, J. D. G. (1986) Design Against Fracture in Welded Structures. *Advances in Marine Structure,* Elsevier Applied Science Publishers.
13. Nishida, S. (1994) *Failure Analysis in Engineering Applications.* Butterworth-Heinemann.
14. Petershagen, H. (1986) Fatigue problems in ship structures. *Advances in Marine Structure,* Elsevier Applied Science Publishers.
15. Smith, C. S. and Chalmers, D. W. (1987) Design of ship superstructures in fibre reinforced plastic. *NA,* May.
16. Hogben, N. and Lumb, F. E. (1967) *Ocean Wave Statistics,* HMSO.
17. Smith, C. S., Anderson, N., Chapman, J. C., Davidson, P. C. and Dowling, P. J. (1992) Strength of Stiffened Plating under Combined Compression and Lateral Pressure. *TRINA.*
18. Violette, F. L. M. (1994) The effect of corrosion on structural detail design. *RINA International Conference on Marine Corrosion Prevention.*

8 Resistance

Although resistance and propulsion are dealt with separately in this book this is merely a convention. In reality the two are closely interdependent although in practice the split is a convenient one. The resistance determines the thrust required of the propulsion device. Then propulsion deals with providing that thrust and the interaction between the propulsor and the flow around the hull.

When a body moves through a fluid it experiences forces opposing the motion. As a ship moves through water and air it experiences both water and air forces. The water and air masses may themselves be moving, the water due to currents and the air as a result of winds. These will, in general, be of different magnitudes and directions. The resistance is studied initially in still water with no wind. Separate allowances are made for wind and the resulting distance travelled corrected for water movements. Unless the winds are strong the water resistance will be the dominant factor in determining the speed achieved.

FLUID FLOW

Classical hydrodynamics[1,2] leads to a flow pattern past a body of the type shown in Figure 8.1.

As the fluid moves past the body the spacing of the streamlines changes, and the velocity of flow changes, because the mass flow within streamlines is constant. Bernouilli's theorem applies and there are corresponding changes in pressure. For a given streamline, if p, ρ, v and

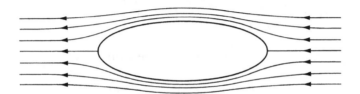

Figure 8.1 Streamlines round elliptic body

h are the pressure, density, velocity and height above a selected datum level, then:

$$\frac{p}{\rho} + \frac{v^2}{2} + gh = \text{constant}$$

Simple hydrodynamic theory deals with fluids without viscosity. In a non-viscous fluid a deeply submerged body experiences no resistance. Although the fluid is disturbed by the passage of the body, it returns to its original state of rest once the body has passed. There will be local forces acting on the body but these will cancel each other out when integrated over the whole body. These local forces are due to the pressure changes occasioned by the changing velocities in the fluid flow.

In studying fluid dynamics it is useful to develop a number of non-dimensional parameters with which to characterize the flow and the forces. These are based on the fluid properties. The physical properties of interest in resistance studies are the density, ρ, viscosity, μ and the static pressure in the fluid, p. Taking R as the resistance, V as velocity and L as a typical length, dimensional analysis leads to an expression for resistance:

$$R = f\left[L^a V^b \rho^c \mu^d g^e p^f\right]$$

The quantities involved in this expression can all be expressed in terms of the fundamental dimensions of time, T, mass, M and length L. For instance resistance is a force and therefore has dimensions ML/T^2, ρ has dimensions M/L^3 and so on. Substituting these fundamental dimensions in the relationship above:

$$\frac{ML}{T^2} = f\left[L^a \left(\frac{L}{T}\right)^b \left(\frac{M}{L^3}\right)^c \left(\frac{M}{LT}\right)^d \left(\frac{L}{T^2}\right)^e \left(\frac{M}{LT^2}\right)^f\right]$$

Equating the indices of the fundamental dimensions on the two sides of the equation the number of unknown indices can be reduced to three and the expression for resistance can be written as:

$$R = \rho V^2 L^2 f\left[\left(\frac{\mu}{\rho VL}\right)^d, \left(\frac{gL}{V^2}\right)^e, \left(\frac{p}{\rho V^2}\right)^f\right]$$

The expression for resistance can then be written as:

$$R = \rho V^2 L^2 \left[f_1\left(\frac{\mu}{\rho VL}\right), f_2\left(\frac{gL}{V^2}\right), f_3\left(\frac{p}{\rho V^2}\right)\right]$$

Thus the analysis indicates the following non-dimensional combinations as likely to be significant:

$$\frac{R}{\rho V^2 L^2}, \quad VL\frac{\rho}{\mu}, \quad \frac{V}{(gL)^{0.5}}, \quad \frac{p}{\rho V^2}$$

The first three ratios are termed, respectively, the *resistance coefficient*, *Reynolds' number*, and *Froude number*. The fourth is related to cavitation and is discussed later. In a wider analysis the speed of sound in water, α and the surface tension, σ, can be introduced. These lead to non-dimensional quantities V/α, and $\sigma/g\,\rho L^2$ which are termed the *Mach number* and *Weber number*. These last two are not important in the context of this present book and are not considered further. The ratio μ/ρ is called the *kinematic viscosity* and is denoted by v. At this stage it is assumed that these non-dimensional quantities are independent of each other. The expression for the resistance can then be written as:

$$R = \rho V^2 L^2 \left[f_1\left(\frac{v}{VL}\right) + f_2\left(\frac{gL}{Vft1^2}\right) \right]$$

Consider first f_2 which is concerned with wave-making resistance. Take two geometrically similar ships or a ship and a geometrically similar model, denoted by subscripts 1 and 2.

$$R_{w1} = \rho_1 V_1^2 L_1^2 f_2\left(\frac{gL_1}{V_1^2}\right) \quad \text{and} \quad R_{w2} = \rho_2 V_2^2 L_2^2 f_2\left(\frac{gL_2}{V_2^2}\right)$$

Hence:

$$\frac{R_{w2}}{R_{w1}} = \frac{\rho_2}{\rho_1} \times \frac{V_2^2}{V_1^2} \times \frac{L_2^2}{L_1^2} \times \frac{f_2(gL_2/V_2^2)}{f_2(gL_1/V_1^2)}$$

The form of f_2 is unknown, but, whatever its form, provided $gL_1/V_1^2 = gL_2/V_2^2$ the values of f_2 will be the same. It follows that:

$$\frac{R_{w2}}{R_{w1}} = \frac{\rho_2 V_2^2 L_2^2}{\rho_1 V_1^2 L_1^2}$$

Since $L_1/V_1^2 = L_2/V_2^2$, this leads to:

$$\frac{R_{w2}}{R_{w1}} = \frac{\rho_2 L_2^3}{\rho_1 L_1^3} \quad \text{or} \quad \frac{R_{w2}}{R_{w1}} = \frac{\Delta_2}{\Delta_1}$$

For this relationship to hold $V_1/(gL_1)^{0.5} = V_2/(gL_2)^{0.5}$ assuming ρ is constant.

Putting this into words, the wave-making resistances of geometrically similar forms will be in the ratio of their displacements when their speeds are in the ratio of the square roots of their lengths. This has become known as *Froude's law of comparison* and the quantity $V/(gL)^{0.5}$ is called the *Froude number*. In this form it is non-dimensional. If g is omitted from the Froude number, as it is in the presentation of some data, then it is dimensional and care must be taken with the units in which it is expressed. When two geometrically similar forms are run at the same Froude number they are said to be run at *corresponding speeds*.

The other function in the total resistance equation, f_1, determines the frictional resistance. Following an analysis similar to that for the wave-making resistance, it can be shown that the frictional resistance of geometrically similar forms will be the same if:

$$\frac{v_1}{V_1 L_1} = \frac{v_2}{V_2 L_2}$$

This is commonly known as *Rayleigh's law* and the quantity VL/v is called the *Reynolds' number*. As the frictional resistance is proportional to the square of the length, it suggests that it will be proportional to the wetted surface of the hull. For two geometrically similar forms, complete dynamic similarity can only be achieved if the Froude number and Reynolds' number are equal for the two bodies. This would require $V/(gL)^{0.5}$ and VL/v to be the same for both bodies. This cannot be achieved for two bodies of different size running in the same fluid.

THE FROUDE NOTATION

In dealing with resistance and propulsion Froude introduced his own notation. This is commonly called the *constant notation* or the *circular notation*. The first description is because, although it appears very odd to modern students, it is in fact a non-dimensional system of representation. The second name derives from the fact that in the notation the key characters are surrounded by circles.

Froude took as a characteristic length the cube root of the volume of displacement, and denoted this by U. He then defined the ship's geometry with the following:

$$Ⓜ = \text{length constant} = \frac{\text{wetted length}}{U}$$

$$\text{(B)} = \text{breadth constant} = \frac{\text{wetted breadth}}{U}$$

$$\text{(D)} = \text{draught constant} = \frac{\text{draught at largest section}}{U}$$

$$\text{(S)} = \text{wetted surface constant} = \frac{\text{wetted surface area}}{U^2}$$

$$\text{(A)} = \text{section area constant} = \frac{\text{section area}}{U^2}$$

In verbal debate (M) and (B) are referred to as 'circular M' and 'circular B' and so on.

To cover the ship's performance Froude introduced:

$$\text{(K)} = \frac{\text{speed of ship}}{\text{speed of wave of length } U/2}$$

$$\text{(L)} = \frac{\text{speed of ship}}{\text{speed of wave of length } L/2}$$

$$\text{(C)} = \frac{1000(\text{resistance})}{\Delta\text{(K)}^2}$$

with subscripts to denote total, frictional or residuary resistance as necessary.

Elements of form diagram

This diagram was used by Froude to present data from model resistance tests. Resistance is plotted as (C) – (K) curves, corrected to a standard 16 ft model. Separate curves are drawn for each ship condition used in the tests. Superimposed on these are curves of skin friction correction needed when passing from the 16 ft model to geometrically similar ships of varying length. The complete elements of form diagram includes, in addition, the principal dimensions and form coefficients, and non-dimensional plottings of the curve of areas, waterline and midship section.

Although Froude's methods and notation are not used nowadays, they are important because of the large volume of data existing in the format.

TYPES OF RESISTANCE

When a moving body is near or on the free surface of the fluid, the pressure variations around it are manifested as waves on the surface. Energy is needed to maintain these waves and this leads to a resistance. Also all practical fluids are viscous and movement through them causes tangential forces opposing the motion. Because of the way in which they arise the two resistances are known as the *wave-making resistance* and the *viscous* or *frictional resistance*. The viscosity modifies the flow around the hull, inhibiting the build up of pressure around the after end which is predicted for a perfect fluid. This effect leads to what is sometimes termed *viscous pressure resistance* or *form resistance* since it is dependent on the ship's form. The streamline flow around the hull will vary in velocity causing local variations in frictional resistance. Where the hull has sudden changes of section they may not be able to follow the lines exactly and the flow 'breaks away'. For instance, this will occur at a transom stern. In breaking away, eddies are formed which absorb energy and thus cause a resistance. Again because the flow variations and eddies are created by the particular ship form, this resistance is sometimes linked to the *form resistance*. Finally the ship has a number of appendages. Each has its own characteristic length and it is best to treat their resistances (they can generate each type of resistance associated with the hull) separately from that of the main hull. Collectively they form the *appendage resistance*.

Because wave-making resistance arises from the waves created and these are controlled by gravity, whereas frictional resistance is due to the fluid viscosity, it is to be expected that the Froude and Reynolds' numbers are important to the two types respectively, as was mentioned above. Because it is not possible to satisfy both the Froude number and the Reynolds' number in the model and the ship, the total resistance of the model cannot be scaled directly to the full scale. Indeed because of the different scaling of the two components it is not even possible to say that, if one model has less total resistance than another, a ship based on the first will have less total resistance than one based on the second. It was Froude who, realizing this, proposed that the model should be run at the corresponding Froude number to measure the total resistance, and that the frictional resistance of the model be calculated and subtracted from the total. The remainder, or *residuary resistance*, he scaled to full scale in proportion to the displacement of the ship to model. To the result he added an assessment of the skin friction resistance of the ship. The frictional resistance in each case was based on that of the equivalent flat plate. Although not theoretically correct this does yield results which are sufficiently accurate and Froude's approach has provided the basis of ship model correlations ever since.

Although the different resistance components were assumed independent of each other in the above non-dimensional analysis, in
practice each type of resistance will interact with the others. Thus the
waves created will change the wetted surface of the hull and the drag it
experiences from frictional resistance. Bearing this in mind, and having
discussed the general principles of ship resistance, each type of
resistance is now discussed separately.

Wave-making resistance

A body moving on an otherwise undisturbed water surface creates a
varying pressure field which manifests itself as waves because the
pressure at the surface must be constant and equal to atmospheric
pressure. From observation when the body moves at a steady speed, the
wave pattern seems to remain the same and move with the body. With a
ship the energy for creating and maintaining this wave system must be
provided by the ship's propulsive system. Put another way, the waves
cause a drag force on the ship which must be opposed by the propulsor if
the ship is not to slow down. This drag force is the *wave-making
resistance.*

A submerged body near the surface will also cause waves. It is in this
way that a submarine can betray its presence. The waves, and the
associated resistance, decrease in magnitude quite quickly with
increasing depth of the body until they become negligible at depths a
little over half the body length.

The wave pattern

The nature of the wave system created by a ship is similar to that which
Kelvin demonstrated for a moving pressure point. Kelvin showed that
the wave pattern had two main features: diverging waves on each side
of the pressure point with their crests inclined at an angle to the
direction of motion and transverse waves with curved crests intersecting
the centreline at right angles. The angle of the divergent waves to the
centreline is $\sin^{-1}\frac{1}{3}$, that is just under $20°$, Figure 8.2.

A similar pattern is clear if one looks down on a ship travelling in a
calm sea. The diverging waves are readily apparent to anybody on
board. The waves move with the ship so the length of the transverse
waves must correspond to this speed, that is their length is $2\pi V^2/g$.

The pressure field around the ship can be approximated by a moving
pressure field close to the bow and a moving suction field near the stern.
Both the forward and after pressure fields create their own wave system
as shown in Figure 8.3. The after field being a suction one creates a
trough near the stern instead of a crest as is created at the bow. The angle

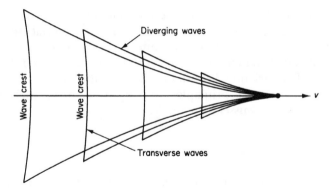

Figure 8.2 Pressure point wave system

of the divergent waves to the centreline will not be exactly that of the Kelvin wave field. The maximum crest heights of the divergent waves do lie on a line at an angle to the centreline and the local crests at the maxima are at about twice this angle to the centreline. The stern generated waves are less clear, partly because they are weaker, but mainly because of the interference they suffer from the bow system.

Interference effects
In addition to the waves created by the bow and stern others may be created by local discontinuities along the ship's length. However the qualitative nature of the interference effects in wave-making resistance are illustrated by considering just the bow and stern systems. The transverse waves from the bow travel aft relative to the ship, reducing in height. When they reach the stern-generated waves they interact with them. If crests of the two systems coincide the resulting wave is of greater magnitude than either because their energies combine. If the crest of one coincides with a trough in the other the resultant energy

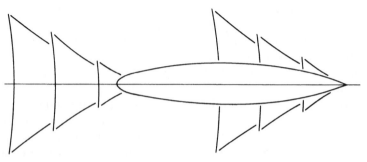

Figure 8.3 Bow and stern wave systems

will be less. Whilst it is convenient to picture two wave systems interacting, in fact the bow wave system modifies the pressure field around the stern so that the waves it generates are altered. Both wave systems are moving with the ship and will have the same lengths. As ship speed increases the wavelengths increase so there will be times when crests combine and others when crest and trough become coincident. The ship will suffer more or less resistance depending upon whether the two waves augment each other or partially cancel each other out. This leads to a series of *humps and hollows* in the resistance curve, relative to a smoothly increasing curve, as speed increases. This is shown in Figure 8.4.

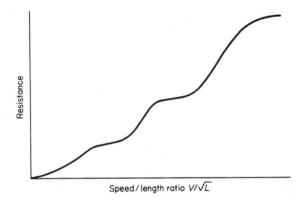

Figure 8.4 Humps and hollows in resistance curve

This effect was shown experimentally by Froude[3] by testing models with varying lengths of parallel middle body but the same forward and after ends. Figure 8.5 illustrates some of these early results. The residuary resistance was taken as the total measured resistance less a calculated skin friction resistance.

Now the distance between the two pressure systems is approximately $0.9L$. The condition therefore that a crest or trough from the bow system should coincide with the first stern trough is:

$$V^2/0.9L = g/N\pi$$

The troughs will coincide when N is an odd integer and for even values of N a crest from the bow coincides with the stern trough. The most pronounced hump occurs when $N = 1$ and this hump is termed the *main hump*. The hump at $N = 3$ is often called the *prismatic hump* as it is greatly affected by the ship's prismatic coefficient.

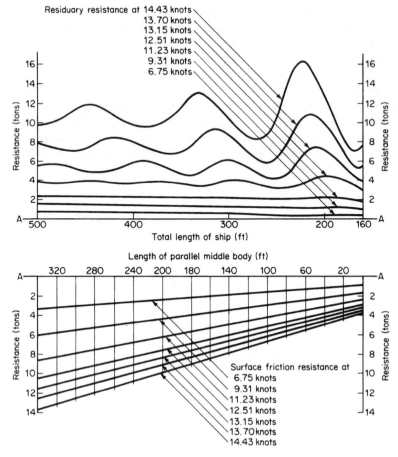

Figure 8.5 Resistance curves

Scaling wave-making resistance

It has been shown that for geometrically similar bodies moving at corresponding speeds, the wave pattern generated is similar and the wave-making resistance can be taken as proportional to the displacements of the bodies concerned. This assumes that wave-making was unaffected by the viscosity and this is the usual assumption made in studies of this sort. In fact there will be some viscosity but its major effects will be confined to the boundary layer. To a first order then, the effect of viscosity on wave-making resistance can be regarded as that of modifying the hull shape in conformity with the boundary layer addition. These effects are relatively more pronounced at model scale than the full scale which means there is some scale effect on wave-making resistance. For the purposes of this book this is ignored.

Frictional resistance

Water is viscous and the conditions for dynamic similarity are geometric similarity and constancy of Reynolds' number. Due to the viscosity the particles immediately adjacent to the hull adhere to it and move at the speed of the ship. At a distance from the hull the water is at rest. There is a velocity gradient which is greatest close to the hull. The volume of water which moves with the body is known as the *boundary layer*. Its thickness is usually defined as the distance from the hull at which the water velocity is 1 per cent of the ship speed.

Frictional resistance is associated with Reynolds because of the study he made of flow through pipes. He showed that there are two distinct types of flow. In the first, *laminar flow*, each fluid particle follows its own streamlined path with no mass transfer between adjacent layers. This flow only occurs at relatively low Reynolds' numbers. At higher numbers the steady flow pattern breaks down and is replaced by a more confused flow pattern called *turbulent flow*.

Reynolds showed that different laws of resistance applied to the two flow types. Further, if care was taken to ensure that the fluid entered the mouth of the pipe smoothly the flow started off as laminar but at some distance along the tube changed to turbulent. This occurred at a critical velocity dependent upon the pipe diameter and the fluid viscosity. For different pipe diameters, d, the critical velocity, V_c, was such that $V_c d/\nu$ was constant. Below the critical velocity, resistance to flow was proportional to the velocity of flow. As velocity increased above the critical value there was an unstable region where the resistance appeared to obey no simple law. At higher velocity again the flow was fully turbulent and resistance became proportional to V raised to the power 1.723.

Reynolds' work related to pipes but qualitatively the conclusions are relevant to ships. There are two flow regimes, laminar and turbulent. The change from one to the other depends on the *critical Reynolds' number* and different resistance laws apply.

Calculations have been made for laminar flow past a flat surface, length L and wetted surface area S, and these lead to a formula developed by Blassius, as:

$$\textit{Specific resistance coefficient} = \frac{R_f}{\frac{1}{2}\rho S V^2} = 1.327 \left(\frac{VL}{\nu}\right)^{-0.5}$$

Plotting the values of C_f against Reynolds' number together with results for turbulent flow past flat surfaces gives Figure 8.6.

In line with Reynolds' conclusions the resistance at higher numbers is turbulent and resistance is higher. The critical Reynolds' number at

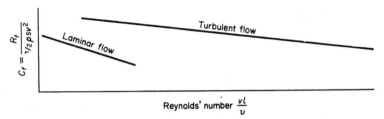

Figure 8.6 Laminar and turbulent flow

which breakdown of laminar flow occurs depends upon the smoothness of the surface and the initial turbulence present in the fluid. For a smooth flat plate it occurs at a Reynolds' number between 3×10^5 and 10^6. In turbulent flow the boundary layer still exists but in this case, besides the molecular friction force there is an interaction due to momentum transfer of fluid masses between adjacent layers. The *transition* from one type of flow to the other is a matter of stability of flow. At low Reynolds' numbers, disturbances die out and the flow is stable. At the critical value the laminar flow becomes unstable and the slightest disturbance will create turbulence. The critical Reynolds' number for a flat plate is a function of the distance, l, from the leading edge and is given by:

Critical Reynolds' number = Vl/v

Ahead of the point defined by l the flow is laminar. At l transition begins and after a *transition region* turbulence is fully established. For a flat plate the critical Reynolds' number is about 10^6. A curved surface is subject to a pressure gradient and this has a marked affect on transition. Where pressure is decreasing transition is delayed. The thickness of the turbulent boundary layer is given by:

$$\frac{\delta x}{L} = 0.37 \, (R_L)^{-0.2}$$

where L is the distance from the leading edge and R_L is the corresponding Reynolds' number.

Even in turbulent flow the fluid particles in contact with the surface are at rest relative to the surface. There exists a very thin *laminar sub-layer*. Although thin, it is important as a body appears smooth if the surface roughness does not project through this sub-layer. Such a body is said to be *hydraulically smooth*.

The existence of two flow regimes is important for model tests conducted to determine a ship's resistance. If the model is too small it may be running in the region of mixed flow. The ship obviously has turbulent flow over the hull. If the model flow was completely laminar this could be allowed for by calculation. However this is unlikely and the small model would more probably have laminar flow forward turning to turbulent flow at some point along its length. To remove this possibility models are fitted with some form of *turbulence stimulation* at the bow. This may be a trip wire, a strip of sandpaper or a line of studs.

Frictional resistance experiments

William Froude carried out the first important experiments in the early 1870s, using a series of planks with different surface roughnesses. He tried fitting the results with a formula such as:

$$R_f = fSV^n$$

where f and n were empirical constants.

He found that both f and n depended upon the nature of the surface. For very rough surfaces n tended towards 2. The value of f reduced with increasing length. For smooth surfaces, at least, n tended to decline with increasing length.

Later his son proposed:

$$R_f = fSV^{1.825}$$

in conjunction with f values as in Table 8.1.

The f values in Table 8.1 apply to a wax surface for a model and a freshly painted surface for a full scale ship.

Within the limits of experimental error, the values of f in the above formula, can be replaced by:

$$f = 0.00871 + \frac{0.053}{8.8 + L}$$

where R_f is in lbf, l in ft, S in ft^2 and V in knots, or:

$$f = 1.365 + \frac{2.530}{2.68 + L}$$

where R_f is in newtons, l in m, S in m^2 and V in m/s.

Table 8.1 R. E. Froude's skin friction constants. f values (metric units): frictional resistance $= fSV^{1.825}$, newtons; wetted surface, S, in metres; ship speed, V, in m/s. Values are for salt water. Values in fresh water may be obtained by multiplying by 0.975

Length (m)	f	Length (m)	f	Length (m)	f
2	1.966	18	1.526	70	1.441
3	1.867	20	1.515	80	1.437
4	1.791	22	1.506	90	1.432
5	1.736	24	1.499	100	1.428
6	1.696	26	1.492	120	1.421
7	1.667	28	1.487	140	1.415
8	1.643	30	1.482	160	1.410
9	1.622	35	1.472	180	1.404
10	1.604	40	1.464	200	1.399
12	1.577	45	1.459	250	1.389
14	1.556	50	1.454	300	1.380
16	1.539	60	1.447	350	1.373

Alternative formulations of frictional resistance

Dimensional analysis suggests that the resistance can be expressed as:

$$C_f = \frac{R_f}{\frac{1}{2}\rho SV^2} = F\left(\frac{vL}{V}\right)$$

Later approaches to the resistance of ships have used this type of formula. The function of Reynolds' number has still to be determined by experiment. Schoenherr[4] developed a formula, based on all the available experimental data, in the form:

$$\frac{0.242}{(C_f)^{0.5}} = \log_{10}(R_n\, C_f)$$

from which Figure 8.7 is plotted.

In 1957 the International Towing Tank Conference (ITTC)[5] adopted a *model-ship correlation line*, based on:

$$C_f = \frac{R_f}{\frac{1}{2}\rho SV^2} = \frac{0.075}{(\log_{10}R_n - 2)^2}$$

The term correlation line was used deliberately in recognition of the fact that the extrapolation from model to full scale is not governed solely by the variation in skin friction. C_f values from Schoenherr and the ITTC line are compared in Figure 8.8 and Table 8.2.

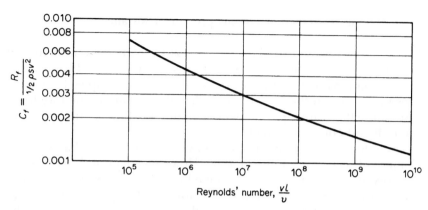

Figure 8.7 Schoenherr line

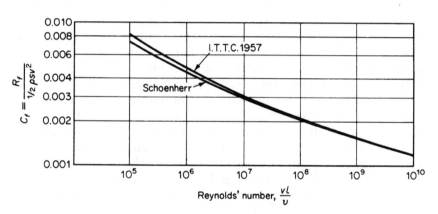

Figure 8.8 Comparison of Schoenherr and ITTC 1957 lines

Table 8.2 Comparison of coefficients from Schoenherr and ITTC formulae

Reynolds' number	*Schoenherr*	*ITTC 1957*
10^6	0.00441	0.004688
10^7	0.00293	0.003000
10^8	0.00207	0.002083
10^9	0.00153	0.001531
10^{10}	0.00117	0.001172

Eddy making resistance or viscous pressure resistance

In a non-viscous fluid the lines of flow past a body close in behind it creating pressures which balance out those acting on the forward part of the body. With viscosity, this does not happen completely and the pressure forces on the after body are less than those on the fore body. Also where there are rapid changes of section the flow breaks away from the hull and eddies are created.

The effects can be minimized by *streamlining* the body shape so that changes of section are more gradual. However, a typical ship has many features which are likely to generate eddies. Transom sterns and stern frames are examples. Other eddy creators can be appendages such as the bilge keels, rudders and so on. Bilge keels are aligned with the smooth water flow lines, as determined in a circulating water channel, to minimize the effect. At other loadings and when the ship is in waves the bilge keels are likely to create eddies. Similarly rudders are made as streamlined as possible and breakdown of flow around them is delayed by this means until they are put over to fairly large angles. In multi-shaft ships the shaft bracket arms are produced with streamlined sections and are aligned with the local flow. This is important not only for resistance but to improve the flow of water into the propellers.

Flow break away can occur on an apparently well rounded form. This is due to the velocity and pressure distribution in the boundary layer. The velocity increases where the pressure decreases and vice versa. Bearing in mind that the water is already moving slowly close into the hull, the pressure increase towards the stern can bring the water to a standstill or even cause a reverse flow to occur. That is the water begins to move ahead relative to the ship. Under these conditions separation occurs. The effect is more pronounced with steep pressure gradients which are associated with full forms.

Appendage resistance

Appendages include rudders, bilge keels, shaft brackets and bossings, and stabilizers. Each appendage has its own characteristic length and therefore, if attached to the model, would be running at an effective Reynolds' number different from that of the main model. Thus, although obeying the same scaling laws, its resistance would scale differently to the full scale. That is why resistance models are run naked. This means that some allowance must be made for the resistance of appendages to give the total ship resistance. The allowances can be obtained by testing appendages separately and scaling to the ship. Fortunately the overall additions are generally relatively small, say 10 to 15 per cent of the hull resistance, and errors in their assessment are not likely to be critical.

Wind resistance

In conditions of no natural wind the air resistance is likely to be small in relation to the water resistance. When a wind is blowing the fore and aft resistance force will depend upon its direction and speed. If coming from directly ahead the relative velocity will be the sum of wind and ship speed. The resistance force will be proportional to the square of this relative velocity. Work at the National Physical Laboratory[6] introduced the concept of an *ahead resistance coefficient* (ARC) defined by:

$$\text{ARC} = \frac{\text{fore and aft component of wind resistance}}{\frac{1}{2}\rho V_R^2 A_T}$$

where V_R is the relative velocity and A_T is the transverse cross section area.

For a tanker, the ARC values ranged from 0.7 in the light condition to 0.85 in the loaded condition and were sensibly steady for winds from ahead and up to 50° off the bow. For winds astern and up to 40° off the stern the values were −0.6 to −0.7. Between 50° off the bow and 40° off the stern the ARC values varied approximately linearly. Two cargo ships showed similar trends but the ARC values were about 0.1 less. The figures allowed for the wind's velocity gradient with height. Because of this ARC values for small ships would be relatively greater and if the velocity was only due to ship speed they would also be greater. Data is also available[7] for wind forces on moored ships.

CALCULATION OF RESISTANCE

Having discussed the general nature of the resistance forces a ship experiences and the various formulations for frictional resistance it is necessary to apply this knowledge to derive the resistance of a ship. The model, or data obtained from model experiments, is still the principal method used. The principle followed is that stated by Froude. That is, the ship resistance can be obtained from that of the model by:

(1) measuring the total model resistance by running it at the corresponding Froude number;
(2) calculating the frictional resistance of the model and subtracting this from the total leaving the residuary resistance;

(3) scaling the model residuary resistance to the full scale by multiplying by the ratio of the ship to model displacements;
(4) adding a frictional resistance for the ship calculated on the basis of the resistance of a flat plate of equivalent surface area and roughness;
(5) calculating, or measuring separately, the resistance of appendages;
(6) making an allowance, if necessary, for air resistance.

ITTC method

The resistance coefficient is taken as $C = $ (Resistance)$/\frac{1}{2}\rho SV^2$. Subscripts t, v, r and f for the total, viscous, residual and frictional resistance components. Using subscripts m and s for the model and ship, the following relationships are assumed:

$$C_{vm} = (1 + k) C_{fm}$$

where k is a form factor.

$$C_{rs} = C_{rm} = C_{tm} - C_{vm}$$
$$C_{vs} = (1 + k) C_{fs} + \delta C_F$$

where δC_F is a roughness allowance.

$$C_{ts} = C_{vs} + C_{rs} + \text{(air resistance)}$$

The values of C_f are obtained from the ITTC model-ship correlation line for the appropriate Reynolds' number. That is, as in Table 8.3:

$$C_f = \frac{0.075}{(\log_{10} R_n - 2)^2}$$

k is determined from model tests at low speed and assumed to be independent of speed and scale.

The roughness allowance is calculated from:

$$\delta C_F = \left[105 \left(\frac{k_s}{L} \right)^{\frac{1}{3}} - 0.64 \right] \times 10^{-3}$$

where k_s is the roughness of hull, i.e., 150×10^{-6} m and L is the length on the waterline.

The contribution of air resistance to C_{ts} is taken as $0.001 A_T/S$ where A_T is the transverse projected area of the ship above water.

Table 8.3 Coefficients for the ITTC 1957 model–ship correlation line

Reynolds' number	C_f	Reynolds' number	C_f
10^5	0.008333	10^8	0.002083
5×10^5	0.005482	5×10^8	0.001671
10^6	0.004688	10^9	0.001531
5×10^6	0.003397	5×10^9	0.001265
10^7	0.003000	10^{10}	0.001172
5×10^7	0.002309	5×10^{10}	0.000991

Froude method
Using Froude's *'circular'* or *'constant' notation*:

$$\text{\textcircled{C}}_F = \frac{1000\,(\text{frictional resistance})}{\Delta \text{\textcircled{K}}^2}$$

$$= \frac{\dfrac{1000}{\rho g U^3}\, fSV^{1.825}}{4\pi V^2/gU}$$

$$= O \text{\textcircled{S}} \text{\textcircled{L}}^{-0.175}$$

where

$$O = \frac{1000f}{4\pi\rho\left(\dfrac{gL}{4\pi}\right)^{0.0875}} = \text{'Circular O'}$$

From which:

$$[\text{\textcircled{C}}_t]_{\text{ship}} = [\text{\textcircled{C}}_t]_{\text{model}} - [O_m - O_s]\,\text{\textcircled{S}}\,\text{\textcircled{L}}^{-0.175}$$

A selection of O and f values are presented in Table 8.4. These apply to a standard temperature of 15°C (59°F). The $\text{\textcircled{C}}_f$ value is increased or decreased by 4.3 per cent for every 10°C (2.4 per cent for every 10°F) the temperature is below or above this value.

The two methods above represent two different philosophies for scaling frictional resistance. Froude based his method on measurements of the resistance of planks extrapolated to ship-like lengths. Schoenherr and the ITTC used Reynolds' number as the basis for scaling.

Table 8.4 R. E. Froude's frictional data. O and f values. Frictional resistance = $fSV^{1.825}$ lbf. Values are for a standard temperature of 15°C. f values are for salt water with S in ft^2, V in knots. Values of f in fresh water may be obtained by multiplying by 0.975.

Length (ft)	O	f	Length (ft)	O	f
5	0.15485	0.012585	80	0.08987	0.009309
10	0.13409	0.011579	90	0.08840	0.009252
15	0.12210	0.010925	100	0.08716	0.009207
20	0.11470	0.010524	200	0.08012	0.008992
25	0.10976	0.010269	300	0.07655	0.008902
30	0.10590	0.010068	400	0.07406	0.008832
35	0.10282	0.009908	500	0.07217	0.008776
40	0.10043	0.009791	600	0.07062	0.008726
45	0.09839	0.009691	700	0.06931	0.008680
50	0.09664	0.009607	800	0.06818	0.008639
60	0.09380	0.009475	1000	0.06636	0.008574
70	0.09164	0.009382	1200	0.06493	0.008524

Table 8.5 $L^{-0.175}$ values

L	$L^{-0.175}$	L	$L^{-0.175}$
0.05	1.6892	1.00	1.0000
0.10	1.4962	1.20	0.9686
0.15	1.3937	1.40	0.9428
0.20	1.3253	1.60	0.9210
0.30	1.2345	1.80	0.9023
0.40	1.1739	2.00	0.8858
0.50	1.1290	2.20	0.8711
0.60	1.0935	2.40	0.8580
0.70	1.0644	2.60	0.8460
0.80	1.0398	2.80	0.8351
0.90	1.0186	3.00	0.8251

The method of extrapolating to the ship from the model is illustrated diagrammatically in Figure 8.9. It will be noted that if the friction lines used are displaced vertically but remain parallel, there will be no difference in the value of total resistance calculated for the ship. That is the actual frictional resistance taken is not critical as long as the error is the same for model and ship and all the elements making up the residuary resistance obey the Froude law of comparison. It is the slope of the skin friction line that is most important.

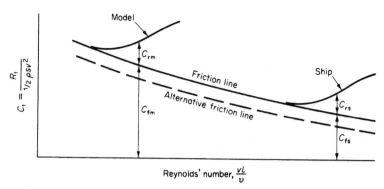

Figure 8.9 Extrapolation to ship

Notwithstanding this, the skin friction resistance should be calculated as accurately as possible so that an accurate wave-making resistance is obtained for comparing results between different forms and for comparing experimental results with theoretical calculations.

Wetted surface area

To obtain the frictional resistance it is necessary to calculate the wetted surface area of the hull. The most direct way of doing this is to plot the girths of the ship at various points along its length to a base of ship length. The area under the curve so produced is approximately the desired wetted surface area. This is the way Froude derived his circular S values and the method should be used when using Froude data. For a more accurate value of the actual wetted surface area some allowance must be made for the inclination of the hull surface to the centreline plane especially towards the ends of the ship. This can be done by assessing a mean hull surface length in each section and applying this as a correction factor to the girth readings. Alternatively an overall mean surface length can be found by averaging the distances round the waterline boundaries for a range of draughts.

A number of approximate formulae are available for estimating wetted surface area from the principal hull parameters. With the usual notation and taking T as the draught, those proposed by various people have been

Denny, $\quad S = L(C_B B + 1.7T)$

Taylor, $\quad S = C(\Delta L)^{0.5}$

where C is a constant depending upon the breadth/draught ratio and the midship section coefficient. With Δ in tons and L in feet C generally lies in the range 15.2 to 16.5.

Haslar has proposed in the circular notation:

$$\circled{S} = 3.4 + \frac{\circled{M}}{2.06}$$

Example 8.1

To illustrate the use of a model in calculating ship resistance a worked example is given here. The ship is 140 m long, 19 m beam, 8.5 m draught and has a speed of 15 knots. Other details are:

Block coefficient	= 0.65
Midship area coefficient	= 0.98
Wetted surface area	= 3300 m^2
Density of sea water	= 1025 kg/m^3
Froude coefficient, f	= 0.421 34

Tests on a geometrically similar model 4.9 m long, run at corresponding speed, gave a total resistance of 19 N in fresh water whose density was 1000 kg/m^3.

Solution

$$\text{Speed of model} = 15 \left(\frac{4.9}{140}\right)^{0.5} = 2.81 \text{ knots} = 1.44 \text{ m/s}$$

$$\text{Wetted surface of model} = 3300 \left(\frac{4.9}{140}\right)^{2} = 4.04 \text{ m}^2$$

Froude coefficient for model (fresh water) = 0.506 36

$$\text{Frictional resistance of model} = 0.506\,36 \times 4.04 \times 2.81^{1.825}$$
$$= 13.481 \text{N}$$

$$\text{Wave resistance of model} = 19 - 13.481 = 5.519 \text{ N}$$

$$\text{Wave resistance of ship} = 5.519 \times \frac{1025}{1000} \times \left(\frac{140}{4.9}\right)^{3}$$
$$= 131\,900 \text{ N}$$

$$\text{Frictional resistance of ship} = 0.421\,34 \times 3300 \times 15^{1.825}$$
$$= 194\,800 \text{ N}$$

$$\text{Total resistance of ship} = 326\,700 \text{ N}$$

If the kinematic viscosity for fresh water is $1.139 \times 10^{-6}\,\text{m}^2/\text{s}$ and that for sea water is $1.188 \times 10^{-6}\,\text{m}^2/\text{s}$, the Reynolds' numbers can be calculated for model and ship.

$$\text{For model } R_\text{n} = \frac{4.9 \times 1.44}{1.139 \times 10^{-6}} = 6.195 \times 10^6$$

$$\text{For ship } R_\text{n} = \frac{140 \times 15 \times 1852}{3600 \times 1.188 \times 10^{-6}} = 9.094 \times 10^8$$

Schoenherr

The values of C_f for model and ship are 3.172×10^{-3} and 1.553×10^{-3} respectively. Now:

$$C_\text{tm} = \frac{R_\text{tm}}{\frac{1}{2}\rho SV^2} = \frac{19}{\frac{1}{2} \times 1000 \times 4.04 \times 1.44^2} = 0.004\,536$$

$$C_\text{fm} \qquad\qquad\qquad\qquad\qquad\qquad = 0.003\,172$$

$$C_\text{wm} = C_\text{ws} \qquad\qquad\qquad\qquad\qquad = 0.001\,364$$

$$C_\text{fs} \qquad\qquad\qquad\qquad\qquad\qquad = 0.001\,553$$

$$C_\text{ts} \qquad\qquad\qquad\qquad\qquad\qquad = 0.002\,917$$

$$V_\text{s} = \frac{15 \times 1852}{3600} = 7.717\,\text{m/s}$$

$$R_\text{ts} = \tfrac{1}{2}\rho SV^2 \times C_\text{ts} = \tfrac{1}{2} \times 1025 \times 3300 \times 7.717^2 \times 0.002\,917$$

$$= 293\,800\,\text{N}$$

This makes no allowance for roughness. The usual addition for this to C_f is 0.0004. This would give a C_ts of 0.003 317 and the resistance would be 334 100 N.

ITTC correlation line

This gives:

$$C_\text{f} = \frac{0.075}{(\log_{10} R_\text{n} - 2)^2}$$

which yields:

For the model $\quad C_\text{fm} = 0.003\,266$

For the ship $\quad\;\; C_\text{fs} = 0.001\,549$

Hence:

$$C_{wm} = C_{ws} = 0.004\,536 - 0.003\,266 = 0.001\,270$$
$$C_{ts} = 0.001\,270 + 0.001\,549 = 0.002\,819$$
$$R_{ts} = \tfrac{1}{2} \times 1025 \times 3300 \times 7.717^2 \times 0.002\,819 = 283\,900\,\text{N}$$

Making the same allowance of 0.0004 for roughness, yields:

$$R_{ts} = 324\,200\,\text{N}$$

METHODICAL SERIES

Apart from tests of individual models a great deal of work has gone into ascertaining the influence of hull form on resistance. The tests start with a *parent form* and then vary systematically a number of form parameters which are considered likely to be significant. Such a series of tests is called a *methodical series* or a *standard series*. The results can show how resistance varies with the form parameters used and are useful in estimating power for new designs before the stage has been reached at which a model can be run. To cover n values of m variables would require m^n tests so the amount of work and time involved can be enormous. In planning a methodical series great care is needed in deciding the parameters and range of variables.

One methodical series is that carried out by Admiral D.W. Taylor.[8] He took as variables the prismatic coefficient, displacement to length ratio and beam to draught ratio. With eight, five and two values of the variables respectively he tested 80 models. Taylor standardized his results on a ship length of 500 ft (152 m) and a wetted surface coefficient of 15.4. He plotted contours of R_f/Δ with $V/L^{0.5}$ and $\Delta/(L/100)^3$ as in Figure 8.10. R_f/Δ was in pounds per ton displacement. Taylor also presented correction factors for length and contours for wetted surface area correction. The residuary resistance, R_r, was plotted in a similar way but with prismatic coefficient in place of $V/L^{0.5}$ as abscissa, see Figure 8.11.

Taylor's data was re-analysed[9] using C_f and C_r instead of resistance in pounds per ton of displacement. Frictional resistance was calculated from the Schoenherr formula rather than being based on the Froude data used by Taylor. A typical chart from the re-analysed data is given in Figure 8.12.

More recent methodical series for merchant ships have been by BSRA[10,11] and DTMB.[12] The former varied block coefficient, length to displacement ratio, breadth to draught ratio and longitudinal position of the LCB. Data was presented in circular C form to a base of block

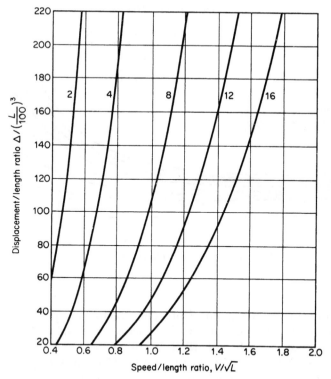

Figure 8.10 Contours of frictional resistance in pounds per ton displacement for 500 ft ship

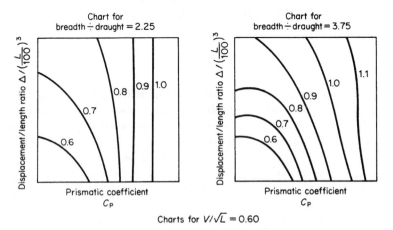

Figure 8.11 Taylor's contours of residuary resistance in pounds per ton displacement

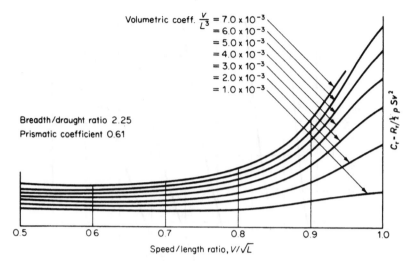

Figure 8.12 Typical chart from re-analysis of Taylor's data

coefficient for various speeds. Correction factors are presented for the variation in the other parameters. The forms represent single screw ships with cruiser sterns. The DTMB data covers the same variables as the BSRA tests. Data is presented in circular C form and uses both the Froude skin friction correction and the ITTC 1957 ship-model correlation line.

A designer must consult the methodical series data directly in order to use it to estimate the resistance of a new design. Unless the new design is of the type and within the general range of the variables covered by the methodical series errors are likely. In this case other data may be available from which to deduce correction factors.

ROUGHNESS

It will be clear that apart from the wetted surface area and speed the major factor in determining the frictional resistance is the roughness of the hull. This is why so many researchers have devoted so much time to this factor. For slowish ships the frictional resistance is the major part of the total and it is important to keep the hull as smooth as possible.

Owing to the increase in boundary layer thickness, the ratio of a given roughness amplitude to boundary layer thickness decreases along the length of the hull. Protrusions have less effect at the after end than forward. In the towing trials of HMS *Penelope*, the hull roughness, measured by a wall roughness gauge, was found to be 0.3 mm mean apparent amplitude per 50 mm. This mean apparent amplitude per 50 mm gauge length is the standard parameter used in the UK to represent hull roughness. Roughness can be considered under three headings:

(1) *Structural roughness.* This depends upon the design and method of construction. In a riveted ship the plate overlaps and edges and the rivet heads constituted roughness. These are avoided in modern welded construction but in welded hulls the plating exhibits a waviness between frames, particularly in thin plating, and this is also a form of roughness.

(2) *Corrosion.* Steel corrodes in sea water creating a roughened surface. Modern painting systems are reasonably effective in reducing corrosion all the while the coating remains intact. If it is abraded in one area then corrosion is concentrated at that spot and pitting can be severe. This is bad from the structural point of view as well as for frictional resistance. Building ships on covered slipways and early plate treatments to reduce corrosion both reduce the initial hull roughness on completion of build. To reduce corrosion during build and in operation, many ships are now fitted with cathodic protection systems, either active or passive. These are discussed briefly under structure.

(3) *Fouling.* Marine organisms such as weed and barnacles can attach themselves to the hull. This would represent a very severe roughening if steps were not taken to prevent it. Traditionally the underwater hull has been coated with anti-fouling compositions. Early treatments contained toxic materials such as compounds of mercury or copper which leached out into the water and prevented the marine growth taking a hold on the hull. Unfortunately these compounds also pollute the general ocean and other treatments are now used. Fouling is very dependent upon the time a ship spends in port relative to its time at sea, and the ocean areas in which it operates. Fouling increases more rapidly in port and in warmer waters. In the *Lucy Ashton* towing trials it was found that the frictional resistance increased by about 5 per cent over 40 days, that is by about $\frac{1}{8}$ of 1 per cent per day. This is a common allowance applied to a ship's frictional resistance to allow for time out of dock.

For an operator the deterioration of the hull surface with time results in a slower speed for a given power or more power being needed for a given speed. This increases running costs which must be set against the costs of docking, cleaning off the underwater hull and applying new coatings.

The Schoenherr and ITTC resistance formulations were intended to apply to a perfectly smooth surface. This will not be true even for a newly completed ship. The usual allowance for roughness is to increase the frictional coefficient by 0.0004 for a new ship. The actual value will depend upon the coatings used. In the *Lucy Ashton* trials two different coatings gave a difference of 5 per cent in frictional resistance. The standard allowance for roughness represents a significant increase in frictional resistance. To this must be added an allowance for time out of dock.

FORM PARAMETERS AND RESISTANCE

There can be no absolutes in terms of optimum form. The designer must make many compromises. Even in terms of resistance one form may be better than another at one speed but inferior at another speed. Another complication is the interdependence of many form factors, including those chosen for discussion below. In that discussion only generalized comments are possible.

Frictional resistance is directly related to the wetted surface area and any reduction in this will reduce skin friction resistance. This is not, however, a parameter that can be changed in isolation from others. Other form changes are likely to have most affect on wave-making resistance but may also affect frictional resistance because of consequential changes in surface area and flow velocities around the hull.

Length
An increase in length will increase frictional resistance but usually reduce wave-making resistance but this is complicated by the interaction of the bow and stern wave systems. Thus while fast ships will benefit overall from being longer than slow ships, there will be bands of length in which the benefits will be greater or less.

Prismatic coefficient
The main effect is on wave-making resistance and choice of prismatic coefficient is not therefore so important for slow ships where it is likely to be chosen to give better cargo carrying capacity. For fast ships the desirable prismatic coefficient will increase with the speed to length ratio.

Fullness of form
Fullness may be represented by the block or prismatic coefficient. For most ships resistance will increase as either coefficient increases. This is

reasonable as the full ship can be expected to create a greater disturbance as it moves through the water. There is evidence of optimum values of the coefficients on either side of which the resistance might be expected to rise. This optimum might be in the working range of high speed ships but is usually well below practical values for slow ships. Generally the block coefficient should reduce as the desired ship speed increases.

In moderate speed ships, power can always be reduced by reducing block coefficient so that machinery and fuel weights can be reduced. However, for given overall dimensions, a lower block coefficient means less payload. A balance must be struck between payload and resistance based on a study of the economics of running the ship.

Slimness
Slimness can be defined by the ratio of the length to the cube root of the volume of displacement (this is Froude's circular M) or in terms of a volumetric coefficient which is the volume of displacement divided by the cube of the length. For a given length, greater volume of displacement requires steeper angles of entrance and run for the waterplane endings. Increase in volumetric coefficient or reduction in circular M can be expected, therefore, to lead to increased resistance. Generally in high speed forms with low block coefficient, the displacement length ratio must be kept low to avoid excessive resistance. For slow ships this is not so important. Fast ships require larger length to beam ratios than slow ships.

Breadth to draught ratio
Generally resistance increases with increase in breadth to draught ratio within the normal working range of this variable. This can again be explained by the angles at the ends of the waterlines increasing and causing a greater disturbance in the water. With very high values of beam to draught ratio the flow around the hull would tend to be in the vertical plane rather than the horizontal. This could lead to a reduction in resistance.

Longitudinal distribution of displacement
Even when the main hull parameters have been fixed it is possible to vary the distribution of displacement along the ship length. This distribution can be characterized by the longitudinal position of the centre of buoyancy (LCB). For a given block coefficient the LCB position governs the fullness of the ends of the ship. As the LCB moves towards one end that end will become fuller and the other finer. There

will be a position where the overall resistance will be minimized. This generally varies from just forward of amidships for slow ships to about 10 per cent of the length aft of amidships for fast ships. In considering the distribution of displacement along the length the curve of areas should be smooth. Sudden changes of curvature could denote regions where waves or eddies will be created.

Length of parallel middle body

In high speed ships with low block coefficient there is usually no parallel middle body. In ships of moderate and high block coefficient, parallel middle body is needed to avoid the ends becoming too full. For a given block coefficient, as the length of parallel middle body increases the ends become finer and vice versa. Thus there will be an optimum value of parallel middle body for a given block coefficient.

Section shape

It is not possible to generalize on the shape of section to adopt but slow to moderate speed ships tend to have U-shaped sections in the fore body and V-shaped sections aft. It can be argued that the U-sections forward keep more of the ship's volume away from the waterline and so reduce wave-making.

Bulbous bow

The principle of the bulbous bow is that it is sized, shaped and positioned so as to create a wave system at the bow which partially cancels out the ship's own bow wave system, so reducing wave-making resistance. This can only be done over a limited speed range and at the expense of resistance at other speeds. Many merchant ships operate at a steady speed for much of their lives so the bulb can be designed for that speed. It was originally applied to moderate to high speed ships but has also been found to be beneficial in relatively slow ships such as tankers and bulk carriers and these ships now often have bulbous bows. The effectiveness of the bulb in the slower ships, where wave-making resistance is only a small percentage of the total, suggests the bulb reduces frictional resistance as well. This is thought to be due to the change in flow velocities which it creates over the hull. Sometimes the bulb is sited well forward and it can extend beyond the fore perpendicular.

Triplets

The designer cannot be sure of the change in resistance of a form, as a result of small changes, unless data is available for a similar form as part of a methodical series. However, changes are often necessary in the early design stages and it is desirable that their consequences should be known. One way of achieving this is to run a set of three models early on. One is the base model and the other two are the base model with one parameter varied by a small amount. Typically the parameters changed would be beam and length and the variation would be a simple linear expansion of about 10 per cent of all dimensions in the chosen direction. Because only one parameter is varied at a time the models are not geometrically similar. The variation in resistance, or its effective power, of the form can be expressed as:

$$\frac{\mathrm{d}R}{R} = \frac{a_1\,\mathrm{d}L}{L} + \frac{a_2\,\mathrm{d}B}{B} + \frac{a_3\,\mathrm{d}T}{T}$$

The values of a_1 etc., can be deduced from the results of the three experiments.

MODEL EXPERIMENTS

Full scale resistance trials are very expensive. Most of the knowledge on ship resistance has been gained from model experiment. W. Froude was the pioneer of the model experiment method and the towing tank which he opened in Torquay in 1872 was the first of its kind. The tank was in effect a channel about 85 m long, 11 m wide and 3 m deep. Over this channel ran a carriage, towed at a uniform speed by an endless rope, and carrying a dynamometer. Models were attached to the carriage through the dynamometer and their resistances were measured by the extension of a spring. Models were made of paraffin wax which is easily shaped and altered. Since Froude's time great advances have been made in the design of tanks, their carriages and the recording equipment. However, the basic principles remain the same. Every maritime nation now has towing tanks.

Early work on ship models was carried out in smooth water. Most resistance testing is still in this condition but now tanks are fitted with wavemakers so that the added resistance in waves can be studied. Wavemakers are fitted to one end of the tank and can generate regular or long crested irregular waves. They may be oscillating paddles or wedges or use varying pneumatic pressure in an enclosed space. For these experiments the model must be free to heave and pitch and these motions are recorded as well as the resistance. In towing tanks, testing is limited to head and following seas. Some discussion of special seakeeping basins was presented in Chapter 6 on seakeeping. Such basins can be used to determine model performance when manoeuvring in waves.

FULL SCALE TRIALS

The final test of the accuracy of any prediction method based on extrapolation from models must be the resistance of the ship itself. This cannot be found from speed trials although the overall accuracy of power estimation can be checked by them as will be explained in Chapter 9. In measuring a ship's resistance it is vital to ensure that the ship under test is running in open, smooth water. That is to say the method of towing or propelling it must not interfere with the flow of water around the test vessel. Towing has been the usual method adopted.

The earliest tests were conducted by Froude on HMS *Greyhound* in 1874.[13] *Greyhound* was a screw sloop and was towed by HMS *Active*, a vessel of about 3100 tonf (30.9 MN) displacement, using a 190 ft (58 m) towrope attached to the end of a 45 ft (13.7 m) outrigger in *Active*. Tests were carried out with *Greyhound* at three displacements ranging from 1161 tonf (11.57 MN) to 938 tonf (9.35 MN), and over a speed range of 3 to 12.5 knots.

The pull in the towrope was measured by dynamometer and speed by a log. Results were compared with those derived from a model of *Greyhound* and showed that the curve of resistance against speed was of the same character as that from the model but somewhat higher. This was attributed to the greater roughness of the ship surface than that assumed in the calculations. Froude concluded that the experiment 'substantially verify the law of comparison which has been propounded by me as governing the relation between the resistance ships and their models'.

In the late 1940s, the British Ship Research Association carried out full scale tests on the former Clyde paddle steamer, *Lucy Ashton*. The problems of towing were overcome by fitting the ship with four jet engines mounted high up on the ship and outboard of the hull to avoid the jet efflux impinging on the ship or its wake.[14-17] Most of the tests were at a displacement of 390 tonf (3.9 MN). Speeds ranged from 5 to 15 knots and the influence of different hull conditions were investigated. Results were compared with tests on six geometrically similar models of lengths ranging from 9 to 30 ft (2.7 to 9.1 m). Estimates of the ship resistance were made from each model using various skin friction formulae, including those of Froude and Schoenherr, and the results compared to the ship measurements.

Generally the Schoenherr formulae gave the better results, Figure 8.13. The trials showed that the full scale resistance is sensitive to small roughnesses. Bituminous aluminium paint gave about 5 per cent less skin friction resistance and 3.5 per cent less total resistance, than red oxide paint. Fairing the seams gave a reduction of about 3 per cent in total resistance. Forty days fouling on the bituminous aluminium hull increased skin frictional resistance by about 5 per cent, that is about $\frac{1}{8}$

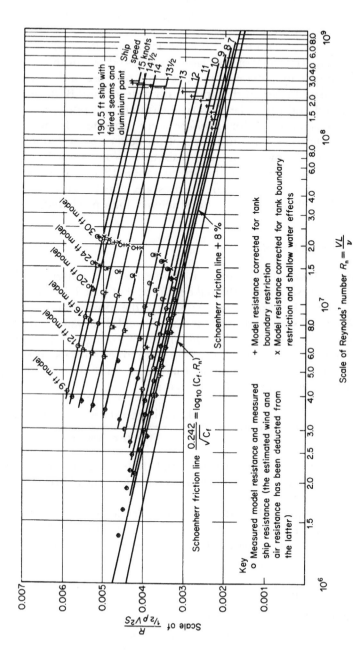

Figure 8.13 Lucy Ashton data

of 1 per cent per day. The results indicated that the interference between skin friction and wave-making resistance was not significant over the range of the tests.

Later trials were conducted on the frigate HMS *Penelope*[18] by the Admiralty Experiment Works. *Penelope* was towed by another frigate at the end of a mile long nylon rope. The main purpose of the trial was to measure radiated noise and vibration for a dead ship. Both propellers were removed and the wake pattern measured by a pitot fitted to one shaft. Propulsion data for *Penelope* were obtained from separate measured mile trials with three sets of propellers. Correlation of ship and model data showed the ship resistance to be some 14 per cent higher than predicted over the speed range 12 to 13 knots. There appeared to be no significant wake scale effects. Propulsion data showed higher thrust, torque and efficiency than predicted.

EFFECTIVE POWER

The *effective power* at any speed is defined as the power needed to overcome the resistance of the naked hull at that speed. It is sometimes referred to as the *towrope power* as it is the power that would be expended if the ship were to be towed through the water without the flow around it being affected by the means of towing. Another, higher, effective power would apply if the ship were towed with its appendages fitted. The ratio of this power to that needed for the naked ship is known as the *appendage coefficient*. That is:

$$\text{the appendage coefficient} = \frac{\text{Effective power with appendages}}{\text{Effective power naked}}$$

Froude, because he dealt with Imperial units, used the term *effective horsepower* or **ehp**. Even in mathematical equations the abbreviation ehp was used.

For a given speed the effective power is the product of the total resistance and the speed. Thus returning to the earlier worked example, the effective powers for the three cases considered, would be:

(1) Using Froude.

Total resistance = 326 700 N

$$\text{Effective power} = \frac{326\ 700 \times 15 \times 1852}{1000 \times 3600}$$

$$= 2521\ \text{kW}$$

(2) Using Schoenherr.

Total resistance = 334 100 N, allowing for roughness

Effective power = 2578 kW

(3) Using the ITTC line.

Total resistance = 324 200 N

Effective power = 2502 kW

As will be seen in Chapter 9, the effective power is not the power required of the main machinery in driving the ship at the given speed. This latter power will be greater because of the efficiency of the propulsor used and its interaction with the flow around the hull. However, it is the starting point for the necessary calculations.

SUMMARY

The different types of resistance a ship experiences in moving through the water have been identified and the way in which they scale with size discussed. In practice the total resistance is considered as made up of frictional resistance, which scales with Reynolds' number, and residuary resistance, which scales with the Froude number. This led to a method for predicting the resistance of a ship from model tests. The total model resistance is measured and an allowance for frictional resistance deducted to give the residuary resistance. This is scaled in proportion to the displacements of ship and model to give the ship's residuary resistance. To this is added an allowance for frictional resistance of the ship to give the ship's total resistance. Various ways of arriving at the skin friction resistance have been explained together with an allowance for hull roughness.

The use of individual model tests, and of methodical series data, in predicting resistance have been outlined. The few full scale towing tests carried out to validate the model predictions have been discussed.

Finally the concept of effective power was introduced and this provides the starting point for discussing the powering of ships which is covered in Chapter 9.

References

1. Milne-Thomson, L. M. *Theoretical hydrodynamics.* MacMillan.
2. Lamb, H. *Hydrodynamics,* Cambridge University Press.
3. Froude, W. (1877) On experiments upon the effect produced on the wave-making resistance of ships by length of parallel middle body. *TINA*

4. Schoenherr, K. E. (1932) Resistance of flat surfaces moving through a fluid. *TSNAME.*

5. Hadler, J. B. (1958) Coefficients for International Towing Tank Conference 1957 Model-Ship Correlation Line. *DTMB*, Report 1185.

6. Shearer, K. D. A. and Lynn, W. M. (1959–60) Wind tunnel tests on models of merchant ships. *TNECI.*

7. Iwai, A. and Yajima, S. (1961) Wind forces acting on ship moored. *Nautical Institute of Japan.*

8. Taylor, D. W. (Out of print) *Speed and power of ships.* United States Shipping Board, revised 1933.

9. Gertler, M. (1954) *A re-analysis of the original test data for the Taylor standard series.* Navy Department, Washington, DC.

10. Moor, D. I., Parker, M. N. and Pattullo, R. N. M. (1961) The BSRA methodical series. An overall presentation. Geometry of forms and variation of resistance with block coefficient and longitudinal centre of buoyancy. *TRINA.*

11. Lackenby, H. (1966) The BSRA methodical series. An overall presentation. Variation of resistance with breadth/draught ratio and length/displacement ratio. *TRINA.*

12. Lackenby, H. and Milton, P. (1972) DTMB Standard Series 60. A new presentation of the resistance data for block coefficient, LCB, breadth/draught ratio and length/breadth ratio variations. *TRINA.*

13. Froude, W. (1874) On experiments with HMS *Greyhound. TINA.*

14. Denny, Sir Maurice E. (1951) BSRA resistance experiments on the *Lucy Ashton*, Part 1; Full scale measurements. *TINA.*

15. Conn, J. F. C., Lackenby, H. and Walker, W. B. (1953) BSRA resistance experiments on the *Lucy Ashton*, Part II; The ship-model correlation for the naked hull condition. *TINA.*

16. Lackenby, H. (1955) BSRA resistance experiments on the *Lucy Ashton*, Part III; The ship-model correlation for the shaft appendage conditions. *TINA.*

17. Livingstone Smith, S. (1955) BSRA resistance experiments on the *Lucy Ashton*, Part IV; Miscellaneous investigations and general appraisal. *TINA.*

18. Canham, H. J. S. (1974) Resistance, propulsion and wake tests with HMS *Penelope. TRINA.*

9 Propulsion

The concept of effective power was introduced in Chapter 8. This is the power needed to tow a naked ship at a given speed and it is the starting point for discussing the propulsion of the ship. In this chapter means of producing the driving force are discussed together with the interaction between the propulsor and the flow around the hull. It is convenient to study the propulsor performance in open water and then the change in that performance when placed close behind a ship. There are many different factors involved so it is useful to outline the general principles before proceeding to the detail.

GENERAL PRINCIPLES

When a propulsor is introduced behind the ship it modifies the flow around the hull at the stern. This causes an augmentation of the resistance experienced by the hull. It also modifies the wake at the stern and therefore the average velocity of water through the propulsor. This will not be the same as the ship speed through the water. These two effects are taken together as a measure of hull efficiency. The other effect of the combined hull and propulsor is that the flow through the propulsor is not uniform and generally not along the propulsor axis. The ratio of the propulsor efficiency in open water to that behind the ship is termed the relative rotative efficiency. Finally there will be losses in the transmission of power between the main machinery and the propulsor. These various effects can be illustrated by the different powers applying to each stage.

Extension of effective power concept

The concept of *effective power* (P_E) can be extended to cover the power needed to be installed in a ship in order to obtain a given speed. If the installed power is the *shaft power* (P_S) then the *overall propulsive efficiency* is determined by the *propulsive coefficient*, where:

$$\text{Propulsive coefficient (PC)} = \frac{P_E}{P_S}$$

The intermediate stages in moving from the effective to the shaft power are usually taken as:

Effective power for a hull with appendages $= P'_E$
Thrust power developed by propulsors $= P_T$
Power delivered by propulsors when propelling ship $= P_D$
Power delivered by propulsors when in open water $= P'_D$

With this notation the overall propulsive efficiency can be written:

$$PC = \frac{P_E}{P_S} = \frac{P_E}{P'_E} \times \frac{P'_E}{P_T} \times \frac{P_T}{P'_D} \times \frac{P'_D}{P_D} \times \frac{P_D}{P_S}$$

The term P_E/P'_E is the inverse of the appendage coefficient. The other terms in the expression are a series of efficiencies which are termed, and defined, as follows:

$P'_E/P_T =$ *hull efficiency* $= \eta_H$
$P_T/P'_D =$ *propulsor efficiency* in open water $= \eta_O$
$P'_D/P_D =$ *relative rotative efficiency* $= \eta_R$
$P_D/P_S =$ *shaft transmission efficiency*

This can be written:

$$PC = \left(\frac{\eta_H \times \eta_O \times \eta_R}{\text{appendage coefficient}} \right) \times \text{Transmission efficiency}$$

The expression in brackets is termed the *quasi-propulsive coefficient* (QPC) and is denoted by η_D. The QPC is obtained from model experiments and to allow for errors in applying this to the full scale an additional factor is needed. Some authorities use a *QPC factor* which is the ratio of the propulsive coefficient determined from a ship trial to the QPC obtained from the corresponding model. Others[1] use a *load factor*, where:

$$\text{load factor} = (1 + x) = \frac{\text{Transmission efficiency}}{\text{QPC factor} \times \text{appendage coefficient}}$$

In this expression the *overload fraction, x,* is meant to allow for hull roughness, fouling and weather conditions on trial.

It remains to establish how the hull, propulsor and relative rotative efficiencies can be determined. This is dealt with later in this chapter.

Propulsors

Propulsion devices can take many forms. They all rely upon imparting momentum to a mass of fluid which causes a force to act on the ship. In the case of air cushion vehicles the fluid is air but usually it is water. By far and away the most common device is the propeller. This may take various forms but attention in this chapter is focused on the fixed pitch propeller. Before defining such a propeller it is instructive to consider the general case of a simple actuator disc imparting momentum to water.

Momentum theory

In this theory the propeller is replaced by an actuator disc, area A, which is assumed to be working in an ideal fluid. The actuator disc imparts an axial acceleration to the water which, in accordance with Bernoulli's principle, requires a change in pressure at the disc, Figure 9.1.

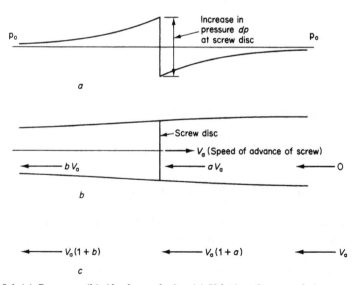

Figure 9.1 (a) Pressure; (b) Absolute velocity; (c) Velocity of water relative to screw

It is assumed that the water is initially, and finally, at pressure p_0. At the actuator disc it receives an incremental pressure increase dp. The water is initially at rest, achieves a velocity aV_a at the disc, goes on accelerating and finally has a velocity bV_a at infinity behind the disc. The disc is moving at a velocity V_a relative to the still water. Assuming the velocity increment is uniform across the disc and only the column of water passing through the disc is affected:

Velocity of water relative to the disc $= V_a(1 + a)$

where a is termed the *axial inflow factor*, and:

Mass of water acted on in unit time $= \rho A V_a(1 + a)$

Since this mass finally achieves a velocity bV_a, the change of momentum in unit time is:

$$\rho A V_a(1 + a) bV_a$$

Equating this to the thrust generated by the disc:

$$T = \rho A V_a^2(1 + a) b$$

The work done by the thrust on the water is:

$$TaV_a = \rho A V_a^3(1 + a) ab$$

This is equal to the kinetic energy in the water column,

$$\frac{\rho A V_a(1 + a)(bV_a)^2}{2}$$

Equating this to the work done by the thrust:

$$\rho A V_a^3(1 + a) ab = \frac{\rho A V_a^3(1 + a) b^2}{2} \quad \text{and} \quad a = \frac{b}{2}$$

That is half the velocity ultimately reached is acquired by the time the water reaches the disc. Thus the effect of a propulsor on the flow around the hull, and therefore the hull's resistance, extends both ahead and astern of the propulsor.

The useful work done by the propeller is equal to the thrust multiplied by its forward velocity. The total work done is this plus the work done in accelerating the water so:

Total work $= \rho A V_a^3 (1 + a)\, ab + \rho A V_a^3 (1 + a)\, b$

The efficiency of the disc as a propulsor is the ratio of the useful work to the total work. That is:

$$\text{efficiency} = \frac{\rho A V_a^3 (1 + a)\, b}{\rho A V_a^3 [\,(1 + a)\, ab + (1 + a)\, b\,]} = \frac{1}{1 + a}$$

This is termed the *ideal efficiency*. For good efficiency a must be small. For a given speed and thrust the propulsor disc must be large, which also follows from general considerations. The larger the disc area the less the velocity that has to be imparted to the water for a given thrust. A lower race velocity means less energy in the race and more energy usefully employed in driving the ship.

So far it has been assumed that only an axial velocity is imparted to the water. In a real propeller, because of the rotation of the blades, the water will also have rotational motion imparted to it. Allowing for this it can be shown[2] that the overall efficiency becomes:

$$\eta = \frac{1 - a'}{1 + a}$$

where a' is the *rotational inflow factor*. Thus the effect of imparting rotational velocity to the water is to reduce efficiency further.

THE SCREW PROPELLER

A screw propeller may be regarded as part of a helicoidal surface which, when rotating, 'screws' its way through the water.

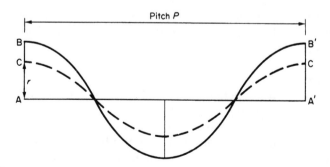

Figure 9.2

A helicoidal surface

Consider a line AB, perpendicular to line AA′, rotating at uniform angular velocity about AA′ and moving along AA′ at uniform velocity. Figure 9.2. AB sweeps out a helicoidal surface. The *pitch* of the surface is the distance travelled along AA′ in making one complete revolution. A propeller with a flat face and constant pitch could be regarded as having its face trace out the helicoidal surface. If AB rotates at N revolutions per unit time, the circumferential velocity of a point, distant r from AA′, is $2\pi Nr$ and the axial velocity is NP. The point travels in a direction inclined at θ to AA′ such that:

$$\tan \theta = \frac{2\pi Nr}{NP} = \frac{2\pi r}{P}$$

If the path is unwrapped and laid out flat the point will move along a straight line as in Figure 9.3.

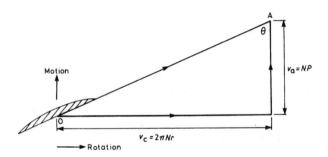

Figure 9.3

Propellers can have any number of blades but three, four and five are most common in marine propellers. Reduced noise designs often have more blades. Each blade can be regarded as part of a different helicoidal surface. In modern propellers the pitch of the blade varies with radius so that sections at different radii are not on the same helicoidal surface.

Propeller features

The *diameter* of a propeller is the diameter of a circle which passes tangentially through the tips of the blades. At their inner ends the blades are attached to a *boss*, the diameter of which is kept as small as possible consistent with strength. Blades and boss are often one casting for fixed pitch propellers. The boss diameter is usually expressed as a fraction of the propeller diameter.

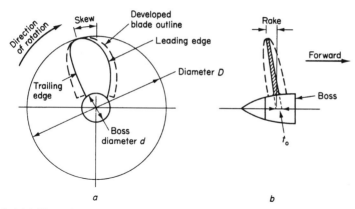

Figure 9.4 (a) View along shaft axis, (b) Side elevation

   The blade outline can be defined by its projection on to a plane normal to the shaft. This is the *projected outline*. The *developed outline* is the outline obtained if the circumferential chord of the blade, that is the circumferential distance across the blade at a given radius, is set out against radius. The shape is often symmetrical about a radial line called the *median*. In some propellers the median is curved back relative to the rotation of the blade. Such a propeller is said to have *skew back*. Skew is expressed in terms of the circumferential displacement of the blade tip. Skew back can be advantageous where the propeller is operating in a flow with marked circumferential variation. In some propellers the face in profile is not normal to the axis and the propeller is said to be *raked*. It may be raked forward or back, but generally the latter to improve the clearance between the blade tip and the hull. Rake is usually expressed as a percentage of the propeller diameter.

Blade sections
A section is a cut through the blade at a given radius, that is it is the intersection between the blade and a circular cylinder. The section can be laid out flat. Early propellers had a flat face and a back in the form of a circular arc. Such a section was completely defined by the blade width and maximum thickness.
   Modern propellers use aerofoil sections. The *median* or *camber line* is the line through the mid-thickness of the blade. The *camber* is the maximum distance between the camber line and the *chord* which is the line joining the forward and trailing edges. The camber and the maximum thickness are usually expressed as percentages of the chord length. The maximum thickness is usually forward of the mid-chord point. In a flat face circular back section the camber ratio is half the

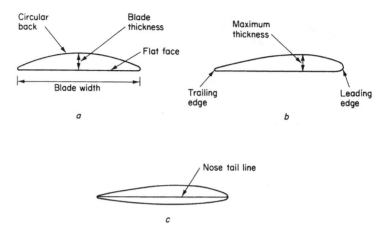

Figure 9.5 (a) Flat face, circular back; (b) Aerofoil; (c) Cambered face

thickness ratio. For a symmetrical section the camber line ratio would be zero. For an aerofoil section the section must be defined by the ordinates of the face and back as measured from the chord line.

The maximum thickness of blade sections decreases towards the tips of the blade. The thickness is dictated by strength calculations and does not necessarily vary in a simple way with radius. In simple, small, propellers thickness may reduce linearly with radius. This distribution gives a value of thickness that would apply at the propeller axis were it not for the boss. The ratio of this thickness, t_o, to the propeller diameter is termed the *blade thickness fraction*.

Pitch ratio
The ratio of the pitch to diameter is called the *pitch ratio*. When pitch varies with radius that variation must be defined. For simplicity a nominal pitch is quoted being that at a certain radius. A radius of 70 per cent of the maximum is often used for this purpose.

Blade area
Blade area is defined as a ratio of the total area of the propeller disc. The usual form is:

$$Developed\ blade\ area\ ratio = \frac{developed\ blade\ area}{disc\ area}$$

In some earlier work, the developed blade area was increased to allow for a nominal area within the boss. The allowance varied with different authorities and care is necessary in using such data. Sometimes the projected blade area is used, leading to a *projected blade area ratio*.

Handing of propellers
If, when viewed from aft, a propeller turns clockwise to produce ahead
thrust it is said to be right handed. If it turns anti-clockwise for ahead
thrust it is said to be left handed. In twin screw ships the starboard
propeller is usually right handed and the port propeller left handed. In
that case the propellers are said to be outward turning. Should the
reverse apply they are said to be inward turning. With normal ship
forms inward turning propellers sometimes introduce manoeuvring
problems which can be solved by fitting outward turning screws.
Tunnel stern designs can benefit from inward turning screws.

Forces on a blade section
From dimensional analysis it can be shown that the force experienced
by an aerofoil can be expressed in terms of its area, A; chord, c, and its
velocity, V, as:

$$\frac{F}{\rho A V^2} = f\left(\frac{v}{Vc}\right) = f(R_n)$$

Another factor affecting the force is the attitude of the aerofoil to the
velocity of flow past it. This is the *angle of incidence* or *angle of attack*.
Denoting this angle by α, the expression for the force becomes:

$$\frac{F}{\rho A V^2} = f(R_n, \alpha)$$

This resultant force F, Figure 9.6, can be resolved into two components.
That normal to the direction of flow is termed the *lift*, L, and the other

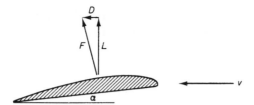

Figure 9.6 Forces on blade section

in the direction of the flow is termed the *drag*, D. These two forces are
expressed non-dimensionally as:

$$C_L = \frac{L}{\frac{1}{2}\rho A V^2} \quad \text{and} \quad C_D = \frac{D}{\frac{1}{2}\rho A V^2}$$

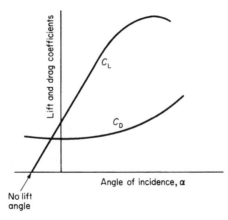

Figure 9.7 Lift and drag curves

Each of these coefficients will be a function of the angle of incidence and Reynolds' number. For a given Reynolds' number they depend on the angle of incidence only and a typical plot of lift and drag coefficients against angle of incidence is presented in Figure 9.7.

Initially the curve for the lift coefficient is practically a straight line starting from a small negative angle of incidence called the *no lift angle*. As the angle of incidence increases further the curve reduces in slope and then the coefficient begins to decrease. A steep drop occurs when the angle of incidence reaches the *stall angle* and the flow around the aerofoil breaks down. The drag coefficient has a minimum value near the zero angle of incidence, rises slowly at first and then more steeply as the angle of incidence increases.

Lift generation
Hydrodynamic theory shows the flow round an infinitely long circular cylinder in a non-viscous fluid is as in Figure 9.8.

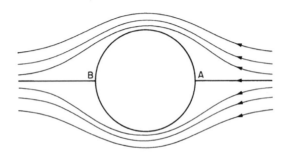

Figure 9.8 Flow round circular cylinder

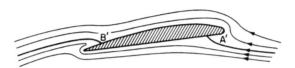

Figure 9.9 Flow round aerofoil without circulation

At points A and B the velocity is zero and these are called *stagnation points*. The resultant force on the cylinder is zero. This flow can be transformed into the flow around an aerofoil as in Figure 9.9, the stagnation points moving to A′ and B′. The force on the aerofoil in these conditions is also zero.

In a viscous fluid the very high velocities at the trailing edge produce an unstable situation due to shear stresses. The potential flow pattern breaks down and a stable pattern develops with one of the stagnation points at the trailing edge, Figure 9.10.

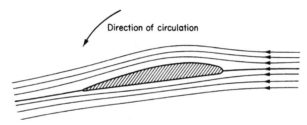

Figure 9.10 Flow round aerofoil with circulation

The new pattern is the original pattern with a *vortex* superimposed upon it. The vortex is centred on the aerofoil and the strength of its circulation depends upon the shape of the section and its angle of incidence. Its strength is such as to move B′ to the trailing edge. It can be shown that the lift on the aerofoil, for a given strength of circulation, τ, is:

$$\text{Lift} = L = \rho V \tau$$

The fluid viscosity introduces a small drag force but has little influence on the lift generated.

Three-dimensional flow
The simple approach assumes an aerofoil of infinite span in which the flow would be two-dimensional. The lift force is generated by the difference in pressures on the face and back of the foil. In practice an

aerofoil will be finite in span and there will be a tendency for the
pressures on the face and back to try to equalize at the tips by a flow
around the ends of the span reducing the lift in these areas. Some
lifting surfaces have plates fitted at the ends to prevent this 'bleeding'
of the pressure. The effect is relatively greater the less the span in
relation to the chord. This ratio of span to chord is termed the *aspect
ratio*. As aspect ratio increases the lift characteristics approach more
closely those of two-dimensional flow.

Pressure distribution around an aerofoil
The effect of the flow past, and circulation round, the aerofoil is to
increase the velocity over the back and reduce it over the face. By
Bernouilli's principle there will be corresponding decreases in pressure
over the back and increases over the face. Both pressure distributions
contribute to the total lift, the reduced pressure over the back making
the greater contribution as shown in Figure 9.11.

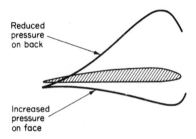

Figure 9.11 Pressure distribution on aerofoil

   The maximum reduction in pressure occurs at a point between the
mid-chord and the leading edge. If the reduction is too great in
relation to the ambient pressure in a fluid like water, bubbles form
filled with air and water vapour. The bubbles are swept towards the
trailing edge and they collapse as they enter an area of higher pressure.
This is known as *cavitation* and is bad from the point of view of noise
and efficiency. The large forces generated when the bubbles collapse
can cause physical damage to the propeller.

PROPELLER THRUST AND TORQUE

Having discussed the basic action of an aerofoil in producing lift, the
action of a screw propeller in generating thrust and torque can be
considered. The momentum theory has already been covered. The

actuator disc used in that theory must now be replaced by a screw with
a large number of blades.

Blade element theory
This theory considers the forces on a radial section of a propeller
blade. It takes account of the axial and rotational velocities at the blade
as deduced from the momentum theory. The flow conditions can be
represented diagrammatically as in Figure 9.12.

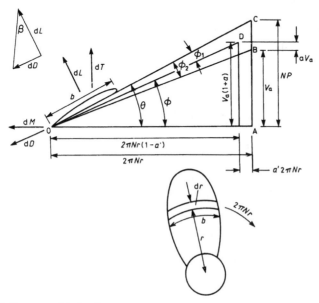

Figure 9.12 Forces on blade element

Consider a radial section at r from the axis. If the revolutions are N
per unit time the rotational velocity is $2\pi Nr$. If the blade was a screw
rotating in a solid it would advance axially at a speed NP, where P is the
pitch of the blade. As water is not solid the screw actually advances at a
lesser speed, V_a. The ratio V_a/ND is termed the *advance coefficient*, and
is denoted by J. Alternatively the propeller can be considered as having
'slipped' by an amount $NP - V_a$. The *slip* or *slip ratio* is:

$$\text{Slip} = (NP - V_a)/NP = 1 - J/p$$

where p is the *pitch ratio* $= P/D$

In Figure 9.12 the line OB represents the direction of motion of the
blade relative to still water. Allowing for the axial and rotational inflow

velocities, the flow is along OD. The lift and drag forces on the blade element, area dA, shown will be:

$$dL = \tfrac{1}{2}\rho V_1^2 C_L \, dA = \tfrac{1}{2}\rho C_L [V_a^2(1 + a)^2 + 4\pi^2 r^2(1 - a')^2] \, b dr$$

where:

$$V_1^2 = V_a^2(1 + a)^2 + 4\pi^2 r^2(1 - a')^2$$

$$dD = \tfrac{1}{2}\rho V_1^2 C_D \, dA = \tfrac{1}{2}\rho C_D [V_a^2(1 + a)^2 + 4\pi^2 r^2(1 - a')^2] \, b dr$$

The contributions of these elemental forces to the thrust, T, on the blade follows as:

$$dT = dL \cos \varphi - dD \sin \varphi = dL \left(\cos \varphi - \frac{dD}{dL} \sin \varphi \right)$$

$$= \tfrac{1}{2}\rho V_1^2 C_L (\cos \varphi - \tan \beta \sin \varphi) \, b dr$$

where $\tan \beta = dD/dL = C_D/C_L$.

$$= \tfrac{1}{2}\rho V_1^2 C_L \frac{\cos (\varphi + \beta)}{\cos \beta} \, b dr$$

Since $V_1 = V_a(1 + a)/\sin \varphi$,

$$dT = \tfrac{1}{2}\rho C_L \frac{V_a^2(1 + a)^2 \cos (\varphi + \beta)}{\sin^2 \varphi \cos \beta} \, b dr$$

The total thrust acting is obtained by integrating this expression from the hub to the tip of the blade. In a similar way, the transverse force acting on the blade element is given by:

$$dM = dL \sin \varphi + dD \cos \varphi = dL \left(\sin \varphi + \frac{dD}{dL} \cos \varphi \right)$$

$$= \tfrac{1}{2}\rho V_1^2 C_L \frac{\sin (\varphi + \beta)}{\cos \varphi} \, b dr$$

Continuing as before, substituting for V_1 and multiplying by r to give torque:

$$dQ = rdM = \tfrac{1}{2}\rho C_L \frac{V_a^2(1 + a)^2 \sin (\varphi + \beta)}{\sin^2 \varphi \cos \beta} \, b r dr$$

The total torque is obtained by integration from the hub to the tip of the blade.

The thrust power of the propeller will be proportional to TV_a and the shaft power to $2\pi NQ$. So the propeller efficiency will be $TV_a/2\pi NQ$. Correspondingly there is an efficiency associated with the blade element in the ratio of the thrust to torque on the element. This is:

$$\text{blade element efficiency} = \frac{V_a}{2\pi Nr} \times \frac{1}{\tan(\varphi + \beta)}$$

But from Figure 9.12,

$$\frac{V_a}{2\pi Nr} = \frac{V_a(1 + a)}{2\pi Nr(1 + a')} \times \frac{1 - a'}{1 + a} = \frac{1 - a'}{1 + a}\tan\varphi$$

This gives a blade element efficiency:

$$\frac{1 - a'}{1 + a} \times \frac{\tan\varphi}{\tan(\varphi + \beta)}$$

This shows that the efficiency of the blade element is governed by the 'momentum factor' and the blade section characteristics in the form of the angles φ and β, the latter representing the ratio of the drag to lift coefficients. If β were zero the blade efficiency reduces to the ideal efficiency deduced from the momentum theory. Thus the drag on the blade leads to an additional loss of efficiency.

The simple analysis ignores many factors which have to be taken into account in more comprehensive theories. These include:

(1) the finite number of blades and the variation in the axial and rotational inflow factors;
(2) interference effects between blades;
(3) the flow around the tip from face to back of the blade which produces a tip vortex modifying the lift and drag for that region of the blade.

It is not possible to cover adequately the more advanced propeller theories in a book of this nature. For those the reader should refer to a more specialist treatise.[2] Theory has developed greatly in recent years, much of the development being possible because of the increasing power of modern computers. So that the reader is familiar with the terminology mention can be made of:

(1) *Lifting line models.* In these the aerofoil blade element is replaced with a single bound vortex at the radius concerned. The strength

of the vortices varies with radius and the line in the radial direction about which they act is called the *lifting line*.

(2) **Lifting surface models.** In these the aerofoil is represented by an infinitely thin bound vortex sheet. The vortices in the sheet are adjusted to give the lifting characteristics of the blade. That is they are such as to generate the required circulation at each radial section. In some models the thickness of the sections is represented by source-sink distributions to provide the pressure distribution across the section. Pressures are needed for studying cavitation.

(3) **Surface vorticity models.** In this case rather than being arranged on a sheet the vortices are arranged around the section. Thus they can represent the section thickness as well as the lift characteristics.

(4) **Vortex lattice models.** In such models the surface of the blade and its properties are represented by a system of vortex panels.

PRESENTATION OF PROPELLER DATA

Dimensional analysis was used in the last chapter to deduce meaningful non-dimensional parameters for studying and presenting resistance. The same process can be used for propulsion.

Thrust and torque
It is reasonable to expect the thrust, T, and the torque, Q, developed by a propeller to depend upon:

(1) its size as represented by its diameter, D;
(2) its rate of revolutions, N;
(3) its speed of advance, V_a;
(4) the viscosity and density of the fluid it is operating in;
(5) gravity.

The performance generally also depends upon the static pressure in the fluid but this affects cavitation and will be discussed later. As with resistance, the thrust and torque can be expressed in terms of the above variables and the fundamental dimensions of time, length and mass substituted in each. Equating the indices of the fundamental dimensions leads to a relationship:

$$T = \rho V^2 D^2 \left[f_1\left(\frac{ND}{V_a}\right), f_2\left(\frac{\nu}{V_a D}\right), f_3\left(\frac{gD}{V_a^2}\right) \right]$$

As required this gives thrust in the units of force and the various expressions in brackets are non-dimensional. f_1 is a function of advance coefficient and is likely to be important. f_2 is a function of Reynolds' number. Whilst relevant to the drag on the propeller blades due to viscous effects its influence is likely to be small in comparison with the other dynamic forces acting. It is therefore neglected at this stage. f_3 is a function of Froude number and is concerned with gravity effects. Unless the propeller is acting close to a free surface where waves may be created, or is being tested behind a hull, it too can be ignored.

Hence for deeply immersed propellers in the non-cavitating condition, the expression for thrust reduces to:

$$T = \rho V_a^2 D^2 \times f_T \left(\frac{ND}{V_a} \right)$$

For two geometrically similar propellers, operating at the same advance coefficient the expression in the brackets will be the same for both. Hence using subscripts 1 and 2 to denote the two propellers:

$$\frac{T_1}{T_2} = \frac{\rho_1}{\rho_2} \times \frac{V_{a1}^2}{V_{a2}^2} \times \frac{D_1^2}{D_2^2}$$

If it is necessary to take Froude number into account:

$$\frac{gD_1}{V_{a1}^2} = \frac{gD_2}{V_{a2}^2}$$

To satisfy both Froude number and advance coefficient:

$$\frac{T_1}{T_2} = \frac{\rho_1}{\rho_2} \times \frac{D_1^3}{D_2^3} = \frac{\rho_1}{\rho_2} \lambda^3$$

where λ is the ratio of the linear dimensions.

Since ND/V_a is constant:

$$\frac{N_1}{N_2} = \frac{V_{a1}}{V_{a2}} \times \frac{D_2}{D_1} = \frac{1}{\lambda^{0.5}}$$

Thus for dynamic similarity the model propeller must rotate faster than the corresponding ship propeller in the inverse ratio of the square root of the linear dimensions.

The thrust power is the product of thrust and velocity and for the same Froude number:

$$\frac{P_{T1}}{P_{T2}} = \frac{\rho_1}{\rho_2} \lambda^{3.5}$$

Correspondingly for torque it can be shown that:

$$Q = \rho V_a^2 D^3 \times f_Q\left(\frac{ND}{V_a}\right)$$

The ratio of torques for geometrically similar propellers at the same advance coefficient and Froude number will be as the fourth power of the linear dimensions. That is:

$$\frac{Q_1}{Q_2} = \frac{\rho_1}{\rho_2} \lambda^4$$

Coefficients for presenting data
It has been shown that:

$$T = \rho V_a^2 D^2 [f_T(J)] \quad \text{and} \quad Q = \rho V_a^2 D^3 [f_Q(J)]$$

Substituting $V_a = NDJ$ in these expressions:

$$T = \rho N^2 D^4 J^2 [f_T(J)] \quad \text{and} \quad Q = \rho N^2 D^5 J^2 [f_Q(J)]$$

$J^2[f(J)]$ is a new function of J, say $F(J)$, and thus:

$$T = \rho N^2 D^4 F_T(J) \text{ and } Q = \rho N^2 D^5 F_Q(J)$$

Non-dimensional coefficients for thrust and torque are:

$$K_T = T/\rho N^2 D^4 = F_T(J) \quad \text{and} \quad K_Q = Q/\rho N^2 D^5 = F_Q(J)$$

The other parameter of concern is the *propeller efficiency* which can be defined as the ratio of output to the input power. Thus:

$$\eta_o = \frac{TV_a}{2\pi QN} = \frac{K_T}{K_Q} \times \frac{J}{2\pi}$$

Thrust and torque coefficients and efficiency when plotted against advance coefficient produce plots as in Figure 9.13. Both thrust and

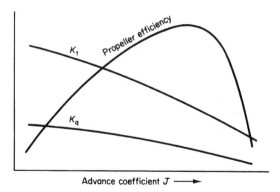

Figure 9.13 Thrust, torque and efficiency curves

torque coefficients decrease with increasing advance coefficient whereas efficiency rises to a maximum and then falls off steeply.

This format is good for presenting the data for a given propeller but not very useful for design purposes. In design the problem is usually to find the diameter and pitch of a propeller to provide the desired power at set revolutions and speed. The thrust power, P_T, is the product of thrust and speed.

$$\text{Thrust power} = TV_a = \rho V_a^3 D^2 f_T(J) = \frac{\rho V_a^5}{N^2 J^2} f_T(J)$$

That is $P_T(N^2/\rho V_a^5) = G(J)$, where G is a new function of J.

Taylor used U to denote thrust power and using seawater as the fluid, dropped ρ and took the square root of the left hand side of the above equation to give a coefficient B_U. He used a corresponding coefficient, B_P, for shaft power which he designated P. That is:

$$B_U = \frac{NU^{0.5}}{V_a^{2.5}} \quad \text{and} \quad B_P = \frac{NP^{0.5}}{V_a^{2.5}}$$

For a series of propellers in which the only parameter varied was pitch ratio, Taylor plotted B_U or B_P against pitch ratio in the form of contours for constant δ values, δ being the reciprocal of the advance coefficient. A typical plot is shown in Figure 9.14.

To use the plot the designer decides upon a value of revolutions for a given power and advance coefficient. This gives B_U or B_P. Erecting an ordinate at this value gives a choice of values of δ from which the diameter is obtained. Associated with each diameter is a value of pitch ratio. For a given B_P the maximum efficiency that can be obtained is

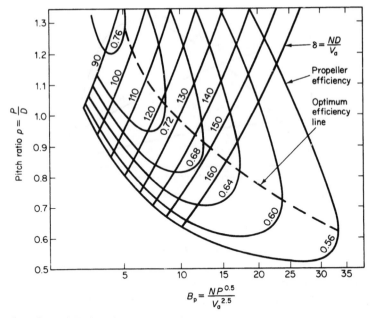

Figure 9.14 Typical Taylor plot

that defined by the efficiency contour which is tangential to the ordinate at that B_P. In other words a line of maximum efficiency can be drawn through the points where the efficiency contours are vertical. Such a line is shown in Figure 9.14. The intersection of this line with the designer's B_P value establishes the pitch and diameter of the most efficient propeller.

Taylor used as units the horse power, speed in knots, N in revolutions per minute and diameter in feet. With these units:

$$B_P = 33.08 \left(\frac{K_Q}{J^5}\right)^{0.5} \quad \text{and} \quad \delta = \frac{ND}{V_a} = \frac{101.27}{J}$$

Keeping speed in knots and N in revolutions per minute, but putting diameter in metres and power in kilowatts:

$$B_P = 1.158 \frac{NP^{0.5}}{V_a^{2.5}} \quad \text{and} \quad \delta = 3.2808 \frac{ND}{V_a}$$

The Taylor method of presentation is widely used for plotting model propeller data for design purposes.

OPEN WATER TESTS

Open water tests of propellers are used in conjunction with tests behind models to determine the wake and relative rotative efficiency. Also methodical propeller testing is carried out in a towing tank. The propeller is powered from the carriage through a streamlined housing. It is pushed along the tank with the propeller ahead of the housing so that the propeller is effectively in undisturbed water. Records of thrust and torque are taken for a range of carriage speeds and propeller revolutions, that is advance coefficient. Such tests eliminate cavitation and provide data on propeller in uniform flow. This methodical series data[3–5] can be used by the designer, making allowance for the actual flow conditions a specific design is likely to experience behind the hull it is to drive.

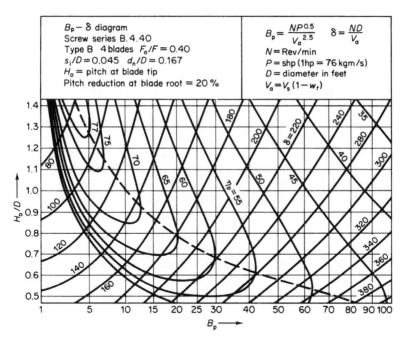

Figure 9.15 Propeller diagram

There have been many methodical series. Those by Froude, Taylor, Gawn, Troost and van Lammeren are worthy of mention. The reader should refer to published data if it is wished to make use of these series. A typical plot for a four bladed propeller from Troost's series is presented in Figure 9.15.

THE PROPELLER BEHIND THE SHIP

So far the resistance of the ship and the propeller performance have been treated in isolation. When the two are brought together there will be interaction effects.

Wake

The presence of the ship modifies the flow conditions in which the propeller works. The water locally will have a velocity relative to the ship and due to this *wake*, as it is called, the average speed of advance of the propeller through the local water will differ from the ship speed. The wake comprises three main elements:

(1) The velocity of the water as it passes round the hull varies, being less than average at the ends.
(2) Due to viscous effects the hull drags a volume of water along with it creating a boundary layer.
(3) The water particles in the waves created by the passage of the ship move in circular orbits.

The first two of these will reduce the velocity of flow into the propeller. The last will reduce or increase the velocity depending upon whether there is a crest or trough at the propeller position. If the net result is that the water is moving in the same direction as the ship the wake is said to be positive. This is the case for most ships but for high speed ships, with a large wave-making component in the wake, it can become negative. The wake will vary across the propeller disc area, being higher close to the hull or behind a structural element such as a shaft bracket arm. Thus the blades operate in a changing velocity field as the propeller rotates leading to a variable angle of incidence. The pitch cannot be constantly varied to optimize the angle and an average value has to be chosen. That is the design of each blade section is based on the mean wake at any radius.

Model tests in a towing tank can be used to study the wake but it must be remembered that the boundary layer thickness will be less relatively in the ship. Model data has to be modified to take account of full-scale measurements as discussed later.

In preliminary propeller design, before the detailed wake pattern is known, an average speed of flow over the whole disc is taken. This is usually expressed as a fraction of the speed of advance of the propeller or the ship speed. It is termed the *wake fraction* or the *wake factor*. Froude used the speed of advance and Taylor the ship speed in deriving the wake fraction, so that if the difference in ship and local water speed is V_w:

Froude wake fraction, $w_F = \dfrac{V_w}{V_a}$ and:

Taylor wake fraction, $w_T = \dfrac{V_w}{V_s}$ where $V_w = V_s - V_a$

These are merely two ways of defining the same phenomenon. Generally the wake fraction has been found to be little affected by ship speed although for ships where the wave-making component of the wake is large there will be some speed effect due to the changing wave pattern with speed. The full-scale towing trials of HMS *Penelope* indicated no significant scale effect on the wake.[6]

The wake will vary with the after end shape and the relative propeller position. The wake fraction can be expected to be higher for a single screw ship than for twin screws. In the former the Taylor wake fraction may be as high as 0.25 to 0.30.

Relative rotative efficiency

The wake fraction was based on the average wake velocity across the propeller disc. As has been explained, the flow varies over the disc and in general will be at an angle to the shaft line. The propeller operating in these flow conditions will have a different efficiency to that it would have if operating in uniform flow. The ratio of the two efficiencies is called the *relative rotative efficiency*. This ratio is usually close to unity and is often taken as such in design calculations.

Augment of resistance, thrust deduction

In the simple momentum theory of propeller action it was seen that the water velocity builds up ahead of the propeller disc. This causes a change in velocity of flow past the hull. The action of the propeller also modifies the pressure field at the stern. If a model is towed in a tank and a propeller is run behind it in the correct relative position, but run independently of the model, the resistance of the model is greater than that measured without the propeller. The propeller causes an augment in the resistance. The thrust, T, required from a propeller will be greater than the towrope resistance, R. The propeller-hull interaction effect can be regarded as an augment of resistance or a reduction in thrust. This leads to two expressions of the same phenomenon.

Augment of resistance, $a = \dfrac{T - R}{R}$

and:

$$\text{Thrust deduction factor, } t = \frac{T - R}{T}$$

Hull efficiency
Using the thrust deduction factor and Froude's notation:

$$T(1 - t) = R \quad \text{and} \quad TV_s(1 - t) = RV_s = TV_a(1 + w_F)(1 - t)$$

Now TV_a is the thrust power of the propeller and RV_s is the effective power for driving the ship, with appendages, at V_s. Thus:

$$P'_E = (P_T)(1 + w_F)(1 - t)$$

Using Taylor's notation, $P'_E = (P_T)(1 - t)/(1 - w_T)$.

In terms of augment of resistance $(1 - t)$ can be replaced by $1/(1 + a)$.

The ratio of P'_E to P_T is called the *hull efficiency* and for most ships is a little greater than unity. This is because the propeller gains from the energy already imparted to the water by the hull. Augment and wake are functions of Reynolds' number as they arise from viscous effects. The variation between model and ship are usually ignored and and the error this introduces is corrected by applying a factor obtained from ship trials.

The factors augment, wake and relative rotative efficiency are collectively known as the *hull efficiency elements*.

Quasi-propulsive coefficient (QPC)
As already explained, this coefficient is obtained by dividing the product of the hull, propeller and relative rotative efficiencies by the appendage coefficient. If the overall *propulsive coefficient* is the ratio of the naked model effective power to the shaft power:

The propulsive coefficient = QPC × transmission efficiency.

The transmission efficiency can be taken[1] as 0.98 for ships with machinery aft and 0.97 for ships with machinery amidships. The difference is due to the greater length of shafting in the latter.

DETERMINING HULL EFFICIENCY ELEMENTS

Having debated in qualitative terms, all the elements involved in propulsion it remains to quantify them. This can be done in a series of model tests. The model is fitted with propellers which are driven through a dynamometer which registers the shaft thrust, torque and revolutions. With the model being towed along the tank at its corresponding speed for the ship speed under study, the propellers are run at a range of revolutions straddling the self-propulsion point for the model. The model would already have been run without propellers to find its resistance. Data from the test can be plotted as in Figure 9.16.

The *self-propulsion point* for the model is the point at which the propeller thrust equals the model resistance with propellers fitted. The difference between this resistance, or thrust, and the resistance of the model alone, is the augment of resistance or thrust deduction.

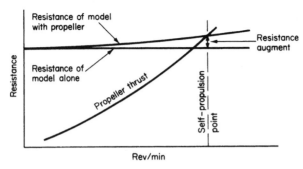

Figure 9.16 Wake and thrust deduction

The propeller is now run in open water and the value of advance coefficient corresponding to the thrust needed to drive the model is determined. This leads to the average flow velocity through the propeller which can be compared to the ship speed corresponding to the self-propulsion point. The difference between the two speeds is the wake assuming an uniform distribution across the propeller disc. The difference in performance due to the wake variation across the disc is given by relative rotative efficiency which is the ratio of the torques needed to drive the propeller in open water and behind the model at the revolutions for self-propulsion.

Although the propellers used in these experiments are made as representative as possible of the actual design, they are small. The thrust and torque obtained are not accurate enough to use directly. The hull efficiency elements obtained are used with methodical series data or specific cavitation tunnel tests to produce the propeller design.

CAVITATION

The lift force on a propeller blade is generated by increased pressure on the face and reduced pressure on the back, the latter making the greater contribution, Figure 9.11. If the reduction in pressure on the back is great enough cavities form and fill up with air coming out of solution and by water vapour. Thus local pressures in the water are important to the study of propellers. In deriving non-dimensional parameters that might be used to characterize fluid flow, it can be shown that the parameter associated with the pressure, p, in the fluid is $p/\rho V^2$. There is always an 'ambient' pressure in water at rest due to atmospheric pressure acting on the surface plus a pressure due to the water column above the point considered. If the water is moving with a velocity V then the pressure reduces to say, p_V, from this ambient value, p_o, according to Bernoulli's principle.

Comparing ship and model under cavitating conditions
For dynamic similarity of ship and model conditions the non-dimensional quantity must be the same for both. That is, using subscripts m and s for model and ship:

$$\frac{p_m}{\rho_m V_m^2} \text{ must equal } \frac{p_s}{\rho_s V_s^2}$$

If the propellers are to operate at the same Froude number, as they would need to if the propeller-hull combination is to be used for propulsion tests:

$$V_m = \frac{V_s}{(\lambda)^{0.5}}$$

where λ is the ratio of the linear dimensions. That is:

$$p_m = \frac{\rho_m}{\rho_s} \times \frac{p_s}{\lambda}$$

Assuming water is the medium in which both model and ship are run, the difference in density values will be negligible. For dynamic similarity the pressure must be scaled down in the ratio of the linear dimensions. This can be arranged for the water pressure head but the atmospheric pressure requires special action. The only way in which this can be scaled is to run the model in an enclosed space in which the pressure can be reduced. This can be done by reducing the air pressure over a ship tank and running a model with propellers fitted at the

correctly scaled pressure as is done in a special *depressurised towing tank*
facility at MARIN in the Netherlands. The tank is 240 m long, 18 m wide
with a water depth of 8 m. The pressure in the air above the water can
be reduced to 0.03 bar. The more usual approach is to use a *cavitation
tunnel.*

Cavitation number

The value $(p_o - p_V)/\rho V^2$ or $(p_o - p_V)/\frac{1}{2}\rho V^2$ is called the *cavitation
number.* Water contains dissolved air and at low pressures this air will
come out of solution and below a certain pressure, the *vapour pressure
of water,* water vapour forms. Hence, as the pressure on the propeller
blade drops, bubbles form. This phenomenon is called *cavitation* and
will occur at a cavitation number given by:

$$\text{cavitation number, } \sigma = (p_o - e)/\tfrac{1}{2}\rho V^2$$

where e is water vapour pressure.

The actual velocity experienced, and the value of p_o, vary with
position on the blade. For a standard, a representative velocity is taken
as speed of advance of the propeller through the water and p_o is taken
at the centre of the propeller hub. For a local cavitation number the
actual velocity at the point concerned, including rotational velocity and
any wake effects, and the corresponding p_o for the depth of the point
at the time must be taken. Blade elements experience different
cavitation numbers as the propeller rotates and cavitation can come
and go.

Occurrence and effects of cavitation

Since cavitation number reduces with increasing velocity cavitation is
most likely to occur towards the blade tips where the rotational
component of velocity is highest. It can also occur near the roots, where
the blade joins the hub, as the angle of incidence can be high there.
The greatest pressure reduction on the back of the blade occurs
between the mid-chord and the leading edge so bubbles are likely to
form there first. They will then be swept towards the trailing edge and
as they enter a region of higher pressure they will collapse. The collapse
of the bubbles generates very high local forces and these can damage
the blade material causing it to be 'eaten away'. This phenomenon is
called *erosion.*

Water temperature, dissolved air or other gases, and the presence of
nuclei to provide an initiation point for bubbles, all affect the pressure at
which cavitation first occurs. Face cavitation usually appears first near the
leading edge of the section. It results from an effective negative angle of
incidence where the wake velocity is low. This face cavitation disappears

as the propeller revolutions and slip increase. Tip vortex cavitation is next to appear, resulting from the low pressure within the tip vortex. As the pressure on the back of the blade falls further the cavitation extends from the leading edge across the back until there is a sheet of cavitation. When the sheet covers the whole of the back of the blade the propeller is said to be fully cavitating or *super-cavitating*. Propellers working in this range do not experience erosion on the back and the drag due to the frictional resistance to flow over the back disappears. Thus when fairly severe cavitation is likely to occur anyway there is some point in going to the super-cavitation condition as the design aim. *Super-cavitating propellers* are sometimes used for fast motor boats.

Flat faced, circular back sections tend to have a less peaky pressure distribution than aerofoil sections. For this reason they have often been used for heavily loaded propellers. However, aerofoil sections can be designed to have a more uniform pressure distribution and this approach is to be preferred. For a given thrust, more blades and greater blade area will reduce the average pressures and therefore the peaks. It will be found that heavily loaded propellers have much broader blades than lightly loaded ones.

A useful presentation for a designer is the *bucket diagram*. This shows, Figure 9.17, for the propeller, the combinations of cavitation number and angle of attack or advance coefficient for which cavitation can be expected. There will be no cavitation as long as the design operates within the bucket. The wider the bucket the greater the range of angle of attack or advance coefficient for cavitation free operation at a given cavitation number.

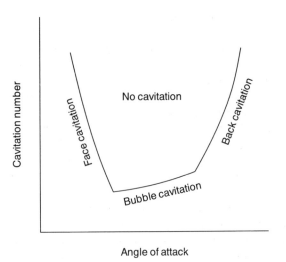

Figure 9.17 Cavitation bucket

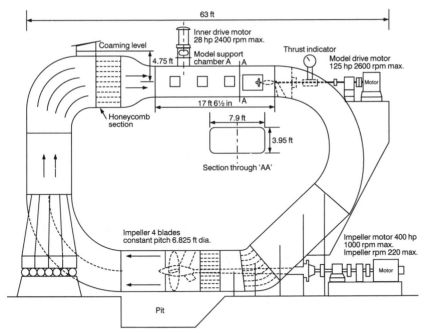

Figure 9.18 Large cavitation tunnel (courtesy RINA)

The cavitation tunnel

A cavitation tunnel is a closed channel in the vertical plane as shown in
Figure 9.18. Water is circulated by means of an impeller in the lower
horizontal limb. The extra pressure here removes the risk of the
impeller itself cavitating. The model propeller under test is placed in a
working section in the upper horizontal limb. The working section is
provided with glass viewing ports and is designed to give uniform flow
across the test section. The water circulates in such a way that it meets
the model propeller before passing over its drive shaft. That is the
propeller is effectively tested in open water. A vacuum pump reduces
the pressure in the tunnel and usually some form of de-aerator is fitted
to reduce the amount of dissolved air and gas in the tunnel water.
Usually the model is tested with the water flow along its axis but there
is often provision for angling the drive shaft to take measurements in
an inclined flow.

A limitation of straight tunnel tests is that the ship wake variations are
not reproduced in the model test. If the tunnel section is large enough
this is overcome by fitting a model hull in the tunnel modified to
reproduce the correctly scaled boundary layer at the test position. In
these cases the flow to the propeller must be past the hull. An
alternative is to create an artificial wake by fixing a grid ahead of the

model propeller. The grid would be designed so that it reduced the water velocities differentially to produce the correctly scaled wake pattern for the hull to which the propeller is to be fitted.

Cavitation tunnel tests
Experiments are usually conducted as follows:

(1) The water speed is made as high as possible to keep Reynolds' number high and reduce scaling effects due to friction on the blades. Since wave effects are not present and the hull itself is not under test the Froude number can be varied.
(2) The model is made to the largest possible scale consistent with avoiding tunnel wall effects.
(3) The shaft revolutions are adjusted to give the correct advance coefficient.
(4) The tunnel pressure is adjusted to give the desired cavitation number at the propeller axis.
(5) A series of runs are made over a range of shaft revolutions, that being a variable which is easy to change. This gives a range of advance coefficients. Tests can then be repeated for other cavitation numbers.

Figure 9.19 shows typical curves of thrust and torque coefficient and efficiency to a base of advance coefficient for a range of cavitation

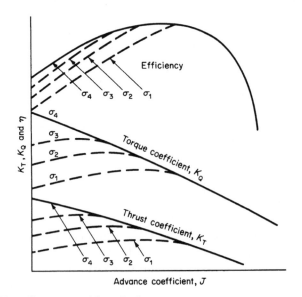

Figure 9.19 Propeller curves with cavitation

number. Compared with non-cavitating conditions values of all three parameters fall off at low advance coefficient, the loss being greater the greater the cavitation number.

When cavitation is present the propeller can be viewed using a stroboscopic light set at a frequency which makes the propeller seem stationary to the human eye. Photographs can be taken to illustrate the degree of cavitation present. A similar technique is used in propeller viewing trials at sea when the operation of the propeller is observed through special glass viewing ports fitted in the shell plating.

The propeller, particularly when cavitating, is a serious noise source. It would be useful to be able to take noise measurements in a cavitation tunnel. This is not possible in most tunnels because of the background noise levels but in recent years a few tunnels have been built which are suited to acoustical measurements.[7]

OTHER PROPULSOR TYPES

So far attention has been focused on the fixed pitch screw propeller as this is the most common form of propulsor. Others are described briefly below.

Controllable pitch propeller

The machinery must develop enough torque to turn the propeller at the revolutions appropriate to the power being developed or the machinery will *lock up*. This matching is not always possible with fixed blades and some ships are fitted with propellers in which the blades can be rotated about axes normal to the drive shaft. These are termed *controllable pitch propellers* (CPPs). The pitch can be altered to satisfy a range of operating conditions which is useful in tugs and trawlers. For such ships there is a great difference in the propeller loading when towing or trawling and when running free. The machinery can be run at constant speed so that full power can be developed over the range of operating conditions.

The pitch of the blades is changed by gear fitted in the hub and controlled by linkages passing down the shaft. Thus the CPP has a larger boss than usual which limits the blade area ratio to about 0.8 which affects cavitation performance. It is also mechanically fairly complex which limits the total power that can be transmitted. By reversing the pitch an astern thrust can be produced thus eliminating the need for a reversing gear box. Variation in thrust for manoeuvring can be more rapid as it only involves changing blade angle rather than shaft revolutions, but for maximum acceleration or deceleration there will be an optimum rate of change of blade angle.

The term controllable pitch propeller should not be confused with a *variable pitch propeller.* The latter term is applied to propellers in which pitch varies with radius, the blades themselves being fixed.

Self pitching propellers

A propeller which has found favour for auxiliary yachts and motorsailers in recent years is the self pitching propeller.[8] The blades are free to rotate through 360° about an axis approximately at right angles to the drive shaft. The angle the blades take up, and therefore their pitch, is dictated solely by the hydrodynamic and centrifugal forces acting.

Shrouded or ducted propellers

The propeller[9] is surrounded by a shroud or duct as depicted in Figure 9.20. The objects are to improve efficiency, avoid erosion of banks in confined waterways and shield noise generated on the blades.

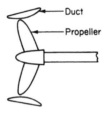

Figure 9.20 Shrouded propeller

The duct can be designed so that it contributes to ahead thrust so offsetting the drag of the shroud and its supports. Most early applications were to ships with heavily loaded propellers like tugs. Its use is now being extended and it is considered suitable for large tankers.

Pump jets

This is an advanced variant of the ducted propeller[10] for use in warships, particularly submarines, where noise reduction is important. A rotor with a large number of blades operates between sets of stator blades the whole being surrounded by a specially shaped duct. The rotational losses in the wake are eliminated, cavitation is avoided and there is no resultant heeling torque acting on the ship. The last point is of significance for single screw submarines.

Contra-rotating propellers

Another way of eliminating the net heeling torque is to use two propellers on the one shaft line rotating in opposite directions. It has been concluded[11] that they can be useful in large tankers where by using slow running contra-rotating propellers the quasi-propulsive coefficient can be increased by up to 20 per cent. In high speed dry cargo ships, where propeller diameter may be restricted by draught, propeller efficiency may be increased by 12 per cent. Like CPPs, contra-rotating propellers introduce mechanical complications.

Azimuthing propellers
These are propellers mounted on a housing which can rotate through a full circle to give thrust in any direction. Drive must be through bevel gearing and the transmissable power is limited. The usual application is to tugs for good manoeuvrability.

Vertical axis propeller
This is essentially a horizontal disc, rotating about a vertical axis, which carries a series of vertical blades which can rotate about their own vertical axes. The individual vertical blades have aerofoil sections and generate lift forces by the same principles as those described for the screw propeller. By controlling the angle of the blades as the horizontal disc turns, a thrust can be produced in any desired direction. Vertical axis propellers are fitted in tugs and ferries for good manoeuvrability. Drive again is usually through bevel gears with a limitation on the power, see Figure 10.10.

Water jet propulsion
This type of propulsion has become more common in recent years for high speed craft. Water is drawn into the ship and then pushed out at the stern to develop thrust. The ejecting unit can be steerable to give a varying thrust direction. It is attractive for craft where it is desired to have no moving parts outside the hull. For this reason early applications were for craft operating in very shallow water. The water jet can be discharged either above or below water. Some hydrofoil craft use the system, discharging above water.

Paddle wheels
A paddle wheel is a ring of paddles rotating about a horizontal transverse axis. In very simple craft the paddles are fixed but in craft requiring greater efficiency their angle is changed as the wheel rotates. When fitted either side of a ship they can exert a large turning moment on the ship by being run one ahead and the other astern. Unfortunately this leads to a wide vessel. For use in narrow waterways the paddle wheel is mounted at the stern giving rise to the *stern wheeler* on the rivers of the USA.

Wind
The wind was the only means, apart from oars, of propelling ships for many centuries. It has always been popular for pleasure craft. The rise in fuel costs and public concern with conserving energy sources has rekindled interest. Some ships have sails to use in place of their engines when wind conditions are suitable. Other applications have harnessed modern technology to use the old idea of rotating cylinders, the *Flettner rotor* concept, more effectively.

SHIP TRIALS

A complete range of trials is carried out on a ship when complete to confirm that the ship meets its specification. Amongst these is a speed trial which has the following uses:

(1) To demonstrate that the desired speed is attained. There are usually penalties imposed if a ship fails to meet the specified speed but it would be uneconomic to provide too much power. This illustrates the importance of a designer being able to predict resistance and powering accurately in the design stages.

(2) To provide a feedback on the effectiveness of prediction methods and provides factors to be applied to overcome any shortcomings in the methods.

(3) To provide data on the relationships between shaft revolutions, ship speed and power for use by the master.

To meet the last two aims it is desirable to gather data at a range of speeds. Therefore trials are run at progressively higher speeds up to the maximum. For that reason they are often called *progressive speed trials*. The engine designer may wish to take readings of a wide range of variables concerned with the performance of the machinery itself. The naval architect, however, is concerned with the shaft revolutions, thrust, torque and speed achieved relative to the water. Thrust is not always measured. It can be measured by a special thrust meter but more commonly by a series of electrical resistance strain gauges fitted to the shaft. Torque is measured by the twist experienced by an accurately known length of shaft. This leaves the problem of determining the speed of the ship.

Speed measurement
Ships are provided with a means of speed measurement, usually in the form of a pitot tube, or *pitot log*, projecting below the keel. This is not

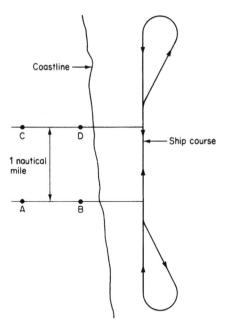

Figure 9.21 Measured mile

accurate enough for speed trial purposes. Indeed the speed trial is often used to calibrate the log.

Traditionally a ship has been taken to a *measured mile* for speed trials although nowadays use can be made of accurate position fixing systems which are available in many areas. The measured mile, Figure 9.21, comprises a number of posts set up on land at known distances apart. These distances are not necessarily exactly one nautical mile but it simplifies analysis if they are. The posts are in parallel pairs clearly visible from the sea. There may be two pairs as in the figure, or three pairs to give a double reading on each run. By noting the time the ship takes to transit between adjacent pairs of posts, the speed relative to land is obtained. For accuracy a number of precautions are needed:

(1) The ship must be travelling at right angles to the line of posts.
(2) The ship must have reached a steady speed for the power used by the time it passes the line of the first pair of posts.
(3) The depth of water must be adequate to avoid the speed being affected due to squat and trim.
(4) A clear day with little or no wind and calm seas is needed.
(5) The ship must be newly out of dock, with a clean bottom. If this condition is not met some allowance may be needed for the increased resistance due to time out of dock.

(6) After passing the last pair of posts the ship must continue on for some way and then turn for the return run, reaching a steady speed before passing the first set of posts. This may involve a run on of several miles and an easy turn to minimize the drop in speed associated with turning.
(7) The displacement must be accurately obtained by measuring the ship's draughts and the density of the water.

If there were no wind, current or tide, one run at each power setting would theoretically be enough and the speed through the water would be the same as that relative to land. In any practical situation a number of runs are needed in each direction so that the results can be analysed to remove current and tidal effects.

Determining speed through the water
It is usually assumed that the current and tide effects will vary with time in accordance with an equation of the type:

$$V_T = a_0 + a_1 t + a_2 t^2$$

where a_0, a_1 and a_2 are constants.

What concerns the ship is the component of tide along the ship's line of transit on the measured mile. This is to be understood when tide is mentioned. Suppose four runs are made, two in each direction. Two will be with the tide and two against. Using subscripts to denote the speeds recorded on the runs:

$$V_1 = V + a_0$$
$$V_2 = V - a_0 - a_1 t_1 - a_2 t_1^2$$
$$V_3 = V + a_0 + a_1 t_2 + a_2 t_2^2$$
$$V_4 = V - a_0 - a_1 t_3 - a_2 t_3^2$$

where V is the speed through the water and the runs are at times zero and t_1, t_2 and t_3.

The four equations can be solved for the three unknowns and the speed relative to the water found. To illustrate this take the simple case where the four runs are made at equal time intervals. In this case t_1 can be taken as t, t_2 as $2t$ and t_3 as $3t$. The equations become:

$$V_1 = V + a_0$$
$$V_2 = V - a_0 - a_1 t - a_2 t^2$$
$$V_3 = V + a_0 + 2a_1 t + 4a_2 t^2$$
$$V_4 = V - a_0 - 3a_1 t - 9a_2 t^2$$

The unknown a_0 can be eliminated by adding successive pairs of equations, yielding three equations for $2V$. Adding successive pairs of these eliminates a_2 and so on, giving, finally:

$$8V = V_1 + 3V_2 + 3V_3 + V_4, \text{ from which } V \text{ follows.}$$

If the tide varied linearly with time three runs would be enough. A higher order equation for tide can be used if more runs are made. Usually four runs are adequate.

Trial condition
Ideally trials would be carried out for each of the likely operating conditions. This would be expensive and time consuming. The key condition is that for which the contract speed is defined which is usually the deep load condition. If this level of loading cannot be achieved some lesser load is specified with a correspondingly higher speed to be obtained. In some ships, oil tankers for instance, the load condition can be achieved by water ballasting.

The trial is carried out in calm conditions which are easy to define for contract purposes but are not representative of the average conditions a ship will meet in service. Increasingly it is realized that it is this speed that is of real interest and this has led to a lot of effort being devoted to obtaining and analysing voyage data. Also the advent of accurate positioning systems facilitates measurement of speed, albeit relative to land, in a whole range of weather conditions during the service life.

Plotting trials data
The results from the ship trial can be plotted as in Figure 9.22. The revolutions will be found to plot as a virtually straight line against

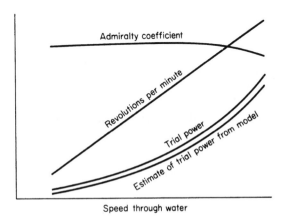

Figure 9.22 Trials data

speed. Power increases rapidly with speed. If enough readings are available the humps and hollows due to the interaction of bow and stern wave systems will be detectable. The figure shows a plot of *Admiralty coefficient*. This coefficient, or constant, is effectively the inverse of circular C and is the given by:

$$\frac{V^3 \Delta^{\frac{2}{3}}}{\text{Power}}$$

A comparison of the power measured on trial and that estimated from model tests, gives a ship-model correlation factor. This data can be used for future similar ships.

Wake fraction from ship trials
If shaft torque is measured a torque coefficient can be calculated from the shaft revolutions and propeller diameter. The advance coefficient can be found from the ship speed and a plot made as in Figure 9.23. From open water propeller tests the value of advance coefficient

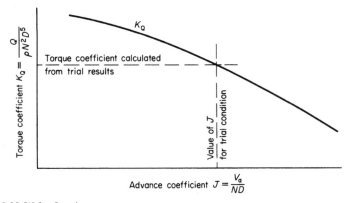

Figure 9.23 Wake fraction

corresponding to any given torque coefficient can be found. This yields a value of V_a. The wake is the difference between the ship speed and V_a. This is the mean wake through the propeller disc. In the absence of open water model tests methodical series data can be used but with less accuracy.

MAIN MACHINERY POWER

The objectives of the resistance and propulsion testing have been to develop an efficient hull form and propulsor design and to establish the main machinery power needed to drive the ship at the design speed. The point has been reached in the analysis where the last aim can be met.

The general principles involved were outlined at the beginning of this chapter. In Chapter 8 an example was given illustrating the calculation of a hull's effective power. This same ship can be used to calculate the machinery power needed to propel it at the 15 knots for which the effective power was 2502 kW allowing for roughness.

Continuing:

P_E for rough hull = 2502 kW

Appendage allowance, say 5 per cent = 125

P'_E in smooth water = 2627

If the hull efficiency elements and the quasi-propulsive coefficient determined from experiment were Taylor wake fraction = 0.27, hull efficiency = 1.15, QPC = 0.75 and relative rotative efficiency = 1.00, then:

Required delivered power = 2627/0.75 = 3503 kW

Transmission loss at say 2 per cent = 70

Required installed power = 3573 kW

This is the power for calm conditions. If 20 per cent is allowed for average service conditions the installed power to maintain 15 knots in these conditions is 4288 kW.

The actual power to be fitted will depend upon the powers of the machinery sets available. For the present example it is assumed that the closest power available is 4275 kW and that the slight difference is accepted by the designer. It follows that:

Power at propeller = 4190 kW

Speed of advance of propeller = 15(1 − 0.27) = 10.95 knots

The choice of propeller revolutions is generally a compromise between propeller performance and machinery characteristics. Propellers are more efficient at low revolutions and machinery is lighter, for a given power, at high revolutions. Reduction gear can be fitted to bridge the gap but the cost and weight must be set against the advantages gained. It is assumed initially that propeller revolutions are to be 100.

$$B_P = \frac{1.158NP^{0.5}}{V_a^{2.5}}$$

$$= \frac{1.158 \times 100 \times (4190)^{0.5}}{(10.95)^{2.5}}$$

$$= 18.89$$

From the propeller curves presented in Figure 9.15, which are for a four bladed propeller of 0.4 blade area ratio:

$\delta = 3.2808ND/V_a = 178$

Pitch ratio $= p = 0.8$

Efficiency $= \eta = 0.655$

These are the values for maximum efficiency. Since $D = (\delta \times V_a)/3.2808N = 5.94$ m.

Pitch $= pD = 4.75$ m.

QPC $=$ (hull efficiency) $\times$ (propeller open η) $\times$ (RRE)

$= 1.15 \times 0.655 \times 1.00 = 0.75$

This QPC happens to be the same as that assumed in the calculation of power. Had it differed significantly then a repeat calculation would have been needed using the new value. The process can be repeated for other propeller revolutions to see how the propeller dimension and QPC would vary. For $N = 110$,

$$B_P = \frac{1.158 \times 110 \times (4190)^{0.5}}{(10.95)^{2.5}} = 20.78$$

From Figure 9.15, $\delta = 183$, $p = 0.78$, $\eta = 0.645$. Hence,

$$\text{diameter} = \frac{183 \times 10.95}{110 \times 3.2808} = 5.55 \text{ m}$$

pitch $= 0.78 \times 5.55 = 4.33$ m,

QPC $= 1.15 \times 0.645 \times 1.00 = 0.74$

For $N = 120$,

$$B_P = \frac{1.158 \times 120 \times (4190)^{0.5}}{(10.95)^{2.5}} = 22.67$$

and:

diameter = 5.29

pitch = 3.97

QPC = 0.73

These results confirm that as expected a higher revving propeller is smaller in diameter and is less efficient.

Figure 9.15 did not allow for cavitation and should cavitation be a problem curves from cavitation tunnel tests should be used.

SUMMARY

As was stated at the beginning of the last chapter, resistance and propulsion are interdependent and the separation of the two is artificial although convenient. It is appropriate therefore in this summary to cover the work of both chapters.

There is resistance to the passage of a ship through the water. The resistance of the naked hull measured in model tests can be considered as comprising two components, the frictional and the residuary resistance. These components scale differently in moving from the model to full-scale. The residuary resistance, for geometrically similar hulls at corresponding speeds, scales as the ratio of the displacements. The frictional resistance component is estimated from experimental data and scaled in relation to Reynolds' number. The naked hull resistance must take account of surface roughness and be increased to allow for appendages. Where necessary an allowance can be made for the resistance of the above water form due to its passage through the air although in the absence of a natural wind this is likely to be small.

Fitting a propulsor modifies the flow around the hull causing an augment in resistance the hull experiences and modifying the wake in which the propulsor must generate its thrust. The flow through the propulsor is not uniform so the efficiency will vary from that found in open water tests. Taking all these factors into account the power to be delivered by the propulsor for a given ship speed can be calculated. The power required of the main propulsion machinery follows after making allowance for transmission losses.

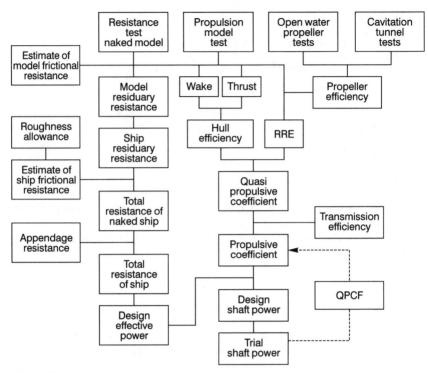

Figure 9.24

This analysis process is illustrated in Figure 9.24, and leads to the power needed in calm seas with no natural wind. This is usually the condition for which the required ship speed is set down in the contract and which is aimed for in the speed trial conducted on completion of the ship. In service the ship will seldom be in these conditions. For more realistic powers and speeds allowance must be made for the wind resistance on the above water form and the effects of waves on the hull resistance and propulsor performance. This involves assessing the average conditions a ship is likely to meet or the range of conditions and their probability of occurrence.

References

1. *Standard procedure for resistance and propulsion experiments with ship models.* National Physical Laboratory Ship Division Report No. 10.
2. Carlton, J. S. (1994) *Marine propellers and propulsion.* Butterworth-Heinemann.
3. Gawn, R. W. (1953) Effect of pitch and blade width on propeller performance. *TINA.*

4. Troost, L. (1950–51) Open water test series with modern propeller forms. *TNECI.*

5. van Lammeren, W. P. A., van Manen, J. D. and Oosterveld, M. W. C. (1969) The Wageningen B-screw series. *TSNAME.*

6. Canham, H. J. S. (1974) Resistance, propulsion and wake tests with HMS *Penelope. TRINA.*

7. Weitsendorf, E.-A., Friesch, J. and Song, C. S. S. (1987) Considerations for the new hydrodynamics and cavitation tunnel (HYCAT) of the Hamburg Ship Model Basin (HSVA). *ASME International Symposium on Cavitation Research Facilities and Techniques,* Boston.

8. Miles, A., Wellicome, J. F. and Molland, A. F. (1993) The technical and commercial development of self pitching propellers. *TRINA.*

9. Ryan, P. G. and Glover, E. J. (1972) A ducted propeller design method: a new approach using surface vorticity distribution technique and lifting line theory. *TRINA.*

10. Heggstad, K. M. (1981) Submarine propellers. *Maritime Defence,* June.

11. Glover, E. J. (1966–67) Contra rotating propellers, for high speed cargo vessels. *TNECI.*

12. Burrill, L. C. and Emerson, A. (1962–63) Propeller cavitation: further tests on 16 in propeller models in the King's College cavitation tunnel. *TNECI.*

10 Manoeuvring

All ships must be able to control their speed and follow an intended course when in transit. Additionally, when entering congested waterways or harbours, they must be able to position themselves accurately. Vessels used for oil drilling or extraction often need to hold a particular position relative to the seabed with great precision.

To achieve this a ship must have the means of producing ahead and astern thrust, turning moments and lateral thrust. The last two are provided by rudders of various types assisted, in some cases, by lateral thrust units at the bow and/or stern. Ahead and astern thrust is usually provided by the main propulsion system as dealt with in Chapter 9 on propulsion. Because rudders are usually sited close to the propulsors there will exist an interaction between the two. Where more than one shaft is fitted, a turning moment can be produced by going ahead on one shaft and astern on the other.

The ease with which a vessel can maintain a straight course, or be made to turn, will depend upon its *directional stability.* Sometimes this characteristic is known as the ship's *dynamic stability* but should not be confused with dynamical stability (see Chapter 5). A number of measures are used to define the manoeuvring characteristics of a ship and these are discussed. They are defined and measured in still water conditions. The influence of wind, waves and current must be allowed for in applying the data to practical sea-going conditions. Wind effects can be very important especially in ships with large superstructures such as cruise liners and ferries. Indeed strong winds may prevent a ship turning into the wind if it has large windage areas aft. When operating close aboard another ship, close to a bank, or in shoaling water, the ship experiences additional forces that may throw it off the intended course.

A submarine is a special case as it operates in three dimensions which brings with it a need to control its position and attitude in depth as well as azimuth. Submarines are dealt with in one section and the rest of the chapter is devoted to surface vessels.

DIRECTIONAL STABILITY AND CONTROL

It was seen in an earlier chapter that when a ship at rest in still water is disturbed in the horizontal plane there are no hydrostatic forces to return it to its original position or to increase the movement. The ship is in neutral equilibrium. When a moving ship is disturbed in yaw it is acted upon by hydrodynamic forces which may be stabilizing or destabilizing. If stabilizing, the ship will take up a new steady line of advance but unless some corrective action is applied, by using the rudder for example, this will not be the original line of advance. The vessel is said to be *directionally stable* in these conditions but clearly this stability differs from that discussed in considering inclinations from the vertical. A ship is said to be directionally stable if, after being disturbed in yaw, it takes up a new straight line path.

An arrow is an example of a directionally very stable body. If gravity is ignored the flight of an arrow is a straight line. If it is disturbed, say by a gust of wind, causing it to take up an angle of attack relative to its line of motion, the aerodynamic forces on its tail feathers will be much greater than those on the shank. The disturbing force will push the arrow sideways and the moment from the force on the tail will reduce the angle of attack. The arrow will oscillate a little and then settle on a new straight line path. The arrow, like a weathercock, has a high degree of directional stability.

For a ship form it is not clear from the lines whether it will be stable or not. By analogy with the arrow, good stability requires that the resultant hydrodynamic moment following a disturbance should tend to reduce yaw. The disturbing force is said to act at the hull's *centre of lateral resistance*. For stability this must be aft of the centre of gravity and it is to be expected that a cut away bow, a large skeg aft and trim by the stern would all tend to improve stability. That is about as much as one can deduce from the general shape at this stage. A degree of directional stability is desirable otherwise excessive rudder movements will be needed to maintain a straight course. Too much stability makes a ship difficult to turn.

Ignoring any longitudinal components, a disturbing force on a ship will lead to a small sideways velocity, v, an angular velocity in yaw, r, and linear and angular accelerations. In addition, in the general case, there will be forces and moments due to the use of the rudder. For small deviations second order terms in the equations of motion can be ignored and the equations become:

$$(m - Y_{\dot{v}})\dot{v} = Y_v v + (Y_r - m)r + Y_{\delta_R}\delta_R$$

$$(I - N_{\dot{r}})\dot{r} = N_v v + N_r r + N_{\delta_R}\delta_R$$

In these equations m is the mass of the ship, Y and N are the lateral force and yawing moment, δ_R is the rudder angle and subscripts denote differentiation with respect to the quantity in the subscript. Other terms have their usual meaning.

These equations look rather complicated but they are only equating the rate of change of momentum to the applied force. The total force and moment are then expressed as the sum of the components due to each variable, that is the force due to lateral velocity is the product of the velocity and the rate of change of force with velocity, and so on.

The equations can be made non-dimensional, the non-dimensional terms being denoted by a prime, giving:

$$(m' - Y'_{\dot{v}})\dot{v}' = Y'_v v' + (Y'_r - m')r' + Y'_{\delta_R}\delta'_R$$

$$(I' - N'_{\dot{r}})\dot{r}' = N'_v v' + N'_r r' + N'_{\delta_R}\delta'_R$$

As an example:

$$Y'_v = \frac{1}{\frac{1}{2}\rho V^2 L^2} \times \frac{\partial Y}{\partial V}$$

The coefficients Y'_v, N'_v etc. are called the *stability derivatives*.

Since the directional stability of a ship relates to its motion with no corrective action the equations defining it are as above with the rudder terms removed. It can then be shown that the condition for positive stability, or *stability criterion*, is:

$$\frac{N'_r}{Y'_r - m'} \text{ must be greater than } \frac{N'_v}{Y'_v}$$

This is the same as saying that the centre of pressure in pure yaw must be ahead of that for pure sway. The centre of pressure for pure sway is often called the *neutral point*. It is kL forward of the centre of gravity where:

$$k = \frac{N'_v}{Y'_v}$$

The value of k is typically $\frac{1}{3}$ so that the neutral point is about $\frac{1}{6}$ of the length aft of the bow. With a lateral force applied at the neutral point the ship continues on its heading but with a steady sideways velocity. That is it is moving at a small angle of attack such that the hydrodynamic forces on the hull balance the applied moment and force. If the applied force is F then the resulting sideways velocity is $v = F/Y_v$. There will be a short period of imbalance before the ship settles down to its new steady state.

If the sideways force is applied aft of the neutral point and to starboard the ship will turn to port. If it is applied forward of the neutral point the ship turns in the direction of the force. The greater the distance the force is from the neutral point the greater the turning moment on the ship. Thus rudders placed aft are more effective than rudders at the bow by a factor of about five for typical hull forms. Aft they can benefit from the propeller race aft as well and are less vulnerable in a collision.

TURNING A SHIP

From simple mechanics it will be appreciated that to cause a ship to move in a circle requires a force to act on it, directed towards the centre of the circle. That force is not provided by the rudder. The rudder exerts a moment on the ship which produces an angle of attack between the ship's heading and its direction of advance. This angle of attack causes relatively large forces to act on the hull and it is the component of these directed towards the centre of the circle that turns the ship. The fore and aft components will slow the ship down which is a noticeable feature of a ship's behaviour in turning.

MEASURES OF MANOEUVRABILITY

These are not easily quantified although there has been much discussion on the matter. Large ocean going ships spend most of their transit time in the open seas, steering a steady course. They can use tugs to assist with manoeuvring in confined waters so the emphasis will probably be on good directional stability. Poor inherent directional stability can be compensated for by fitting an auto pilot but the rudder movements would be excessive and the steering gear would need more maintenance. For ships such as short haul ferries the designer would aim for good rudder response to help the ships avoid collision and to assist berthing and unberthing.

If possible the parameters used to define manoeuvrability should be directly related to the performance the master desires. This is not easy and use is made of a number of standard manoeuvres which can be carried out full scale and during model experiments. Other movements can be created in a model for measuring the stability derivatives, that cannot be directly simulated at full scale. The measures commonly studied are now described.

The turning circle

The motion of a ship turning in a circle is shown in Figure 10.1.

As the rudder is put over there is a force which pushes the ship sideways in the opposite direction to which it wishes to turn. As the hydrodynamic forces build up on the hull the ship slows down and

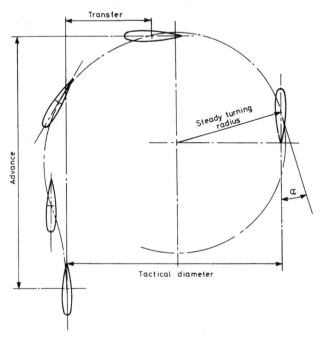

Figure 10.1 Turning circle

starts to turn in a steadily tightening circle until a steady state speed and radius of turn is reached. A number of parameters are used to define the turning performance. They are:

(1) the *drift angle*, which at any point is the angle between the ship's head and its direction of motion. This varies along the length, increasing the further aft it is measured. Unless otherwise specified the drift angle at the ship's centre of gravity is to be understood.

(2) the *advance*, which is the distance travelled by the ship's centre of gravity, in the original direction of motion, from the instant the rudder is put over. Usually the advance quoted is that for a 90° change of heading although this is not the maximum value.

(3) the *transfer* which is the lateral displacement of the ship's centre of gravity from the original path. Usually transfer is quoted for 90° change of heading.

(4) the *tactical diameter* which is the value of the transfer for 180° change of heading although this is not the maximum transfer. It is usual to quote a *tactical diameter to length ratio, TD/L*. Modern frigates at high speed and full rudder turn with a *TD/L* of about 3. For smaller turning circles such as may be required of a mine countermeasures vessel lateral thrust units or azimuthing propellers would be used. A value of 4.5 would be regarded as good for most merchant ships but a value greater than 7 as very poor.

(5) the *diameter of the steady turning circle*. The steady state is typically reached at some point between 90° and 180° change of heading.

(6) the *steady speed on turn*. Due to the fore and aft component of the hydrodynamic forces the ship slows down during the turn. Unless engine power is increased it may be only 60 per cent of the approach speed. The steady speed is reached as the diameter steadies. If a ship does need to reverse direction, as might be the case of a frigate hunting a submarine, the time to turn through 180° is likely to be more important than a really small diameter of turn. Because of the loss of speed on turn such ships would choose a lesser rudder angle to get round quickly and to avoid the need to accelerate so much after the turn.

(7) the *turning rate*. The quickest turn might not be the tightest. A frigate would turn at about 3° per second. Half this rate would be good for merchant ships and values of 0.5–1 would be more typical.

(8) the *pivoting point*. This is the foot of the perpendicular from the centre of the turning circle to the middle line of the ship, extended if necessary. This is the point at which the drift angle will be zero and it is typically about $\frac{1}{6}$ of the length from the bow.

(9) the *angle of heel during the turn*. A ship typically heels in to the turn as the rudder is initially applied. On the steady turn it heels outwards, the heeling moment being due to the couple produced by the athwartships components of the net rudder and hull hydrodynamic forces and the acceleration force acting at the centre of gravity which is caused by the turning of the ship. It is countered by the ship's stability righting moment.

If the steady radius of turn is R, Figure 10.2, and the steady heel is φ and the transverse components of the forces on the hull

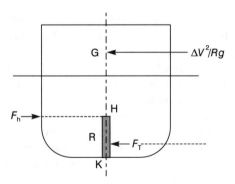

Figure 10.2 Ship heeling in turn

and rudder are F_h and F_r, acting at KH and KR above the keel then:

$$F_h - F_r = \frac{\Delta V^2}{Rg}$$

and the heeling moment is:

$$\frac{\Delta V^2}{Rg} KG + F_r(\text{KR}) - F_h(KH) = (F_h - F_r)(KG - KH) - F_r(KH - KR)$$

For most ships $(KH - KR)$ will be small and the heeling moment becomes $(F_h - F_r) GH$. This leads to an angle of heel such that:

$$\Delta GM \sin \varphi = (F_h - F_r) GH = \frac{\Delta V^2}{Rg} GH \text{ , giving } \sin \varphi = \frac{GH}{GM} \times \frac{V^2}{Rg}$$

This is only an approximation to the angle as it is difficult to estimate the centre of lateral resistance for a heeled hull. In some high speed turns the heel can be quite pronounced. It is important in passenger carrying ships and may influence the choice of metacentric height.

The zig-zag manoeuvre

A ship does not often turn through large angles and seldom through even a half circle. Thus the turning circle is not realistic in terms of movements of a ship in service. It is also difficult to measure the initial reaction to the rudder accurately in this manoeuvre. On the other hand a ship does often need to turn through angles of 10° to 30°. It is

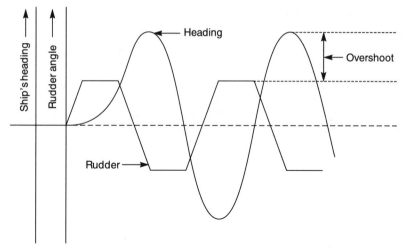

Figure 10.3 Zig-zag manoeuvre

the initial response of the ship to the rudder being put over that can be vital in trying to avoid a collision. This initial response is studied in the *zig-zag manoeuvre*. In it the ship proceeds on a straight course at a steady speed, a rudder angle of 20° is applied and held until the ship's head has changed by 20° and then the rudder is reversed to 20° the other way and held until the ship's head has changed 20° in the opposite direction. The manoeuvre is repeated for different speeds, rudder angles and heading changes.

The important measurements from the manoeuvre, Figure 10.3, are:

(1) the *overshoot* angle. This is the amount the heading increases by after the rudder is reversed. Large angles would represent a ship in which the helmsman would have difficulty in deciding when to take rudder off to check a turn. Values of 5.5 and 8.5° would be reasonable aims for ships at 8 and 16 knots respectively, varying roughly with speed. The angle does not depend upon ship length.

(2) the times to the first rudder reversal and the first maximum heading change. It has been suggested[1] that for reasonable designs, times to change heading by 20° would be of the order of 80 to 30 seconds for a 150 metre ship over the range 6 to 20 knots. The time would be roughly proportional to length.

(3) the steady overshoot angle and the period of the cycle once a steady condition is reached.

The spiral manoeuvre

This is a manoeuvre aimed at giving a feel for a ship's directional stability. From an initial straight course and steady speed the rudder is put over say 15° to starboard. After a while the ship settles to a steady rate of turn and this is noted. The rudder angle is then reduced to 10° starboard and the new steady turn rate noted. This is repeated for angles of 5°S, 5°P, 10°P, 15°P, 10°P and so on. The resulting steady rates of turn are plotted against rudder angle.

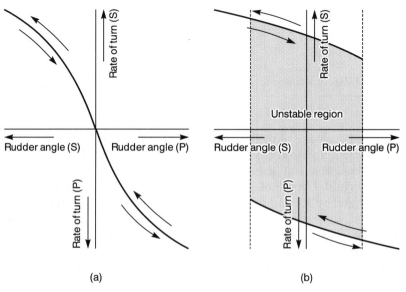

(a)   (b)

Figure 10.4 Spiral manoeuvre

If the ship is stable there will be a unique rate of turn for each rudder angle. If the ship is unstable the plot has two 'arms' for the smaller rudder angles, depending upon whether the rudder angle is approached from above or below the value. Within the rudder angles for which there is no unique response it is impossible to predict which way the ship will turn, let alone the turn rate, as this will depend upon other disturbing factors present in the ocean. The manoeuvre does not give a direct measure of the degree of stability, although the range of rudder angles over which response is indeterminate is a rough guide. To know the minimum rudder angle needed to ensure the ship turns in the desired direction is very useful.

The pull-out manoeuvre

This manoeuvre[1] is also related to the directional stability of the ship. The rudder is put over to a certain angle and held until the ship is turning at a steady rate. The rudder is returned to amidships and the change in the turn rate with time is noted. For a stable ship the turn rate will reduce to zero and the ship takes up a new steady straight line course. A plot of the log of the rate of turn against time is a straight line after a short transition period. If the ship is unstable the turn rate will not reduce to zero but there will remain some steady rate of turn. The area under the plot of turn rate against time gives the total heading change after the rudder angle is taken off. The smaller this is the more stable the ship.

If the ship is conducting turning trials it will be in a state of steady turning at the end of the run. If the rudder is centred the pull-out manoeuvre can be carried out immediately for that speed and rudder angle.

MANOEUVRING DEVICES

Rudder forces and torques

Rudder forces
Rudders are streamlined to produce high lift with minimum drag. They are symmetrical to produce the same lift characteristics whichever way they are turned. The force on the rudder, F, depends upon the cross-sectional shape, area A, the velocity V through the water and the angle of attack α.

$$F = \text{Const.}\rho A V^2 f(\alpha)$$

The constant depends upon the cross section and the rudder profile, in particular the ratio of the rudder depth to its chord length and the degree of rounding off on the lower corners. The lift is also sensitive to the clearance between the upper rudder surface and the hull. If this is very small the lift is augmented by the mirror image of the rudder in the hull. $f(\alpha)$ increases roughly linearly with α up to the stall angle which is typically about $35°$. $f(\alpha)$ will then decrease.

Various approximate formulae have been proposed for calculating F. An early one was:

$$F = 577 \, AV^2 \sin \alpha \text{ newtons}$$

In this an allowance was made for the effect of the propeller race by multiplying V by 1.3 for a rudder immediately behind a propeller and by 1.2 for a centreline rudder behind twin screws. Other formulations based on the true speed of the ship are:

$F = 21.1 \, AV^2 \, \alpha$ newtons for ahead motion
$F = 19.1 \, AV^2 \, \alpha$ newtons for astern motion
$F = 18.0 \, AV^2 \, \alpha$ newtons

The first two were proposed for twin rudders behind twin screws and the third for a centreline rudder behind a single screw.

If wind or water tunnel data is available for the rudder cross section this should be used to calculate the lift and the centre of pressure position.

Typically the rudder area in merchant ships is between $\frac{1}{60}$ and $\frac{1}{70}$ of the product of length and draught.

Rudder torques

To establish the torque needed to turn a rudder it is necessary to find the position on the rudder at which the rudder force acts. That position is the *centre of pressure*. For a rectangular flat plate of breadth B at angle of attack α, this can be taken as $(0.195 + 0.305 \sin \alpha) \, B$ aft of the leading edge. For a typical rudder section it has been suggested[2] that the centre of pressure for a rectangular rudder can be taken at $K \times$ (chord length) aft of the leading edge, where:

$K = 0.35$ for a rudder aft of a fin or skeg, the ship going ahead.
$ = 0.31$ for a rudder in open water.

The open water figure is used for both configurations for a ship going astern.

For a non-rectangular rudder an approximation to the centre of pressure position can be obtained by dividing the rudder into a number of rectangular sections and integrating the individual forces and moments over the total area. This method can also be used to estimate the vertical location of the centre of pressure, which dictates the bending moment on the rudder stock or forces on the supporting pintles.

Example 10.1

A rudder with an area of $20 \, \text{m}^2$ when turned to $35°$ has the centre of pressure 1.2 m from the stock centreline. If the ship speed is 15 knots, and the rudder is located aft of the single propeller, calculate the diameter of the stock able to take this torque, assuming an allowable stress of $70 \, \text{MN/m}^2$.

Solution

Using the simple formula from above to calculate the rudder force and a factor of 1.3 to allow for the screw race:

$$F = AV^2 \sin \alpha$$

$$= 577 \times 20 \times (15 \times 1.3 \times 0.5144)^2 \times \sin 35°$$

$$= 0.666 \, \text{MN}$$

Torque on rudder stock $= 0.666 \times 1.2 = 0.799 \, \text{MNm}$

This can be equated to qJ/r where r is the stock radius, q is the allowable stress, and J is the second moment of area about a polar axis equal to $\pi r^4/2$. Hence

$$r^3 = 2T/\pi q = \frac{0.799 \times 2}{70\pi} = 0.007\,27$$

$r = 0.194 \, \text{m}$ and diameter of stock $= 0.388 \, \text{m}$

In practice it would be necessary to take into account the shear force and bending moment on the stock in checking that the strength was adequate. The bending moment and shear forces will depend upon the way the rudder is supported. If astern speeds are high enough the greatest torque can arise then as the rudder is less well balanced for movements astern.

Rudder types

The rudder is the most common form of manoeuvring device fitted in ships. Its action in causing the ship to turn has already been discussed. In this section it is proposed to review briefly some of the more common types.

Conventional rudders
These have a streamlined section to give a good lift to drag ratio and are of double-plate construction. They can be categorized according to the degree of balance. That is how close the centre of pressure is to the rudder axis. A balanced rudder will require less torque to turn it. They are termed *balanced*, *semi-balanced* or *unbalanced*. The other method of categorization is the arrangement for suspending the rudder from the

hull. Some have a pintle at the bottom of the rudder, others one at about mid depth and others have no lower pintle. The last are termed *spade rudders* and it is this type which is most commonly fitted in warships.

Different rudder types are shown in Figures 10.5 to 10.7. The arrangements are self explanatory.

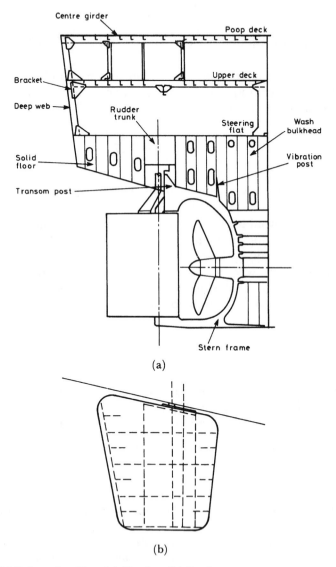

(a)

(b)

Figure 10.5 Balanced rudders (a) Simplex; (b) Spade

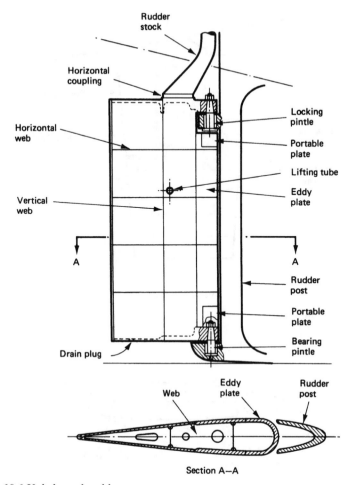

Figure 10.6 Unbalanced rudder

Special rudders

A number of special rudders have been proposed and patented over the years. The aim is usually to improve the lift to drag ratio achieved. A *flap rudder*, Figure 10.8, uses a flap at the trailing edge to improve the lift by changing aerofoil shape. Typically, as the rudder turns, the flap goes to twice the angle of the main rudder but in some rudders the flaps can be moved independently. A variant is the *Flettner rudder* which uses two narrow flaps at the trailing edge. The flaps move so as to assist the main rudder movement reducing the torque required of the steering gear.

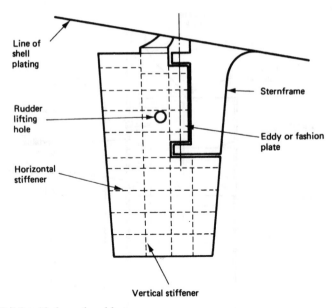

Figure 10.7 Semi-balanced rudder

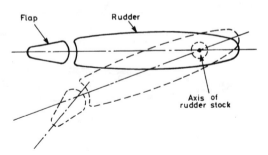

Figure 10.8 Flap rudder

In semi-balanced and unbalanced rudders the fixed structure ahead of the rudder can be shaped to help augment the lateral force at the rudder.

Active rudders
These are usually spade type rudders but incorporating a faired housing with a small electric motor driving a small propeller. This provides a 'rudder' force even when the ship is at rest when the hydrodynamic forces on the rudder would be zero. It is used in ships requiring good manoeuvrability at very low speeds.

The Kitchen rudder

This rudder is a two-part tube shrouding the propeller and turning about a vertical axis. For ahead propulsion the two halves of the tube are opened to fore and aft flow. For turning the two halves can be moved together to deflect the propeller race. The two halves can be moved to block the propeller race and reverse its flow.

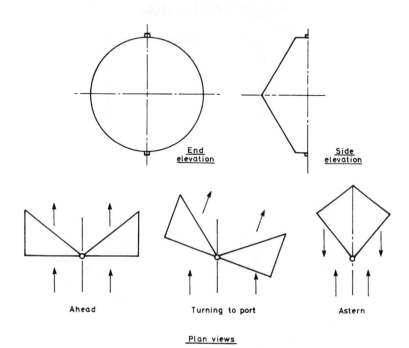

Figure 10.9 Kitchen rudder

Vertical axis propeller

This type of propeller is essentially a horizontal disc carrying a number of aerofoil shaped vertical blades. As the disc turns the blades are caused to turn about their vertical axes so that they create a thrust. For normal propulsion the blades are set so that the thrust is fore and aft. When the ship wishes to turn the blades are adjusted so that the thrust is at an angle. They can produce lateral thrust even at low ship speed.

Lateral thrust units

It is sometimes desirable to be able to control a ship's head and course independently. This situation can arise in mine countermeasure vessels which need to follow a certain path relative to the ground in conditions

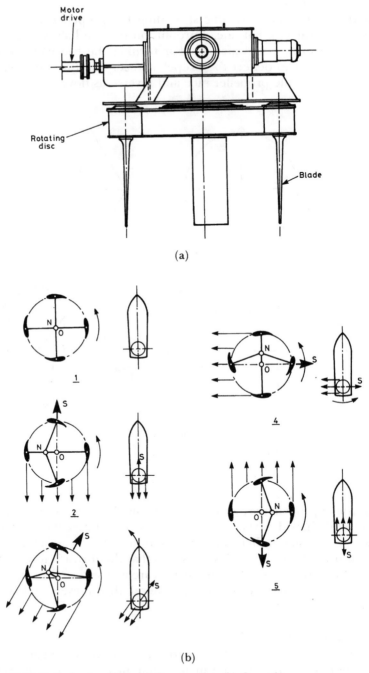

(a)

(b)

Figure 10.10 Vertical axis rudder (a) Construction (b) Operation

of wind and tide. Other vessels demanding good positional control are offshore rigs. This leads to a desire to have the ability to produce lateral thrusts at the bow as well as the stern. It has been seen that bow rudders are likely to be ineffective because of their proximity to the neutral point. The alternative is to put a thrust unit, usually a contra-rotating propeller, in a transverse tube. Such devices are called *lateral thrust units* or *bow thrust units* when fitted forward. Their efficiency is seriously reduced by a ship's forward speed, the thrust being roughly halved at about two knots. Some offshore rigs have dynamic positional control provided by a number of computer controlled lateral thrust units.

SHIP HANDLING

Several aspects of the handling of a ship are not brought out by the various manoeuvres discussed above.

Handling at low speed
At low speed any hydrodynamic forces on the hull and rudders are small since they vary as the square of the speed. The master must use other means to manoeuvre the ship, including:

(1) Using one shaft, in a twin shaft ship, to go ahead while the other goes astern.
(2) When leaving, or arriving at, the dockside a stern or head rope can be used as a pivot while going ahead or astern on the propeller.
(3) Using the so-called *paddle wheel effect* which is a lateral force arising from the non-axial flow through the propeller. The force acts so as to cause the stern to swing in the direction it would move had the propeller been a wheel running on a hard surface. In twin screws the effects generally balance out when both shafts are acting to provide ahead or astern thrust. In coming alongside a jetty a short burst astern on one shaft can 'kick' the stern in towards the jetty or away from it depending which shaft is used.
(4) Using one of the special devices described above. For instance a Kitchen rudder, a vertical axis propeller or a lateral thruster.

Interaction between ships
As discussed in Chapter 8 on resistance a ship creates a pressure field as it moves through the water. The field shows a marked increase in pressure near the bow and stern with a suction over the central portion of the ship. This pressure field acts for quite an area around

the ship. Anything entering and disturbing the pressure field will cause a change in the forces on the ship, and suffer forces on itself. If one ship passes close to another in overtaking it, the ships initially repel each other. This repulsion force reduces to zero as the bow of the overtaking ship reaches the other's amidships and an attraction force builds up. This is at a maximum soon after the ships are abreast after which it reduces and becomes a repelling force as the two ships part company. When running abreast the ships experience bow outward moments. As they approach or break away they suffer a bow inward moment[3]. Such forces are very important for ships when they are replenishing at sea[4].

Similar considerations apply when a ship approaches a fixed object. For a vertical canal bank or jetty the ship experiences a lateral force and yaw moment. Open structure jetties will have much less effect than a solid one. In shallow water the reaction is with the sea bed and the ship experiences a vertical force and trimming moment resulting in a bodily sinkage and trim by the stern. This can cause a ship to ground in water which is nominally several feet deeper than the draught[5].

The sinkage is known as *squat*. This phenomenon has become more important with the increasing size of tankers and bulk carriers. Squat is present even in deep water due to the different pressure field around the ship at speed. It is accentuated, as well as being more significant, in shallow water. In a confined waterway a *blockage* effect occurs once the ship's sectional area exceeds a certain percentage of the waterway's cross section. This is due to the increased speed of the water which is trying to move past the ship.

For narrow channels a *blockage factor* and a *velocity-return factor*[6] have been defined as:

$$\text{Blockage factor, } S = \frac{\text{Ship's breadth} \times \text{draught}}{\text{Canal breadth} \times \text{depth}} = \frac{A_s}{A_c}$$

$$\text{Velocity-return factor, } S_v = \frac{A_s}{A_c - A_s} = \frac{S}{1 - S}$$

A formula for estimating squat at speed V in open or confined waters is:

$$\text{Maximum squat} = \frac{C_B \times S_v^{\frac{2}{3}} \times V^{2.08}}{30} \text{ metres}$$

C_B being the block coefficient.

A simplified formula for open water[7] is:

$$\text{Maximum squat} = \frac{C_B \times V^2}{100} \text{ metres}$$

Other approximate approaches[8] are to take squat as 10 per cent of the draught or as 0.3 metres for every five knots of speed.

DYNAMIC STABILITY AND CONTROL OF SUBMARINES

Modern submarines can travel at high speed although sometimes their function requires them to move very slowly. These two speed regimes pose quite different situations as regards their *dynamic stability* and control in the vertical plane. The submarine's static stability dominates the low speed performance but has negligible influence at high speed. For motions in the horizontal plane the submarine's problems are similar to those of a surface ship except that the submarine, when deep, experiences no free surface effects. At periscope depth the free surface becomes important as it affects the forces and moments the submarine experiences, but again mainly in the vertical plane.

A submarine must avoid hitting the sea bed or exceeding its safe diving depth and, to remain covert, must not break surface. It has a layer of water in which to manoeuvre which is only about two or three ship lengths deep. At high speed there is little time to take corrective action should anything go wrong. By convention submarines use the term pitch angle for inclinations about a transverse horizontal axis (the trim for surface ships) and the term trim is used to denote the state of equilibrium when submerged. To trim a submarine it is brought to neutral buoyancy with the centres of gravity and buoyancy in line.

The approach to the problem is like that used for the directional stability of surface ships but bearing in mind that:

(1) The submarine is positively stable in pitch angle. So if it is disturbed in pitch while at rest it will return to its original trim angle.
(2) The submarine is unstable for depth changes due to the compressibility of the hull.
(3) It is not possible to maintain a precise balance between weight and buoyancy as fuel and stores are used up.

The last two considerations mean that the control surfaces must be able to provide a vertical force to counter any out of balance force and moment in the vertical plane. To control depth and pitch separately

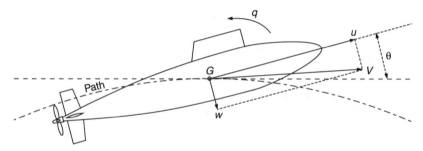

Figure 10.11 Submarine in vertical plane

requires two sets of control surface, the *hydroplanes*, one forward and one aft.

Consider a submarine turning in the vertical plane as in Figure 10.11. Taking the combined effects of the two sets of hydroplanes as represented by a term in δ_H the equations of motion for the vertical plane are given by:

$$wZ_w + qZ_q + mqV + \delta_H Z_{\delta_H} = 0$$

$$wM_w + qM_q + \delta_H M_{\delta_H} - mgBG\theta = 0$$

These are similar to the equations for the directional stability of a surface ship. In this case Z and M are the vertical force and pitching moment. Subscripts w, q and δ_H denote differentiation with respect to the variable concerned. In these equations:

mqV is a centrifugal force term

$mgBG\theta$ is a statical stability term, BG being the distance between B and G.

This stability term is constant for all speeds whereas the moments M vary with the square of the velocity. The stability term can normally be ignored at speeds greater than 10 knots. Ignoring this term for the time being and eliminating w between the two equations leads to the condition that for the submarine to have positive dynamic stability:

$M_q Z_w - M_w(Z_q + mV)$ must be greater than zero.

This is termed the *high speed stability criterion*. If this criterion is met and the submarine is statically stable, it will be stable at all speeds. If the criterion is not met then a statically stable submarine will develop a diverging oscillation at forward speeds above some critical value.

The equations can be manipulated[9] to derive a number of interesting relationships:

(1) The steady path in the vertical plane cannot be a circle unless BG is zero.
(2) The rate of change of depth is zero if

$$V = \frac{mgBG}{M_w - M_{\delta_H} \dfrac{Z_w}{Z_{\delta_H}}}$$

(3) The pitch angle is zero if $M_{\delta_H}/Z_{\delta_H} = M_w/Z_w$ but the depth rate is not zero but given by $\delta_H Z_{\delta_H}/Z_w$.
(4) The ratio M_w/Z_w defines the distance forward of G of a point known as the *neutral point*. A vertical force applied at this point causes a depth change but no change in pitch angle.
(5) A second point, known as the *critical point*, is distant $mgBG/VZ_w$ aft of the neutral point. A vertical force applied at the critical point will cause no change of depth but will change the pitch angle. A downward force forward of the critical point will increase depth, a downward force aft of the critical point will reduce depth. Thus at this point there is a reversal of the expected result of applying a vertical force.
(6) As speed drops the critical point moves aft. At some speed, perhaps two or three knots, the critical point will fall on the after hydroplane position. The speed at which this happens is termed the *critical speed*.

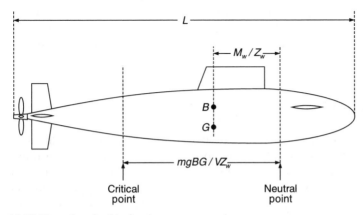

Figure 10.12 Neutral and critical points

MODIFYING THE MANOEUVRING PERFORMANCE

As with other aspects of ship performance it is difficult, and sometimes dangerous, to generalize on the effect of design changes on a ship's manoeuvring qualities. This is because so many factors interact and what is true for one form may not be true for another. Broadly however it can be expected that:

(1) Stern trim improves directional stability and increases turning diameter.
(2) A larger rudder can improve directional stability and give better turning.
(3) Decrease in draught can increase turning rate and improve directional stability. This is perhaps due to the rudder becoming more dominant relative to the immersed hull.
(4) Higher length to beam ratios lead to a more stable ship and greater directional stability.
(5) Quite marked changes in metacentric height, whilst affecting the heel during a turn, have little effect on turning rate or directional stability.
(6) For surface ships at a given rudder angle the turning circle increases in diameter with increasing speed but rate of turn can increase. For submarines turning diameters are little affected by speed.
(7) A large skeg aft will increase directional stability and turning circle diameter.
(8) Cutting away the below water profile forward can increase directional stability.

By and large the hull design of both a surface ship and a submarine is dictated by considerations other than manoeuvring. If model tests show a need to change the manoeuvring performance this would normally be achieved by modifying the areas and positions of the control surfaces and skegs.

SUMMARY

The reasons a ship requires certain levels of manoeuvrability have been discussed and the difficulties in defining any standard parameters for studying the matter pointed out. Various standard manoeuvres used in defining a vessel's directional stability and turning performance have been described. A number of rudder types and other devices for manoeuvring ships have been reviewed. The special case of a submarine moving in three dimensions has been touched upon together with the action of the control forces in controlling pitch angle and depth.

References

1. Burcher, R. K. (1991) The prediction of the manoeuvring characteristics of vessels. *The Dynamics of Ships*. The Royal Society, London.
2. Gawn, R. W. (1943) Steering experiments, Part 1. *TINA*.
3. Newton, R. N. (1960) Some notes on interaction effects between ships close aboard in deep water. *First symposium on ship manoeuvrability, David Taylor Model Basin*.
4. Chislett, H. W. J. (1972) Replenishment at sea. *TRINA*.
5. Dand, I. W. (1981) On ship-bank interaction. *TRINA*.
6. Dand, I. W. and Ferguson, A. M. (1973) The squat of full ships in shallow water. *TRINA*.
7. Barrass, C. B. (1978) Ship squat, *Polytech International*.
8. Dand, I. W. (1977) The physical causes of interaction and its effects. *Nautical Institute Conference on Ship Handling*.
9. Nonweiler, T. R. F. (1961) The stability and control of deeply submerged submarines. *TRINA*.

11 Vibration, noise and shock

Ships must be designed so as to provide a suitable environment for the continuous, efficient and safe working of equipment and crew. Also the environment should be one in which crew and passengers will be comfortable. Vibration, noise and shock are all factors in that environment.

A ship responds to any applied force. For some responses, for instance those of roll, pitch and heave in a seaway, it is acceptable to regard the ship as a rigid body. In all cases however there will be some flexing of the structure and the total response will include movements of one part of the structure relative to others. These can be termed the elastic body responses or degrees of freedom and they can be very important. Even in ship motions slamming must be treated as a dynamic, vibratory response. The vibratory stresses can increase the overall hull stresses quite considerably and must be taken into account, particularly in fatigue studies. Vibration, noise and shock are all manifestations of the ship's elastic responses.

VIBRATION

In this chapter general vibrations of ships are considered. The most common sources of vibration excitation are propellers and main machinery. All vibration is undesirable. It can be unpleasant for people on board and can be harmful to equipment. It must be reduced as much as possible but it cannot be entirely eliminated. The designer of systems and equipment to be fitted must allow for the fact that they will have to operate in a vibratory environment, fitting special anti-vibration mounts, if necessary, for especially sensitive items.

Vibration levels of machinery can be used to decide when a machine needs attention and often vibration measuring devices are fitted as a form of 'health monitoring'. If vibration levels start to rise the cause can be investigated.

A ship is a complex structure and a full study of its vibration modes and levels is very demanding. Indeed, in some cases it is necessary to resort to physical modelling of parts of the ship to confirm results of finite element analyses. However the basic principles involved are not too difficult and these are explained.

Simple vibrations

The simplest case of oscillatory motion is where the restoring force acting on a body is proportional to its displacement from a position of stable equilibrium. This is the case of a mass on a spring which is the fundamental building block from which the response of complex structures can be arrived at, by considering them as combinations of many masses and springs. In the absence of any damping the body, once disturbed, would oscillate indefinitely. Its distance from the equilibrium position would vary sinusoidally and such motion is said to be *simple harmonic*. This type of motion was met earlier in the study of ship motions in still water. The presence of *damping*, due say to friction or viscous effects, causes the motion to die down with time. The motion is also affected by *added mass* effects due to the vibrating body interacting with the fluid around it. These are not usually significant for a body vibrating in air but in water they can be important. There are many standard texts to which the reader can refer for a mathematical treatment of these motions. The important findings are merely summarized here.

The motion is characterized by its amplitude, A, and period, T. For undamped motions the displacement at any time, t, is given by:

$$A \sin \left[\left(\frac{k}{M} \right)^{0.5} t + \delta \right]$$

where:

M is the mass of the body,
k is the force acting per unit displacement, and
δ is a phase angle.

The *period* of this motion is $T = 2\pi (M/k)^{0.5}$, and its *frequency* is $n = 1/T$. These are said to be the system's natural period and frequency.

Damping

All systems are subject to some damping, the simplest case being when the damping is proportional to the velocity. The effect is to modify the period of the motion and cause the amplitude to diminish with time.

The period becomes $T_d = 2\pi/[(k/M) - (\mu/2M)^2]^{0.5}$, frequency being $1/T_d$, where μ is a damping coefficient such that damping force equals μ (velocity).

Successive amplitudes decay according to the equation

$A \exp[-(\mu/2M)t]$.

As the damping increases the number of oscillations about the mean position will reduce until finally the body does not overshoot the equilibrium position at all. The system is then said to be *dead beat.*

Regular forced vibrations

Free vibrations can occur when for instance, a structural member is struck an instantaneous blow. More generally the disturbing force will continue to be applied to the system for a longish period and will itself fluctuate in amplitude. The simplest type of disturbing force to assume for analysis purposes is one with constant amplitude varying sinusoidally with time. This would be the case where the ship is in a regular wave system. The differential equation of motion, taking x as the displacement at time t, becomes:

$$M\frac{dx^2}{dt^2} + \mu\frac{dx}{dt} + kx = F_0 \sin \omega t$$

The solution of this equation for x is the sum of two parts. The first part is the solution of the equation with no forcing function. That is, it is the solution of the damped oscillation previously considered. The second part is an oscillation at the frequency of the applied force. It is $x = B \sin(\omega t - \gamma)$.

After a time the first part will die away leaving the oscillation in the frequency of the forcing function. This is called a *forced oscillation.* It is important to know its amplitude, B, and the phase angle, γ. These can be shown to be:

$$B = \frac{F_0}{k} \times \frac{1}{[(1 - \Lambda^2)^2 + (\mu^2\Lambda^2/Mk)]^{0.5}}$$

and

$$\tan \gamma = \frac{\mu \Lambda}{(Mk)^{0.5}} \times \frac{1}{(1 - \Lambda^2)}$$

In these expressions Λ is called the *tuning factor* and is equal to $\omega/(k/M)^{0.5}$. That is the tuning factor is the ratio of the frequency of the applied force to the natural frequency of the system. Since k represents the stiffness of the system, F_0/k is the displacement which would be caused by a static force F_0. The ratio of the amplitude of the dynamic

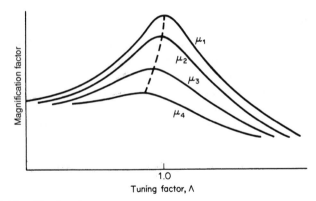

Figure 11.1 Magnification factor

displacement to the static displacement is termed the *magnification factor*, Q. Q is given by:

$$Q = \left[(1 - \Lambda^2)^2 + \frac{\mu^2 \Lambda^2}{Mk} \right]^{-0.5}$$

Curves of magnification factor can be plotted against tuning factor for a range damping coefficients as in Figure 11.1. At small values of Λ, Q tends to unity and at very large values it tends to zero. In between these extremes the response builds up to a maximum value which is higher the lower the damping coefficient. If the damping were zero the response would be infinite. For lightly damped systems the maximum displacement occurs very close to the system's natural frequency and the tuning factor can be taken as unity. Where the frequency of the applied force is equal to the system's natural frequency it is said that there is *resonance*. It is necessary to keep the forcing frequency and natural frequency well separated if large amplitude vibrations are to be avoided. At resonance the expression for the phase angle gives $\gamma = \tan^{-1} \infty$, giving a phase lag of 90°.

In endeavouring to avoid resonance it is important to remember that many systems have several natural frequencies associated with different deflection profiles or *modes* of vibration. An example is a vibrating beam that has many modes, the first three of which are shown in Figure 11.2. All these modes will be excited and the overall response may show more than one resonance peak.

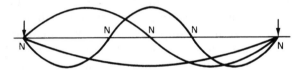

Figure 11.2 Vibration modes

Irregular forcing function

In the above the forcing function was assumed sinusoidal and of constant amplitude. The more general case would be a force varying in an irregular way. In this case the force can be analysed to obtain its constituent regular components as was done for the waves in an irregular sea. The vibratory response of the system to the irregular force can then be taken as the sum of its responses to all the regular components.

SHIP VIBRATION

The disturbing forces

A ship is an elastic structure and will vibrate when subject to oscillating forces. The forces may arise from within the ship or be imposed upon it by external factors. Of the former type the unbalanced forces in main and auxiliary machinery can be important. Rotating machinery such as turbines and electric motors generally produce forces which are of low magnitude and relatively high frequency. Reciprocating machinery on the other hand produces larger magnitude forces of lower frequency. Large main propulsion diesels are likely to pose the most serious problems particularly where, probably for economic reasons, 4 or 5 cylinder engines are chosen. These can have large unbalance forces at frequencies equal to the product of the running speed and number of cylinders. These forces can be at frequencies of the same order as those of the hull vibrations. Thus quite severe vibration can occur unless the engines are very well balanced. Auxiliary diesels tend to run at higher speeds. Their frequencies are higher and may excite local vibrations. Vibration forces transmitted to the ship's structure can be much reduced by flexible mounting systems. In more critical cases vibration neutralizers can be fitted in the form of sprung and damped weights which absorb energy or active systems can be used which generate forces equal but in anti-phase to the disturbing forces.

Misalignment of shafts and propeller imbalance can cause forces at a frequency equal to the shaft revolutions. With modern production methods the forces involved should be small. A propeller operates in a non-uniform flow and is subject to forces varying at blade rate frequency, that is the product of the shaft revolutions and the number of blades. These are unlikely to be of concern unless there is resonance with the shafting system or ship structure. Even in uniform flow a propulsor induces pressure variations in the surrounding water and on the ship's hull in the vicinity. The variations are more pronounced in non-uniform flow particularly if cavitation occurs. Stable cavitation over a relatively large area is equivalent to an increase in blade thickness and the blade rate pressures increase accordingly. If cavitation is unstable pressure variations may be many times greater. The number of blades directly affects frequency but has little effect on pressure amplitude. The probability of vibration problems in single screw ships can be reduced by using bulbous or U sections rather than V in the after body, avoiding near horizontal buttock lines above the propeller, and by providing good tip clearance between propeller and hull. Good tip clearance is important for all ships although smaller clearances are generally acceptable the greater the number of blades. Shallow immersion of the propeller tips should be avoided to reduce the possibility of air drawing. Generally the wake distribution in twin screw ships is less likely to cause vibration problems. If A-brackets are used the angle between their arms must not be the same as that between the propeller blades or the propeller will experience enhanced pressure fluctuations as the blades pass through the wake of the arms.

A ship in waves is subject to varying hull pressures as the waves pass. The ship's rigid body responses were dealt with under seakeeping. Some of the wave energy is transferred to the hull causing main hull and local vibrations. The main hull vibrations are usually classified as *springing* or *whipping*. The former is a fairly continuous and steady vibration in the fundamental hull mode due to the general pressure field. The latter is a transient caused by slamming or shipping green seas. Generally vertical vibrations are most important because the vertical components of wave forces are dominant. However, horizontal and torsional vibrations can become large in ships with large deck openings or of relatively light scantlings such as container ships or light aircraft carriers. The additional bending stresses due to vibration may be significant in fatigue because of their frequency. The stresses caused by whipping can be of the same order of magnitude as the wave bending stresses.

The ship responses

Having considered the various disturbing forces likely to be met, it is necessary to consider the ship's oscillatory responses and their frequencies.

Vibrations are dealt with as either *local vibrations* or *main hull vibrations*. The former are concerned with a small part of the structure, perhaps an area of deck. The frequencies are usually higher, and the amplitudes lower, than the main hull vibrations. Because there are so many possibilities and the calculations can be complex they are not usually studied directly during design except where large excitation forces are anticipated. Generally the designer avoids machinery which generate disturbing frequencies close to those of typical ship type structures. Any faults are corrected as a result of trials experience. This is often more economic than carrying out extensive design calculations as the remedy is usually a matter of adding a small amount of additional stiffening.

Main hull vibrations are a different matter. If they do occur the remedial action may be very expensive. They must therefore be looked at in design. The hull may bend as a beam or twist like a rod about its longitudinal axis. These two modes of vibration are called *flexural* and *torsional* respectively. Flexing may occur in a vertical or horizontal plane but the vertical flexing is usually the more worrying. Except in lightly structured ships the torsional mode is not usually too important.

Flexural vibrations
When flexing in the vertical or horizontal planes the structure has an infinite number of degrees of freedom and the mode of vibration is described by the number of *nodes* which exist in the length. The fundamental mode is the two-node as shown in Figure 11.3.

This yields a displacement at the ends of the ship since there is no rigid support there. This is often referred to as a *free-free* mode and differs from that which would be taken up by a structural beam where there would be zero displacement at one end at least. The next two higher modes have three and four nodes. All are free-free and can occur in both planes. Associated with each mode is a natural

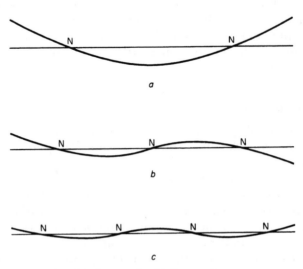

Figure 11.3 (a) Two-node; (b) Three-node; (c) Four-node

Table 11.1 Typical ship vibration frequencies

Ship type	Length (m)	Condition of loading	Frequency of vibration						
			Vertical				Horizontal		
			2 node	3 node	4 node	5 node	2 node	3 node	4 node
Tanker	227	Light	59	121	188	248	103	198	297
		Loaded	52	108	166	220	83	159	238
Passenger ship	136		104	177			155	341	
Cargo ship	85	Light	150	290			230		
		Loaded	135	283			200		
Cargo ship	130	Light	106	210			180	353	
		Loaded	85	168			135	262	
Destroyer	160	Average action	85	180	240		120	200	

frequency of free vibration, the frequency being higher for the higher modes. If the ship were of uniform rigidity and uniform mass distribution along its length and was supported at its ends, the frequencies of the higher modes would be simple multiples of the fundamental. In practice ships differ from this although perhaps not as much as might be expected, as is shown in Table 11.1[1]. It will be noted that the greater mass of a loaded ship leads to a reduction in frequency.

Torsional vibration
In this case the displacement is angular and a one-node mode of vibration is possible. Figure 11.4 shows the first three modes.

Coupling
It is commonly assumed for analysis purposes that the various modes of vibration are independent and can be treated separately. In some circumstances, however, vibrations in one mode can generate vibration in another. In this case the motions are said to be *coupled*. For instance in a ship a horizontal vibration will often excite torsional vibration because of the non-uniform distribution of mass in the vertical plane.

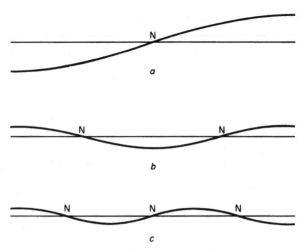

Figure 11.4 (a) One-node; (b) Two-node; (c) Three-node

Flexing of a beam

Before proceeding to the ship it is instructive to consider the flexural vibration of a simple beam. Take a beam of negligible mass of length l, supported at its ends and carrying a mass M at its centre. Under static conditions the deflection at mid span will be $Mgl^3/48EI$.

If the beam is deflected y from its equilibrium position the restoring force will be $y(48EI)/l^3$. Thus $48EI/l^3$ is equivalent to the spring stiffness k considered earlier. It follows that the frequency of vibration will be:

$$\frac{1}{2\pi}\left(\frac{48EI}{Ml^3}\right)^{0.5} = 1.103\left(\frac{EI}{Ml^3}\right)^{0.5}$$

It can be shown that if the mass M is uniformly distributed along the beam the frequency of vibration becomes:

$$n^2\frac{\pi}{2}\left(\frac{EI}{Ml^3}\right)^{0.5}$$

where n is any integer. For $n = 1$, the frequency is $1.57(EI/Ml^3)^{0.5}$. The frequency in which a beam vibrates depends upon the method of support. For vibrations in the free-free mode the frequency becomes:

$$\frac{n^2}{2\pi}\left(\frac{EI}{Ml^3}\right)^{0.5}$$

where $n = 4.73, 7.85$ and 10.99 for the two-, three- and four-node modes respectively.

Formulae for ship vibration

The formulae for uniform beams suggests that for the ship an approximation will be given by a formula of the type:

$$\text{Frequency} = \text{Const.} \left(\frac{EI}{Ml^3} \right)^{0.5}$$

Assuming the hull is made of various grades of steel, for which E is effectively constant, this can be represented by:

$$\text{Frequency} = \text{Const.} \left(\frac{I_a}{\Delta L^3} \right)^{0.5}$$

where I_a is the moment of inertia of the midships section.

This formulation was first proposed by Schlick[2]. Suggestions for the value of the constant for different ship types have been made[3] but these can only be very approximate because of the many variables involved in ships. The most important are:

(1) Mass and stiffness distribution along the length.
(2) Departure from ordinary simple theory due to shear deflection and structural discontinuities.
(3) Added mass.
(4) Rotary inertia.

Shear deflection
Simple bending theory assumes that when a beam is bent sections which were plane and perpendicular to the neutral axis before bending remain so after. For this condition there can be no shear stress in the beam. The influence of shear stresses is two-fold:

(1) The stress is no longer simply proportional to the distance from the neutral axis.
(2) Additional deflection of the beam occurs, the *shear deflection.*

To illustrate the effects of shear consider again the massless beam carrying a mass M at its centre. If the beam has a solid rectangular cross section the deflection due to shear alone is given by $3Mgl/10bdG$, where b and d are the breadth and depth of the beam and G is the *Modulus of rigidity.*

In this case the total deflection due to bending and shear becomes:

$$\frac{Mgl^3}{48EI} \left(1 + \frac{6Ed^2}{5Gl^2}\right) = \text{Bending deflection} \times (1 + r_s)$$

where $r_s = (6Ed^2/5Gl^2)$ and the frequency of vibration becomes:

$$\frac{1}{2\pi} \left[\frac{48EI}{Ml^2 (1 + r_s)}\right]^{0.5}$$

Thus the effect of shear is to reduce the frequency. In this simple example it was seen that r_s depended upon the square of the ratio of the depth of the beam to its length. For shallow beams its effects are therefore small. Unfortunately a ship is not a shallow beam and the ship's structure is akin to a box girder which influences greatly the value of the shear correction factor. Based on the work of Taylor[4,5] and Johnson[6] the value of r_s can be taken as:

$$r_s = 2.5 \frac{D^2}{L^2} \left(\frac{3a^3 + 9a^2 + 12a + 1.2}{3a + 1}\right)$$

where D, B and L are the depth, beam and length of the ship and a = B/D.

In this formula if D/L is 0.1 and a is 1.7 then $r_s = 0.256$ and the factor affecting frequency is $1/(1.256)^{0.5} = 0.892$.

The frequency as calculated by simple bending theory would be reduced by about 11 per cent for two-node vibration. It can be shown that for higher modes the effect is much greater. In fact at higher modes the shear deflection can become dominant.

Structural discontinuities

Full scale experiments have shown that where the structure is continuous the distribution of stress over depth is reasonably linear apart from the influence of shear. When there are abrupt changes in section, in way of superstructures for instance, the picture becomes much more complex and there is no easy way to determine how the stress varies.

The complication with superstructures arises essentially because plane sections no longer remain plane and the stress level the superstructure can take is reduced. It can take no stress at the ends but towards the centre of a long superstructure it may become reasonably effective against bending. The effect was touched upon in considering the efficiency of superstructures in Chapter 7 on strength. A large finite element analysis would be required to study the problem fully.

Added mass
When a body vibrates in any fluid its motion causes a movement of the fluid. The total kinetic energy of the system is the kinetic energies of the body and the fluid it has set in motion. If the fluid is air the kinetic energy in it is low because of its very low density. The effect on frequency can be safely ignored. When the fluid is water, as in the ship case, the water density is much larger and the kinetic energy of the water cannot be neglected.

As a section of the ship moves into the water it pushes fluid aside and as it moves out of the water the fluid returns to fill the void. The water is thus in a constant state of oscillation and this effect is transmitted out to the surrounding water. The phenomena is often termed the *entrained water effect* and is equivalent to an increase in mass of the system. This increase is referred to as the *added virtual mass* or simply *added mass*. It can be shown that for a horizontal circular cylinder, immersed to half its diameter, and executing small vertical oscillations, the virtual added mass is equal to the mass of the cylinder. That is, the effect of the added mass is to double the mass of the system. An effect of possibly this magnitude must be allowed for in calculating vibratory behaviour.

Virtual added mass for ship forms
The theory used for the oscillating cylinder can be adapted to a typical ship section. It is reasonable to assume that the added mass will depend upon the slenderness of the section in the direction of motion, that is the breadth to draught ratio. If it assumed the section has an area A, a waterline breadth of b and a depth t then the cylinder case suggests that the added mass for that section will be approximated by $\rho A(b/2t)$. It gives the correct result for a circular cylinder and allows for the section shape. For the complete ship this gives:

$$\text{Added virtual mass} = \int \rho A \frac{b}{2t} \, dx$$

integrated over the ship length.

It would be reasonable, following this general train of thought, to say that the total virtual mass of a ship should be able to be expressed in terms of the ship's beam and draught. That is

$$\text{total virtual mass } M_v = M\left(1 + \frac{kB}{T}\right)$$

where M is the mass of the ship.

k is a constant which Burrill[7] suggested should be 0.5. Todd[3] on the other hand suggested:

$$M_v = M\left(1.2 + \frac{B}{3T}\right)$$

The Todd formula gives consistently lower values than Burrill, ranging from 93 to 86 per cent for B/T values ranging from 2.0 to 3.5 respectively.

Lewis[8] made a detailed study of added virtual mass of near ship shape sections. He arrived at an added virtual mass per unit length of $\pi\rho B^2 C/2$. He plotted C for various beam to draught ratios and for sections of differing fullness, Figure 11.5.

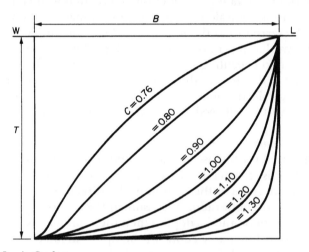

Figure 11.5 Lewis C values

The application of these results to ship shapes involves two interpolations, for C and B/T values between those specifically used for the curves. A more convenient presentation is to plot C_V, that is the coefficient for vertical oscillations, against a cross-sectional area coefficient for a range of beam/draught ratios[9] as in Figure 11.6. Values of C_H are shown in Figure 11.7 for horizontal oscillations[9]. Using these:

added virtual mass for vertical oscillation $= \dfrac{\pi\rho B^2 C_V}{2}$

added virtual mass for horizontal oscillation $= \dfrac{\pi\rho B^2 C_H}{2}$

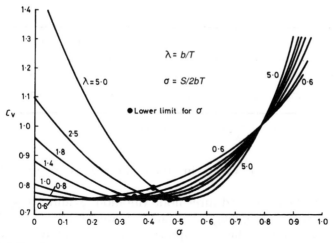

Figure 11.6 C_V values

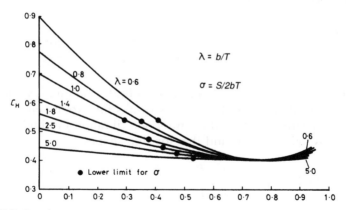

Figure 11.7 C_H values

Three dimensional flow

The work of Lewis and others was based on long cylinders oscillating. Under these conditions it is reasonable to assume that the flow is two-dimensional in the section in the plane of motion. For a ship's hull the flow will be three-dimensional because of the variation in section shape along the length. Also away from the nodes the displacements are rather greater than assumed in uniform oscillations and there will be more movement of water. The overall effect of the three-dimensional flow is to reduce the virtual added mass per unit length. A *three-dimensional added virtual mass factor, J* is used, *J* being the ratio of the

Table 11.2

L/B	5	6	7	8	9	10	11	12	13	14	15
J_2	.700	.752	.787	.818	.840	.858	.872	.887	.900	.910	.919
J_3	.621	.675	.720	.758	.787	.811	.830	.845	.860	.872	.883

Note J_2 and J_3 are for two- and three-node vibrations respectively.

kinetic energies of water in three-dimensions relative to two-dimensions.

Values of J for two- and three-node vibration (J_2 and J_3 respectively) of ellipsoids of varying length to beam ratio were calculated[8] to be as in Table 11.2. These J values are applied to the total virtual added mass calculated on the basis of two-dimensional flow. They are necessarily an approximation and other researchers have proposed different values. Taylor[10] proposed lower J values as follows:

L/B	6.0	7.0	8.0	9.0	10.0
J_2	.674	.724	.764	.797	.825
J_3	.564	.633	.682	.723	.760

Research using models has been done to find added mass values. One such investigation[11] found the Lewis results for two-dimensional flow agreed well with experiment for two-node vibration but higher modes agreed less well. It was found that for ship shapes:

$$J_n = 1.02 - 3\left(1.2 - \frac{1}{n}\right)\frac{B}{L}$$

where:

n = number of nodes
J_n = J value for n nodes.

These J values associated with the Lewis results for two-dimensional flow should give a good estimate of virtual added mass for ship forms in various vibration modes.

Rotary inertia

The simple formulae given above for a beam with a concentrated mass assumed that the masses executed linear oscillations only. In the relatively deep ship hull the rotation of the mass about a transverse axis is also important. A correction is applied based on the ratio of the rotational energy to translational energy, r_r. The correction to the frequency of vibration calculated ignoring rotation, is $1/(1 + r_r)^{0.5}$.

Direct calculation of vibration

Empirical formulae enable a first shot to be made at the frequency of vibration. The accuracy will depend upon the amount of data available from ships on which to base the coefficients. It is desirable to be able to calculate values directly taking account of the specific ship characteristics and loading. These days a full finite element analysis could be carried out to give the vibration frequencies, including the higher order modes. Before such methods became available there were two methods used for calculating the two-node frequency:

(1) The *deflection method* or *full integral method*.
(2) The *energy method*.

The deflection method
In this method the ship is represented as a beam vibrating in simple harmonic motion in which, at any moment, the deflection at any position along the length is $y = f(x) \sin pt$. The function $f(x)$ for non-uniform mass and stiffness distribution is unknown but it can be approximated by the curve for the free-free vibration of a uniform beam.

Differentiating y twice with respect to time gives the acceleration at any point as proportional to y and the square of the frequency. This leads to the dynamic loading. Integrating again gives the shear force and another integration gives the bending moment. A double integration of the bending moment curve gives the deflection curve. At each stage the constants of integration can be evaluated from the end conditions. The deflection curve now obtained can be compared with that originally assumed for $f(x)$. If they differ significantly a second approximation can be obtained by using the derived curve as the new input to the calculation.

In using the deflection profile of a uniform beam it must be remembered that the ship's mass is not uniformly distributed, nor is it generally symmetrically distributed about amidships. This means that in carrying out the integrations for shear force and bending moment the curves produced will not close at the ends of the ship. In practice there can be no force or moment at the ends so corrections are needed. A bodily shift of the base line for the shear force curve and a tilt of the bending moment curve are used.

In the calculation the mass per unit length must allow for the mass of the entrained water using one of the methods described for dealing with added virtual mass. The bending theory used ignores shear deflection and rotary inertia effects. Corrections for these are made at the end by applying factors, based on r_s and r_r, to the calculated frequency as discussed earlier.

The energy method
This method uses the principle that, in the absence of damping, the total energy of a vibrating system is constant. Damping exists in any real system but for ships it is acceptable to ignore it for the present purpose. Hence the sum of the kinetic and potential energies is constant.

In a vibrating beam the kinetic energy is that of the moving masses and initially this is assumed to be due to linear motion only. Assuming simple harmonic motion and a mass distribution, the kinetic energy is obtained from the accelerations deduced from an assumed deflection profile and frequency. The potential energy is the strain energy of bending.

When the beam is passing through its equilibrium position the velocity will be a maximum and there will be no bending moment at that instant. All the energy is kinetic. Similarly when at its maximum deflection the energy is entirely potential. Since the total energy is constant the kinetic energy in the one case can be equated to the potential energy in the other.

As in the deflection method the initial deflection profile is taken as that of a uniform bar. As before allowance is made for shear deflection and for rotary inertia. Applying this energy method to the case of the simply supported, uniform section, beam with a concentrated mass M at mid-span and assuming a sinusoidal deflection curve, yields a frequency of:

$$\frac{1}{2\pi}\left(\frac{\pi^4 EI}{2Ml^3}\right)^{0.5} \text{ compared with } \frac{1}{2\pi}\left(\frac{48EI}{Ml^3}\right)^{0.5} \text{ for the exact solution.}$$

Since $\pi^4/2$ is 48.7 the two results are in good agreement. This simple example suggests that as long as the correct end conditions are satisfied there is considerable latitude in the choice of the form of the deflection profile.

Calculation of higher modes
It might be expected that the frequencies of higher modes could be obtained by the above methods by assuming the appropriate deflection profile to match the mode needed. Unfortunately, instead of the assumed deflection curve converging to the correct one it tends to

diverge with successive iterations. This is due to the profile containing a component of the two-node profile which becomes dominant. Whilst ways have been developed to deal with this, one would today choose to carry out a finite element analysis.

Approximate formulae

It has been seen that the mass and stiffness distributions in the ship are important in deriving vibration frequencies. Such data is not available in the early design stages when the designer needs some idea of the frequencies for the ship. Hence there has always been a need for simple empirical formulae. The Schlick formula had severe limitations and various authorities have proposed modifications to it.

Burrill[7] suggested one allowing for added mass and shear deflection. The frequency was given as:

$$\frac{\text{Const.} \times \left(\dfrac{I}{\Delta L^3}\right)^{0.5}}{\left(1 + \dfrac{B}{2T}\right)^{0.5} (1 + r_s)^{0.5}}$$

where r_s is the deflection correction factor.

With Δ in tonf, dimensions in ft and I in in^{2}ft^2 the constant had a value of about 200 000 for a number of different ship types if L is between perpendiculars. For length overall the constant became about 220 000.

Todd adapted Schlick to allow for added mass, the total virtual displacement being given by:

$$\Delta_v = \Delta \left(\frac{B}{3T} + 1.2\right)$$

He concluded that I should allow for superstructures in excess of 40 per cent of the ship length. For ships with and without superstructure the results for the two-node vibration generally obeyed the rule:

$$\text{Frequency} = 110\,000 \left(\frac{I}{\Delta_v L^3}\right)^{0.5} + 29$$

The constant would become 238 660 if I is in m^4, dimensions in m and Δ_v is in MN.

By approximating the value of I, Todd proposed:

$$\text{Frequency} = \text{Const.} \times \left(\frac{BD^3}{\Delta_v L^3} \right)^{0.5}$$

Typical values of the constant in SI units with Imperial units in parenthesis, were found to be

Large tankers (full load)	11 000	(61 000)
Small tankers (full load)	8 150	(45 000)
Cargo ships (60 per cent load)	9 200	(51 000)

Many other approximate formulae have been suggested. The simpler forms are acceptable for comparing ships which are closely similar. The designer must use the data available to obtain the best estimate of frequency allowing for the basic parameters which control the physical phenomenon.

Amplitudes of vibration

It has been seen that the amplitude of oscillation of a simple mass spring combination depends upon the damping and magnification factor. The situation for a ship is more complex. Allowance must be made for at least the first three or four modes, superimposing the results for each. This can be done by finite element analysis and once the amplitude has been obtained the corresponding hull stress can be evaluated.

The question then arises as to whether the amplitude of vibration is acceptable. Limitations may be imposed by the reactions of humans, equipment or by strength considerations. Sensitive equipment can be protected by placing them on special mounts and this is done quite extensively in warships in particular. Human beings respond mainly to the vertical acceleration they experience. Curves are published[12] indicating the combinations of frequency and displacement that are likely to be acceptable.

Checking vibration levels

It will be appreciated by now that accurate calculation of vibration levels is difficult. It is possible to put a check upon the levels likely to be achieved as the ship nears structural completion by using a vibration exciter. The exciter is simply a device for generating large vibratory forces by rotating an out of balance weight. Placed at appropriate positions in the ship it can be activated and the stuctural response to known forces measured.

Reducing vibration

Ideally vibration would be eliminated completely but this is not a realistic goal. In practice a designer aims to:

(1) Balance all forces in reciprocating and rotary machinery and in the propeller.
(2) Provide good flow into the propeller and site it clear of the hull.
(3) Avoid resonance by changing the stiffness of components or varying the exciting frequencies.
(4) Use special mounts to shield sensitive equipment from the vibration.
(5) Fit a form of vibration damper[3], either active or passive[13].

The two main sources of vibration are the machinery and propellers[14,15].

Table 11.3 Vibration response and endurance test levels for surface warships

Ship type	Region	Standard test level Peak values and frequency range	Endurance tests
Minesweeper size and above	Masthead	1.25 mm, 5 to 14 Hz 0.3 mm, 14 to 23 Hz 0.125 mm, 23 to 33 Hz	1.25 mm, 14 Hz 0.3 mm, 23 Hz 0.125 mm, 33 Hz Each 1 hour
	Main	0.125 mm, 5 to 33 Hz	0.125 mm, 33 Hz For 3 hours
Smaller than minesweeper	Masthead and main	0.2 mm or a velocity of 63 mm/s whichever is less. 7 to 300 Hz	0.2 mm, 50 Hz For 3 hours
	Aftermost $\frac{1}{8}$ of ship length	0.4 mm or a velocity of 60 mm/s whichever is less. 7 to 300 Hz	0.4 mm, 24 Hz For 3 hours

Vibration testing of equipment

Most equipments are fitted in a range of ships and in different positions in a ship. Thus their design cannot be tailored to too specific a vibration specification. Instead they are designed to standard criteria and then samples are tested to confirm that the requirements have been met. These tests include endurance testing for several hours in the vibration environment. Table 11.3 gives test conditions for naval equipments to be fitted to a number of warship types.

In Table 11.3 the masthead region is that part of the ship above the main hull and superstructure. The main hull includes the upper deck, internal compartments and the hull.

NOISE

The internationally agreed unit for *sound intensity* is 10^{-16} watts/cm^2. At 1000 Hz this is close to the threshold of hearing. Noise levels are expressed in *decibels*, dB. If two noise sources have intensities of w_1 and w_2, the number of decibels denoting their ratio is:

$$n = 10 \log_{10} \frac{w_1}{w_2} \text{ db}$$

In saying that a noise source had a certain dB value, w_2 would be taken at the reference level of 10^{-16} watts/cm^2.

Instruments recording noise levels in air record sound pressure so that:

$$n = 10 \log_{10} \frac{w_1}{w_2} = 10 \log_{10} \left(\frac{p_1}{p_2}\right)^2 = 20 \log_{10} \frac{p_1}{p_2}$$

In this expression the pressure is measured in dynes/cm^2 (0.1 N/m^2) and p_2 would correspond to the threshold of hearing $p_2 = 2 \times 10^{-5}$ N/m^2. A sound pressure level of 1 dyne/cm^2 is equivalent to a noise level of 20 log (1/0.0002) dB = 74 dB.

In the open, sound intensity falls off inversely as the square of the distance from the source. At half the distance the intensity will be quadrupled and the difference in dB level will be 10 log 4, which is effectively 6 dB. Doubling the distance will reduce the dB level by 6. The combination of two equal noise sources results in an increase of 3 dB. Sound levels are subjective and for the noise level to seem to a human to have doubled requires a dB increase of 10.

This subjectivity arises because a typical noise contains many components of different frequency and these will affect the human ear differently. To define a noise fully the strength of each component and its frequency must be specified. This is done by presenting a spectral plot of the noise. This approach is needed for instance in considering the importance of radiated noise in terms of its likely detection by enemy sensors or weapons. For human reactions to noise an alternative is to express noise levels in dB(A). The A weighted decibel is a measure of the total sound pressure modified by weighting factors which vary with frequency. The end result reflects more closely a human's subjective appreciation of noise. Humans are more sensitive to high (1000 Hz and over) than low (250 Hz and less) freqencies and this is reflected in the weighting factors.

Primary sources of noise are the same as those which generated vibration, that is machinery, propulsors, pumps and fans. Secondary sources are fluids in systems, electrical transformers and the sea and waves interacting with the ship. Noise from a source may be transmitted through the air surrounding the source or through the structure to which it is attached. The structure on which a machine is mounted can have a marked influence on the amounts of noise transmitted. The actions are complex[16]. Not only is it difficult to predict the transmision losses in typical structures but airborne noise may excite structure on which it impacts and directly excited structure will radiate noise to the air. For machinery, combustion forces, impact forces and rapidly changing pressures generate structural wave motions in the machine which radiate to the air or travel through the mounting system into the ship's structure. For a propulsor much of the noise will be transmitted into the water. That represented by pressure fluctuations on the adjacent hull will cause the structure to vibrate transmitting noise both into the ship and back into the water. Other transmission paths will be through the shaft and its bearings. At low powers noise will arise from the hydrodynamic forces generated by the propulsor working in a non-uniform wake. At higher powers, or when manoeuvring, cavitation can occur and then the noise increases dramatically. For pumps and fans the impeller produces noise which can travel through the fluid along the pipe or trunk or be radiated from the conduit.

A designer will be concerned to limit noise because:

(1) Internal noise levels can affect the performance of the crew and the comfort of passengers.
(2) Noise transmitted into the water can betray the presence of the ship. It can trigger off enemy mines or provide a signal on which weapons can home. It can reduce the effectiveness of the ship's own sensors.

It is the former effects which are of primary concern here. The importance of the latter for the signature of warships is discussed

Table 11.4

Location	Permitted noise level (dBA)
Engine room	110
Workshops	85
Bridge	65
Mess room	65
Recreation space	65
Cabins	60

briefly in Chapter 12. Apart from noise making it hard to hear and be heard, crew performance can fall off because prolonged exposure to noise can cause fatigue and disorientation. It can annoy and disturb sleep. High levels (about 130 to 140 dB) will cause pain in the ear and higher levels can cause physical harm to a person's hearing ability. Thus noise effects can range from mere annoyance to physical injury. The IMO lay down acceptable noise levels in ships according to a compartment's use, Table 11.4.

Noise calculations
There are a number of acoustical calculations a designer can apply to ship noise estimation and for the design of noise control systems[16]. Both finite element and statistical energy analysis methods are used. Since the level of structure borne noise from a machine depends upon the forces in the machine and the structure on which it is mounted the concept of *structural mobility* is introduced. This is the ratio of velocity to force at the excitation point. The structural mobility, velocity and force will all vary with frequency. For a machine mounted rigidly on a plate, the structural mobility depends upon the mass per unit area and thickness of the plate and upon the velocity of longitudinal waves in the plate and wide variation can be expected throughout the frequency range. This factor can be used to deduce the flow of power into the structure. This will be proportional to the mean square vibration velocities of structural elements to which the subsequent sound radiation is proportional. The level of power flow can be minimized by avoiding resonances. In theory this can be done either by decreasing greatly the structural mobility, that is making the seating very stiff, or increasing it greatly which can be achieved by fitting a flexible mount. In practice it is impossible to make a seating stiff enough to avoid resonance over the whole frequency range and a flexible mount is the better solution. When a flexible mount is used the structural mobility approach can be used to measure its isolation effectiveness. Another

useful concept is that of *radiation efficiency* which relates the sound power radiated to the mean square vibration velocity of the surface. It is frequency dependent.

It is not possible to go into the theory of noise generation and transmission in a book such as this but the reader should be aware of the general factors involved[17].

Reducing noise levels

Generally anything that helps reduce vibration will also reduce emitted noise. Machinery can be isolated, the isolating system preventing excessive vibration of the machine and transmission of large forces to the seating. The system must attenuate high frequency vibration and protect against shock. That is it must take account of vibration, noise and shock. Because of the different frequencies at which these occur the problem can be very difficult. For instance a mount designed to deal with shock waves may actually accentuate the forces transmitted in low frequency hull whipping. Dual systems may be needed to deal with this problem. Air borne noise can be prevented from spreading by putting noisy items into sound booths or by putting sound absorption material on the compartment boundaries. Care must be taken to ensure such treatments are comprehensive. To leave part of a bulkhead unclad can negate to a large degree the advantage of cladding. Flow noise from pipe systems can be reduced by reducing fluid speeds within them, by avoiding sudden changes of direction or cross section and by fitting resilient mounts. Inclusion of a mounting plate of significant mass in conjunction with the resilient mount can improve performance significantly.

Where noise mounts are fitted to noisy machinery care is needed to see that they are not 'short circuited' by connecting pipes and cables. The similarities for vibration and shock isolation will be apparent.

In recent years active noise cancellation techniques have been developing[13]. The principle used is the same as that for active vibration control. The system generates a noise of equivalent frequency content and volume but in anti-phase to the noise to be cancelled. Thus to cancel the noise of a funnel exhaust a loudspeaker could be placed at the exhaust outlet. For structure borne noise from a machine force generators could be used at the mounting. Systems have been made to work efficiently but it is not always easy to get the necessary masses, and other equipment, into the space available.

SHOCK

All ships are liable to collisions and in wartime they are liable to enemy attack. The most serious threat to a ship's survival is probably an

underwater explosion[18]. The detonation of the explosive leads to the
creation of a pulsating bubble of gas containing about half the energy
of the explosion. This bubble migrates towards the sea surface and
towards the hull of any ship nearby. It causes pressure waves which
strike the hull. The frequency of the pressure waves is close to the
fundamental hull frequencies of small ships such as frigates and
destroyers, and can cause considerable movement and damage. A
particularly severe vibration, termed *whipping*, occurs when the
explosion is set off a little distance below the keel. The pressure waves
act on a large area of the hull and the ship *whips*[19]. This whipping
motion can lead to buckling, and perhaps breaking, of the hull
girder.

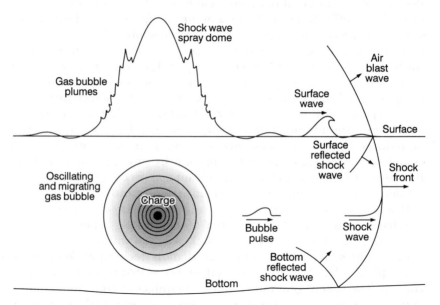

Figure 11.8 Underwater explosion (courtesy RINA[18])

Another major feature of any underwater explosion is the shock wave
containing about a third of the total energy of the explosion. This
shock wave is transmitted through the water, and so into and through
the ship's structure. It causes shock and may lead to hull rupture. The
intensity of shock experienced depends upon the size, distance and
orientation of the explosion relative to the ship. These factors are
combined to produce a shock factor[18]. The *shock factor* related to the
keel is:

$$\frac{(W)^{0.5}(1 + \cos \theta)}{2R}$$

where:

W is the charge weight
R is the distance from charge to the keel
θ is the angle between the line joining charge to keel and the normal to the keel plate.

Since this expression is not non-dimensional and different formulations exist, care is needed when using shock factors. Various explosives are in use and they are usually related to an equivalent weight of TNT in deducing shock factors and comparing results of explosive testing. In addition to the shock factor, the intensity of shock experienced by an item of equipment depends upon its weight, rigidity, position in the ship and method of mounting. For critical systems, perhaps one vital to the safety of the ship, it may be necessary to calculate the shock likely to be felt at a specific position in a given design. This can be done by calculation and/or model experiment using methods validated by full scale trials.

More generally equipments are fitted to more than one design and in different positions in any one ship so they must be able to cope with a range of shock conditions. The approach is to design to generalized shock grade curves. The overall design can be made more robust by providing shock isolation mounts for sensitive items and by siting system elements in positions where the structure offers more shock attenuation. This has the advantages that the item itself does not have to be so strong and the mounts can assist in attenuating any noise the equipment produces, reducing its contribution to the underwater noise signature.

The reaction of equipment to shock is a dynamic problem and the response will depend upon an item's flexibility. This must be allowed for in calculating its ability to survive and function. As a guide, designers should avoid cantilevered components, avoid brittle materials, mount flexibly and ensure that movements in response to the shock are not impeded by pipe or cable connections or cause impact with hard structure. It is important to allow for the behaviour of materials used when subject to high rates of strain. In plating subject to collision or shock loading the maximum strain rates are estimated[20] to lie between 2 and 20 sec^{-1}. This compares with a strain rate of about 10^{-4} sec^{-1} when the hull girder is bending under wave action. Some materials, notably mild steel, exhibit an increase in yield point by a factor up to two when subject to these high strain rates.

In warships essential equipment is designed to remain operable up to a level of shock at which the ship is likely to be lost by hull rupture. The first of class of each new design of warship is subjected to a *shock trial* in which its resistance to underwater shock is tested by exploding large charges, up to 500 kg, fairly close to the hull.

SUMMARY

The three closely related phenomena of vibration, noise and shock have been reviewed. Each topic is important in ship design and levels of vibration and noise must meet internationally agreed standards. Shock is especially important for warships which must be able to withstand enemy attack. Considerable advances have been made in recent years in applying finite element analysis and statistical energy analysis to these problems but the mathematics is beyond the scope of this book and it has only been possible to outline the main features of each and how the designer can deal with them. Having calculated, during design, the vibration amplitudes expected, these can be checked as the build nears completion, by setting up and running a vibration generator on board. Finally the ship's acceptance trials are the final demonstration of how successful a designer has been in reducing vibration and noise levels to acceptable limits. In vibration some simplified formulae are given upon which preliminary design assessments can be based.

References

1. Dieudonne, J. (1959) Vibration in ships. *TINA.*
2. Schlick, O. (1884) Vibration of steam vessels. *TINA.*
3. Todd, F. H. (1961) *Ship hull vibration.* Arnold.
4. Taylor, J. L. (1924–5) The theory of longitudinal bending of ships. *TNECIES.*
5. Taylor, J. L. (1927–8) Ship vibration periods. *TNECIES.*
6. Johnson, A. J. (1950–1) Vibration tests on all welded and riveted 10 000 ton dry cargo ships. *TNECIES.*
7. Burrill, L. C. (1934–5) Ship vibration: simple methods of estimating critical frequencies. *TNECIES.*
8. Lewis, F. M. (1929) The inertia of water surrounding a vibrating ship. *TSNAME.*
9. Landweber, L. and deMacagno, M. C. (1957) Added mass of two dimensional forms oscillating in a free surface. *Journal of Ship Research, SNAME.*
10. Taylor, J. L. (1930) Vibration of ships. *TINA.*
11. Townsin, R. L. (1969) Virtual mass reduction factors: J values for ship vibration calculations derived from tests with beams including ellipsoids and ship models. *TRINA.*
12. BS 6634: 1985. ISO 6954: 1984. Overall evaluation of vibration in merchant ships.
13. Warnaka, G. E. (1982) Active attenuation of noise – the state of the art. *Noise Control Engineering.*

14. Ward, G. and Willshare, G. T. (1975) Propeller excited vibration with particular reference to full scale measurements. *TRINA*.

15. Morel, P., Beghin, D. and Baudin, M. (1995) Assessment of the vibratory behaviour of ships. *RINA Conference on noise and vibration*. London.

16. Morrow, R. T. (1989) Noise reduction methods for ships. *TRINA*.

17. ISO 6954: 1984. *Guidelines for the overall evaluation of vibration in merchant ships*.

18. Greenhorn, J. (1989) The assessment of surface ship vulnerability to underwater attack. *TRINA*.

19. Hicks, A. N. (1986) Explosion induced hull whipping. *Advances in Marine Structures*. Elsevier Applied Science Publishers.

20. Sumpter, J. D. G., Bird, J., Clarke, J. D. and Caudrey, A. J. (1990) Fracture toughness of ship steels. *TRINA*.

12 Ship design

Ship design is perhaps the most demanding of all engineering tasks. A ship is a large, complex artifact. In this it can be likened to a large civil engineering product which must float and move on the interface between water and air. It is usually much larger than an aircraft and often has many more people on board. The ship designer seldom has the advantage of a prototype whereas the aircraft or land vehicle designer usually has several prototypes during the trials of which, any design faults can be detected and rectified. In aircraft for instance, one or more complete fuselages will be tested to destruction to determine strength and fatigue qualities. On the other hand the naval architect has the advantage of many 'type' ships already at sea from which he can learn if he is so minded.

This chapter shows how the various aspects of naval architecture discussed earlier, are brought together in the design process. It is not possible to describe that process in detail but the aim is to give the reader a feel for its nature; what is important, why compromise is necessary and why certain vessels work out the way they do. In particular, those aspects of the design and the design process that impinge upon the safety of the ship will be outlined. Before the designer can start the owner must specify the nature of the ship needed, the areas of operation and any special considerations.

The designer then attempts to create an *effective, efficient* and *safe* ship. To be effective it must meet the owner's needs as laid down in the ship requirements. To be efficient it must carry out its functions reliably and economically. To be safe it must be able to operate under the expected conditions without incident and to survive more extreme conditions and accidents within an agreed level of risk. It must not be unduly vulnerable to the unexpected.

EFFECTIVENESS

Design requirements

The owner must specify what is required of a new vessel. It may have to operate to tight schedules, use specific ports, use the same machinery system as ships already in service, and so on. The owner may employ a naval architect to facilitate this discussion but the aim should be to state the 'operational' needs and leave the designer to decide upon the best means of achieving them. Thus in seakeeping any desired limits on rolling motion should be stated, leaving the designer to decide whether roll stabilizers are necessary and, if so, which would be the best type. On the other hand, the owner may specify that the main machinery is to be of a certain type because there are already a number of ships with this machinery in the company's fleet. To adopt different machinery would complicate the training of personnel and make logistic support more costly. Ideally there will be close collaboration between the designer and owner to ensure that the requirements specified are sensible, taking account of past practice but also taking advantage of developing technology. Thus new outer bottom coatings may make it possible to adopt longer intervals between dockings.

In the case of British warships it is the naval staff of the Ministry of Defence (MOD) who set out the requirements for new ships. Initial discussion with the MOD's own designers will lead to a series of design studies. These are taken by high level committees and gradually the basis for the new design emerges.[1]

Some design features

Capacity and size

Usually there will be a certain volume of goods the ships of a fleet need to carry. This may have been established by a market survey. The 'goods' may be cargo, people or weaponry. The amount to be carried in an individual ship will depend upon the rate at which goods become available. This will depend in turn upon the supporting transport systems on land. Taking ferries as an example, one super ferry sailing each day from Dover to Calais, capable of carrying one day's load of lorries, cars and passengers, would not be popular. Transit for most would be delayed, large holding areas would be needed at the ports and the ship would be idle for much of the time. Whilst such an extreme case is clearly undesirable it is not easy to establish an optimum balance between size of ship and frequency of service. Computer modelling, allowing for the variability of the data, is used to compare different options and establish parameters such as the expected average waiting time, percentage of ship capacity used, and so on.

There may be limits imposed on size by external factors such as the geographical features, and facilities of the ports to be used and the need to use canals. The Suez Canal may limit the draught and the Panama Canal the maximum beam.

Cargo handling

In deciding what cargo handling equipment to fit, a balance is needed between giving a ship the ability to load and discharge its own cargo and reliance upon the terminal port facilities. If the ship is to operate between well defined ports the balance may be clear. If the ship is to operate more flexibly it may not be able to rely on specialist unloading equipment and have to carry more of its own.

The development of the container ship was closely linked to the development of special container ports and the supporting road and rail networks for moving the containers inland. Similarly crude oil carriers can expect good facilities at the loading port and the refinery terminal.

Influence of nature of goods carried

Particularly for those goods where large volumes are to be shipped, the nature of the cargo has come to dictate the main features of the ship. The wool clippers on the Australian run were an early example. More recently tankers have come to the fore and with the growing demand for oil and its by-products, the size of tanker grew rapidly. The major influences are the possible storage methods and the means of loading and discharging. Oil can be carried in large tanks and can be pumped out. Some particulate cargoes can be handled similarly or by conveyor belts and huge grabs. This has led to bulk carriers for grain, iron ore and coal.

Mixed cargoes are often placed in containers of a range of standard sizes. This improves the security in transit and reduces time in port. In other cases the cargo is brought to the ship in the land transport system units. First came the train ferries and then the roll on/roll off ships. Cars can be driven on and off for delivery of new cars around the world or for people taking their cars on holiday.

Perishable goods have led to the refrigerated ships, the *reefers*. Bulk carriage of gas has been possible with a combination of refrigeration and pressurized tanks.

Speed

Speed can be an emotive issue. Some authorities regard high speed as a status symbol but it is expensive of power and fuel and if pitched too high can lead to an inefficient ship. It is an important input to the analysis referred to above. Faster ships can make more journeys in a given time period. Passengers like short passage times and are often prepared to pay a premium to get them as in the case of high speed catamaran ferries. Some goods need to be moved relatively quickly. They may be perishable and a balance must be struck between refrigeration and a fast transit. For other products speed may be of little consequence. For instance, as long as enough oil is arriving in port each day it does not matter to the customer how long it has been on passage. It is important to the ship owner and a balance is needed between speed, size and number of ships required to achieve the desired flow rate economically.

For high speed ships wavemaking resistance is a major factor and the design will have a finer form. At low speeds frictional resistance will dominate and fuller, bluffer forms can be used with greater cargo carrying ability on a given length. When considering speed, allowance must be made for the average voyage conditions expected. Two ships capable of the same still water maximum speed may differ significantly in their ability to maintain speed in rough weather. The conditions that might restrict a ship's speed were discussed under seakeeping.

Manoeuvrability
Manoeuvrability is not too important for a ship in the open ocean. In restricted waters it can be critical. Stopping distances of the huge supertankers are very large. Astern power must be adequate to give the desired deceleration. A balance must be struck between giving a ship very good manoeuvrability and relying upon tugs for assistance in port. What is meant by good manoeuvrability and means of providing it in a ship were discussed in Chapter 10 on manoeuvrability. Twin shafts, azimuthing propellers and lateral thrust units are some of the means. These cost money and the cost must be set against the cost and delays of using tugs, remembering they might not always be available when needed. Ferries which frequently berth and unberth will normally be designed to operate without the assistance of tugs except in exceptional weather conditions. For long haul ships providing a high degree of manoeuvrability could be uneconomic.

Floating oil drilling rigs require exceptionally good abilities in maintaining their position relative to the ground and for that reason they are provided with dynamic positioning systems. A series of thrusters under computer control are constantly correcting the position against the effects of wind, current and waves. In such vessels fin stabilizers are of little use for reducing roll and some form of tank system would be fitted if needed. Mine countermeasure ships also need to be able to maintain an accurate path over the ground if a suspected minefield is to be swept with the minimum number of passes and in maximum safety.

Machinery
The power installed depends upon the speed required under typical operating conditions and the hull form, as discussed in Chapter 9 on propulsion. The type of machinery chosen will reflect a balance

between cost, weight, volume, reliability and maintenance load. Here not just the machinery but such things as fuel, gearing, seatings, uptakes and downtakes must be taken into account. The final decision, however, may be strongly influenced by the type of machinery fitted in others of the owner's ships. If the others all have diesels, say, it would be expensive to change to gas turbine because of the added training and logistic costs.

General

It would be possible to discuss many other features of the design here but the above should give the reader a feeling for the considerations involved. Some special features associated with different ship types are discussed later.

EFFICIENCY

To be efficient a ship must be able to carry out its intended functions economically[2,3] and be available when needed.

Economy

Costs are always important. Unless those of a merchant ship are less than the revenue they can earn the ship will be a liability. For warships, which cannot 'earn' in the commercial sense[4,5] the cost effectiveness of a design is harder to define let alone assess. In the end the warship designer can only inform the naval staff of the cheapest way to meet the requirement. It has then to be decided whether this amount of money can be allocated from the defence budget against the competing bids of other requirements. If not, then the requirement must be reduced till an acceptable balance is achieved between need and affordability. The costs should be the *through life* costs, not just the build costs. Thus it might be better to use more mechanization to reduce crew size if the cost of mechanizing is less than the associated crew costs over the life of the ship.[6] These are not easy balances to assess. The crew not only need to be paid, they must be trained, they need space on board and so on. Mechanization will bring with it initial and maintenance costs, with the need for maintainers offsetting other crew reductions.

Assuming the ship can earn revenue this can be assessed for the years ahead using the anticipated freight rates. Build costs will arise early on and then operating costs, including costs of crew, bunkering, port charges, refitting and repair, will be spread over the life cycle. At the end of the day the owner hopes there will be a profit. Depreciation must be allowed for although it is not an item of cash flow.

All the cash flow elements must be brought to a common basis by treating them as though they occurred simultaneously. This is because cash has a time value in that it might be used more profitably in some other way. It is usual to apply *discounted cash flow* methods to establish a *net present value* for comparison of different design options. A compound interest rate is used to determine the 'present' value of money to be spent in later years. The net present value must be positive if it is to be acceptable. The higher it is for any option the better that option is from an economic point of view. The process can be inverted to give the freight rate needed to give a net present value of zero.

Availability

An owner wants a vessel to be available for use when needed. This is not necessarily all the time. Many ships have a quiet season when time can be found for refitting without risk to the planned schedules. Ferries are often refitted in winter months for that reason. *Availability* can be regarded as a function of *reliability* and *maintainability*.[7,8]

Reliability can be defined as the probability of an artifact performing adequately for the time intended under the operating conditions encountered. This implies that components must have a certain *mean time between failures* (MTBFs). If the MTBF is too low for a given component that component will need to be duplicated so that its failure does not jeopardize the overall operation.

Maintenance is preferably planned. That is items are refurbished or replaced before they fail. By carrying out *planned maintenance* in quiet periods the availability of the ship is unaffected. The MTBF data can be used to decide when action is needed. To plan the maintenance requires knowledge of the *mean time to repair* (MTR) of components. Both MTBF and MTR data are assessed from experience with the components, or similar, in service. The other type of maintenance is *breakdown maintenance* which is needed when an item fails in service. Unless the item is duplicated the system is out of action until repair is effected.

The time taken to maintain can be reduced by adopting a policy of *refit or repair by replacement*. Under this scheme complete units or sub-units are replaced rather than being repaired in situ. Frigates with gas turbine propulsion are designed so that the gas turbines can be replaced as units, withdrawal being usually through the uptakes or downtakes. The used or defective item can then be repaired as convenient without affecting the ship's availability.

Another advantage is that repairs can be carried out under better conditions, often at the manufacturer's plant. The disadvantage is that stocks of components and units must be readily available at short notice. To carry such stocks can be quite costly. But then an idle ship is a costly item. It has been estimated that a frigate costs about £100 000 for each day of seatime. It is a matter of striking the right balance between conflicting factors. To help in making these decisions the technique of *availability modelling* can be used.

In availability modelling the various ship capabilities are set down. Then the equipments involved in conferring that ability on the ship are noted in a diagram showing how they contribute. Some components of the diagram will be in series and others in parallel. One capability might be the ability to move. This requires the main engines, gearing, propulsor, shafting, bearings and so on. There will also be a number of supporting functions such as lub-oil pumps, machinery seatings and bearings as well the need for electrical supplies and fuel. Large items such as the main machinery can be broken down into their constituent components. For each item the MTBF can be assessed together with the probability of a failure in a given time span. These individual figures can be combined to give the overall reliability of a system using an approach similar to the way the total resistance of an electric circuit is calculated from the individual resistances of items in series or parallel. High reliability of components is needed when many are used in a system. Ten components, each with a reliability of 99 per cent, when placed in series lead to an overall reliability of $(0.99)^{10} = 0.905$. Ten units in parallel would have a reliability of $1-(0.1)^{10}$, effectively 100 per cent.

Such analyses can highlight weak links which the designer can improve by fitting more reliable components or duplication. They also provide guidance on which spares should be stocked and in what quantities, that is the *range and scale* of spares.

In some cases, and the ability to move is one, the capability may exist at more than one level. For instance loss of one shaft of a twin shaft ship will reduce the available power to 50 per cent. If more than one diesel drives one shaft, the loss of one is not as critical as losing all the power on the shaft.

SAFETY

A great deal of attention is paid to the safety of ships by national and international regulations and during design and operation. However, a ship can be designed to meet all existing regulations and yet not be as safe as it could, and should, be. This is partly because regulations have to be agreed by many authorities and are often a compromise between what is regarded by many as the best practice and what others feel to be unduly restrictive or are prepared to accept for economic reasons. Partly the difference is due to the time lag between failures being experienced, analysed, the corrective action decided upon, agreed and implemented. Also advancing technology and changing trade requirements can lead to ships with new features, and operating patterns, which have not been fully proven. Testing of hydrodynamic or structural models and of materials in representative conditions can help but the final proof of the soundness of a design is its performance at sea.

A ship can be seriously damaged by, or lost because of:

(1) Water entering as a result of damage or human error in not having watertight boundaries sealed. This can lead to capsize or foundering.
(2) Fire or explosion.
(3) Structural failure due to overloading, fatigue or fracture, possibly brittle in nature. Failure may be of the overall hull girder or local, say in way of a hatch cover, so permitting the ingress of water.
(4) Loss of propulsive power or steering, leading to collision or grounding.

A designer should produce a *safety case*, identifying how a ship might suffer damage, the probability of occurrence and the potential consequences. With such data an informed judgement can be made on the level of risk it is reasonable to accept for the design in question, and what safety systems should be fitted on board. Such analysis might show a need for external support in some situations. For instance, escort tugs[9] might be deemed desirable in confined waters or areas of special ecological significance. Many of the factors involved can be quantified, but not all, making good judgement an essential element in all such analyses. The important thing is that a process of logical thought is applied, exposed to debate and decisions monitored as the design develops. Some of the decisions will depend upon the master and crew taking certain actions and that information should be declared to the command so that the design intent is understood.

Safety is no academic exercise. Many ships are lost as is shown by the annual analysis of ship losses published by Lloyd's Register. In the early 1990s some 200 ships were lost each year from all causes, the gross registered tonnage being about a million per year. In some cases the reason for loss is unknown, suggesting some rapid overwhelming of the ship. One such case, that aroused a lot of debate, was the loss of the *MV Derbyshire*, a British OBO carrier of 192 000 tonne displacement. Too many trawlers have been lost from unknown causes.

Vulnerability

A ship might be quite safe while it remains intact but be very likely to suffer extensive damage, or loss, as a result of a relatively minor incident. For instance, a ship with no internal subdivision could operate safely until water entered by some means. It would then sink. Such a design would be unduly *vulnerable*. This is why in the safety case the designer must consider all the ways in which the ship may suffer damage.

Because they expect to suffer damage in action, vulnerability is an important consideration for warships.[10,11] Each new design is the subject of a vulnerability assessment to highlight any weak elements. This considers the probability of each of the various methods of attack an enemy may deploy, their chances of success and the likely effect upon the ship. The likelihood of retaining various degrees of *fighting capability*, and finally surviving, is calculated. A fighting capability would be a function such as being able to destroy an incoming enemy missile. The contribution of each element of the ship and its systems to each fighting capability is noted. For instance, to destroy a missile would require some detection and classification radar, a launcher and weapon, as well as electrics and chilled water services and a command system. Some elements will contribute to more than one capability. For each form of attack the probability of the individual elements being rendered non-operative is assessed using a blend of calculation, modelling and full scale data. If one element is particularly liable to be damaged, or especially important, it can be duplicated to reduce the overall vulnerability. This modelling is similar to that used for reliability assessments. The assessments for each form of attack can be combined, allowing for the probability of each form, to give an overall vulnerability for the design and the computations can become quite lengthy. Some judgements are very difficult to make and the results must be interpreted with care. For instance, reduced general services such as electricity may be adequate to support some but not all fighting capabilities. What then happens, in a particular battle, will depend upon which capabilities the command needs to deploy at that moment. For this reason the vulnerability results are set in the context of various engagement scenarios. In many cases, the full consequences of an attack will depend upon the actions taken by the crew in damage limitation. For instance how effectively they deal with fire, how rapidly they close doors and valves to limit flooding. Recourse must be made to exercise data and statistical allowances made for human performance.

Whilst such analyses may be difficult they can highlight design weaknesses early in the design process when they can be corrected at little cost. The same techniques can be used for merchant ships, taking the natural hazards and human failings into account rather than deliberate enemy action.

In such studies the statistics of past accidents are very valuable. For instance, from the data on the damaged length in collisions and groundings the probability of a certain fraction of the ship's length being damaged in this way in some future incident, can be assessed. This is the basis of the latest IMO approach to merchant ship vulnerability. The probability of two events occurring together is obtained from the product of their individual probabilities. Thus the designer can combine the probabilities of a collision occurring (it is more likely in the English Channel than in the South Pacific), that the ship will be in a particular loading condition at the time, that the impact will occur at a particular position along the length and that a given length will be damaged. The crew competence in dealing with an incident is again a factor. The IMO have proposed standard shapes for the probability density functions for the position of damage, length of damage, permeability at the time and for the occurrence of an accident. There is a steady change to these probabilistic methods of vulnerability assessment and passenger and cargo ships are now studied in this way.

It must be accepted, however, that no ship can be made absolutely safe under all possible conditions. Unusual combinations of circumstances can occur and freak conditions of wind and waves will arise from time to time. In 1973 the *Benchruachen*, with a gross tonnage of 12 000, suffered as a result of a freak wave. The whole bow section 120 ft forward of the break in forecastle was bent downwards at 7°. When an accident does occur the question to be asked is whether the design was a reasonable one in the light of all the circumstances applying. No matter how tragic the incident the design itself may have been sound. At the same time the naval architect must be prepared to learn as a result of experience.

THE DESIGN PROCESS

Some of the various factors a designer must take into account have been discussed. How then does the designer go about developing the design? What is the design process? Different authorities use different terms for the various design stages. For the present purposes the terms *feasibility studies, contract design* and *full design* will be used.

Feasibility studies
The starting point is usually a *type ship*. That is one which is carrying out all or most of the functions asked of the new ship and which is judged

to be close to the size needed. From this base the designer can get a first approximation to the principal dimensions of the new ship. Allowance would be made for different capacities, perhaps higher speed, smaller crew and so on. A feel for the size of the ship will be obtained from the weight or volume of cargo. The type ship will then give a guide to the ratio of the dimensions but these can be modified to give the form coefficients (block, prismatic, etc.) desired. The values of ratios such as length to beam or draught need to be checked as being within the usually accepted limits. Absolute dimensions must be compared with limiting values for ports and waterways the ship is to use.

From the principal dimensions first assessments of draughts, stability, power, etc., can be made. Each of these will lead to a better picture of the design. It is an iterative process which has been likened by some to a spiral. This analogy is helpful in that each ship feature must be considered more than once and at the end of a cycle the designer should have approached the final design more closely. However it gives the impression that design is a steady progression which it is not. It ignores the step functions that occur such as when a larger machinery set has to be fitted or an extra bulkhead added. A better analogy might be a network which showed the many interdependencies present in the design. This network would really be a combination of a large number of interactive loops.

Not all design features will be considered during every cycle of the design process. Initial stability would be considered early on, large angle stability would follow later but damaged stability would not be dealt with until the design was better defined. The first estimate of power, and hence machinery required, would be likely to be changed and this might introduce a step change in machinery weight and volume. There would be corresponding changes in structural weight and so the design develops. Some of the initial assessments, possibly that of the longitudinal bending moment, would be by using approximate formulae. When the design is reasonably defined more advanced computer programs can be employed.

When a reasonably conventional ship is being built to the rules of a classification society the scantlings of the structure can be obtained from the rules. For merchant ships of novel design, and for warships, it is necessary to carry out a full strength investigation. Even when classification society rules have been used, a still water bending moment calculation will often be demanded. When the structure has been determined and approved a final check can be made of its weight.

The aim at the feasibility stage is to confirm that a design to meet the requirements is possible with the existing technology and to a size and cost likely to be acceptable to the owner. Several design options will usually be produced showing the trade-offs between various conflicting requirements or to highlight features that are unduly costly to achieve and may not be vital to the function of the ship.

Contract design

Once the owner has agreed to the general size and character of the ship more detailed designing can go on. The *contract design*, as its name implies, is produced to a level that it can be used to order the ship from a shipbuilder, or for a contract price to be quoted. At this stage all major features of the ship will be fixed. Usually some model testing will have been carried out to confirm the main performance parameters. Layout drawings will have been produced to confirm spaces allocated to various functions are adequate. The power and type of machinery will have been decided and the electrical power, chilled water, air conditioning, hydraulic and compressed air system capacities defined. The basic ship design drawings will be supported by a mass of supporting specifications which will control the development of the final design.

Full design

The detailing of the design can now proceed leading to the drawings, or with computerized production systems, computer tapes, which are needed by the production department to build the ship. Included in this documentaion will be the detailed specification of tests to be carried out including an inclining experiment to check stability and the sea trials needed to show that the ship meets the conditions of contract and the owner's stated requirements. These are not necessarily the same. For instance, for warships *contractor's sea trials* are carried out to establish that the contract has been met. Then, after acceptance, the Ministry of Defence carries out further trials on weapon and ship performance in typical sea-going conditions.

Also specified will be the shipyard tests needed to be carried out as fabrication proceeds. Thus the testing of structure to ensure watertight and structural integrity will be defined. Tests of pipe systems will lay down the test fluid and the pressures to be used, the time they are to be held and any permissible leakage.

Then there is the mass of documentation produced to define the ship for the user and maintainers. There are lists of spares and many handbooks. Much of this data is carried in micro-form on the ship to facilitate usage and to save weight and space.

The impact of computers

Computers have made a great impact upon the design, production and operation of ships.[12] That impact is felt in a number of ways:

(1) Many individual calculations are possible which otherwise could not be undertaken. For instance, ship motion predictions by theory and the use of finite element analysis for structural strength. Design optimisation techniques[13] are increasingly being proposed and developed.

(2) A number of programs can be combined to form a computer aided design system where the output from one program provides a direct input into others. Revisions of the data base as the design develops can be used to up-date automatically the results of calculations carried out earlier. Thus changes in scantlings occasioned by the strength calculations can up-date displacement and stability estimates. The end result of the hull fairing process leads to a tape which can be supplied to the shipbuilder instead of the lines plan and table of offsets.

(3) Many more design options can be studied and compared and these can be in greater detail.

(4) The computer can develop pictures of what the finished ship will look like, internally as well as externally. These can be used instead of mock-ups to assist in achieving efficient layouts. The colours and textures of different materials can be shown. An owner can effectively be taken for a walk through the ship before it leaves the drawing board.[14]

(5) In production the computer can help with routine matters like stock control. It can control cutting and welding machines ensuring greater accuracy of fit and facilitating more extensive pre-fabrication and reducing built-in stress levels.

(6) On board it can control machinery and monitor its performance to give early warning of incipient failure.

(7) It can help the command with decision making. For instance it can advise on loading sequences to eliminate the possibility of overloading the structure. It can assist warship captains when under enemy attack by suggesting the optimum actions to take in defence.

(8) Computer based simulators can assist in training navigators, machinery controllers and so on.

The outcome

Having dealt, albeit only in outline, with the factors involved in design, and the design process, it is time to look at the end product, the ship. Not surprisingly these differ considerably in look and size depending upon the function they have to fulfill. Hence there is a need to look at a number of ship types.

MERCHANT SHIPS

It has been seen that the development of merchant ship types has been dictated largely by the nature of the cargo. The range of ships are listed in a number of publications. An annual publication[15] of the RINA reviews the more interesting and significant ships of the previous year. Designs can be divided broadly into general cargo, bulk cargo and passenger vessels.

The general cargo carrier is a flexible design of vessel which will go anywhere and carry anything. Specialist forms include container ships, roll on/roll off ships and barge carriers. Bulk cargoes may be liquid, solid or liquefied gas. Particular designs of vessel exist for the carriage of each. Passenger-carrying vessels include cruise liners and ferries.

General cargo ships

The general cargo ship has several large clear open cargo-carrying spaces or holds. One or more decks may be present within the holds. They are known as 'tween decks and provide increased flexibility in loading and unloading, permit cargo segregation and improved stability. Access to the holds is by openings in the deck known as hatches.

Hatches are made as large as strength considerations permit in order to reduce the amount of horizontal movement of cargo within the ship. Hatch covers are, nowadays, made of steel although old vessels used wood. They must be watertight and rest upon coamings around the hatch. The coamings of the upper or weather deck hatches are raised above the deck to reduce the risk of flooding in heavy seas.

A double bottom is fitted along the ship's length, divided into various tanks. These may be used for fuel, lubricating oils, fresh water or ballast sea water. Fore and aft peak tanks are fitted and may be used to carry ballast and to trim the ship. Deep tanks are often fitted and used to carry liquid cargoes or water ballast. Water ballast tanks can be filled when the ship is only partially loaded in order to provide a sufficient draught for stability, better weight distribution for longitudinal strength and better propeller immersion. There is usually one hold aft of the accommodation and machinery space to improve the trim of the vessel when partially loaded. General cargo ships are typically from 2000 to 15 000 tonne displacement with speeds from 12 to 18 knots.

Refrigerated cargo ships

A refrigeration system provides low temperature holds for carrying perishable cargoes. The holds are insulated to reduce heat transfer. The cargo may be carried frozen or chilled and holds are at different

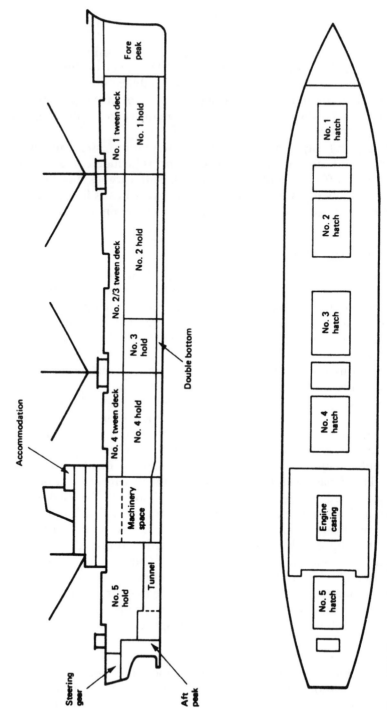

Figure 12.1 General cargo ship

temperatures according to requirements. The possible effect of the low temperatures on surrounding structure must be considered. These vessels are usually faster than general cargo ships with speeds up to 22 knots and up to 12 passengers are carried on some.

Container ships

Containers are re-usable boxes of 2435 mm by 2435 mm section, with lengths of 6055, 9125 or 12 190 mm. They are used for most general cargoes and liquid-carrying and refrigerated versions are in use. The latter may have their own independent cooling plant or be supplied with cooled air from the ship's refrigeration system.

The cargo-carrying section of the ship is divided into several holds with the containers racked in special frameworks and stacked one upon the other within the hold space. Cargo handling is by vertical movement of the containers by a special quayside crane. Containers may also be stacked on hatch covers and secured by special lashing arrangements. Cargo holds are separated by a deep web-framed structure to provide the ship with transverse strength. The structure outboard of the container holds is a box-like arrangement of wing tanks providing longitudinal strength. The wing tanks may be used for water ballast and can be used to counter the heeling of the ship when discharging containers. A double bottom is fitted which adds to the longitudinal strength and provides additional ballast space.

Accommodation and machinery spaces are usually located aft leaving the maximum length of full-bodied ship for container stowage. Cargo-handling equipment is rarely fitted, since these ships travel between specially equipped terminals to ensure rapid loading and discharge. Container ships have carrying capacities from 1000 to 2500 TEUs or more. The *twenty foot equivalent unit* (TEU) represents a 20 ft (6055 mm) 'standard' container. Container ships are faster than most general cargo ships, with speeds up to 30 knots.

Barge carriers are a variant of the container ship. Standard barges are carried into which the cargo has been previously loaded. The barges, once unloaded, are towed away by tugs and return cargo barges are loaded. Minimal or even no port facilities are required and the system is particularly suited to countries with extensive inland waterways.

Roll on/roll off ships

These vessels are designed for wheeled cargo, usually in the form of trailers. The cargo can be rapidly loaded and unloaded through stern or bow doors and sometimes sideports for smaller vehicles. Some have been adapted to carry containers.

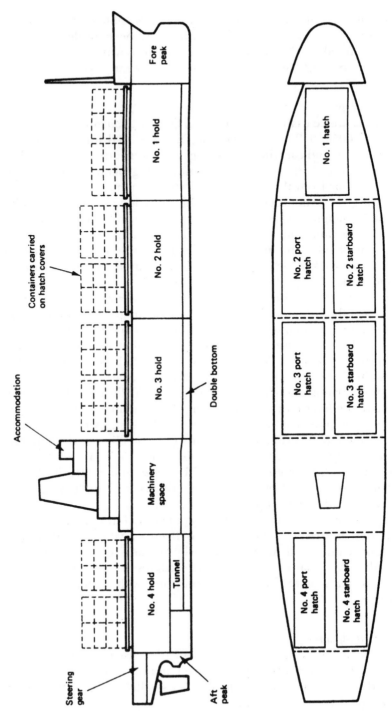

Figure 12.2 Container ship

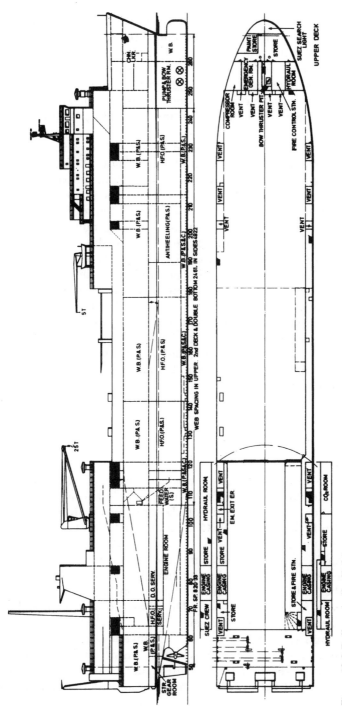

Figure 12.3 Roll on/roll off ship

The cargo-carrying section of the ship is a large open deck with a loading ramp usually at the after end. Internal ramps lead from the loading deck to the other 'tween deck spaces. The cargo may be driven aboard under its own power or loaded by straddle carriers or fork lift trucks. One or more hatches may be provided for containers or general cargo, served by deck cranes. Where cargo, with or without wheels, is loaded and discharged by cranes the term lift-on lift-off (Lo-Lo) is used.

The structure outboard of the cargo decks is a box-like arrangement of wing tanks to provide longitudinal strength. A double bottom is fitted along the complete length. The machinery space and accommodation are located aft. Only a narrow machinery casing actually penetrates the loading deck. Sizes range considerably with about 16 000 dwt (28 000 displacement tonne) being quite common. High speeds in the region of 18 to 22 knots are usual.

When used as ferries, vehicles usually enter at one end and leave at the other. This speeds up loading and unloading but requires two sets of doors. There has been considerable debate on the vulnerability of Ro-Ro ships should water get on to their vehicle decks. Various means of improving stability in the event of collision and to cater for human error in not securing entry doors, have been proposed. Since the loss of the *Herald of Free Enterprise* regulations have been tightened up. The later loss of the *Estonia* gave an additional impetus to a programme of much needed improvements.

Bulk cargo carriers

Oil tankers

Oil tankers, in particular crude carriers, have significantly increased in size in order to obtain the economies of scale and to respond to the demands for more and more oil. Designations such as ULCC (Ultra Large Crude Carrier) and VLCC (Very Large Crude Carrier) have been used for these huge vessels. Crude oil tankers with deadweight tonnages in excess of half a million have been built although the current trend is for somewhat smaller (100 000 – 150 000 dwt) vessels. After the crude oil is refined the various products obtained are transported in product carriers. The refined products carried include gas oil, aviation fuel and kerosene.

The cargo carrying section of the tanker is divided into tanks by longitudinal and transverse bulkheads. The size and location of these cargo tanks is dictated by the International Maritime Organisation Convention MARPOL 1973/78 which became internationally accepted in 1983. These regulations require the use of segregated ballast tanks

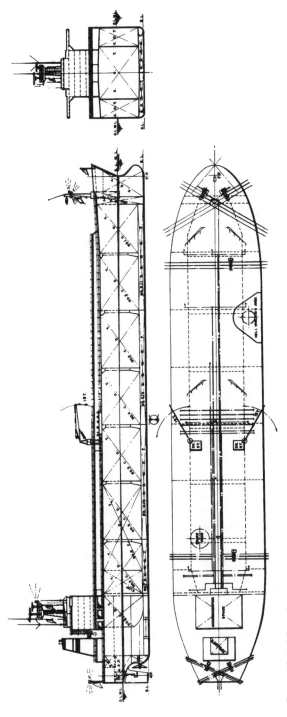

Figure 12.4 Oil tanker

and their location such that they provide a barrier against accidental oil spillage. An oil tanker when on a ballast voyage must use only its segregated ballast tanks in order to achieve a safe operating condition.

One arrangement of a 105 000 dwt crude oil tanker which satisfies these requirements is shown in Figure 12.4. The cargo carrying tanks include the seven centre tanks, four pairs of wing tanks and two slop tanks. The segregated ballast tanks include all the double bottom tanks beneath the cargo tanks, two pairs of wing tanks and the fore and aft peak tanks. Each tank is discharged by cargo pumps fitted in the aft pump room. Each tank has its own suction arrangement which connects to the pumps, and a network of piping discharges the cargo to the deck from where it is pumped ashore. Hose-handling derricks are fitted port and starboard near the manifolds. The accommodation and machinery spaces are located aft and separated from the tank region by a cofferdam. The range of sizes for crude oil tankers is enormous, beginning at about 20 000 dwt and extending beyond 500 000 dwt. Speeds range from 12 to 16 knots.

Product carriers are tankers which carry the refined products of crude oil. The cargo tank arrangement is again dictated by MARPOL 73/78. Individual 'parcels' of various products may be carried at any one time which results in several separate loading and discharging pipe systems. The tank surfaces are usually coated to prevent contamination and enable a high standard of tank cleanliness to be achieved after discharge. Sizes range from about 18 000 up to 75 000 dwt with speeds of about 14 to 16 knots.

Bulk carriers
The economies of scale have also been gained in the bulk carriage of cargoes such as grain, sugar and ore. A bulk carrier is a single-deck vessel with the cargo carrying section of the ship divided into holds or tanks. The hold or tank arrangements vary according to the range of cargoes to be carried. Combination carriers are bulk carriers which have been designed to carry any one of several bulk cargoes on a particular voyage, e.g., ore, crude oil or dry bulk cargo.

In a general-purpose bulk carrier, Figure 12.5, only the central section of the hold is used for cargo. The partitioned tanks which surround the hold are used for ballast purposes. This hold shape also results in a self-trimming cargo. During unloading the bulk cargo falls into the space below the hatchway facilitating the use of grabs or other mechanical unloaders. Large hatchways are a particular feature of bulk carriers. They reduce cargo handling time during loading and unloading.

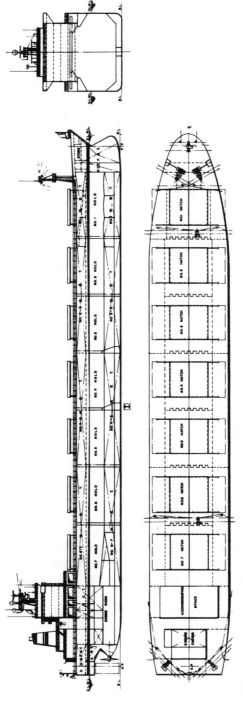

Figure 12.5 General purpose bulk carrier

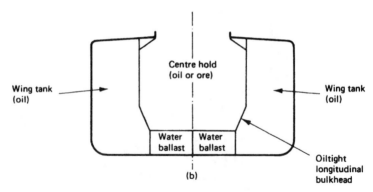

Figure 12.6 Section of oil/ore carrier

An ore carrier has two longitudinal bulkheads which divide the cargo section into wing tanks and a centre hold which is used for ore. A deep double bottom is fitted. Ore, being a dense cargo, would have a very low centre of gravity if placed in the hold of a normal ship leading to an excess of stability in the fully loaded condition. The deep double bottom raises the centre of gravity and the behaviour of the vessel at sea is improved. The wing tanks and the double bottoms provide ballast capacity. The cross section would be similar to that for an ore/oil carrier shown in Figure 12.6.

An ore/oil carrier uses two longitudinal bulkheads to divide the cargo section into centre and wing tanks which are used for the carriage of oil. When ore is carried, only the centre tank section is used for cargo. A double bottom is fitted but used only for water ballast.

The ore/bulk/oil (OBO) bulk carrier is currently the most popular combination bulk carrier. It has a cargo carrying cross section similar to the general bulk carrier but the structure is significantly stronger. Only the central hold carries cargo, the other tanks being for ballast, except the double bottoms which may carry oil fuel or fresh water.

Large hatches facilitate rapid cargo handling. Many bulk carriers do not carry cargo handling equipment, since they trade between special terminals with special equipment. Combination carriers handling oil cargoes have their own cargo pumps and piping systems for discharging oil. They are required to conform to the requirement of MARPOL 73/78. Deadweight capacities range from small to upwards of 200 000 tonnes. Speeds are in the range of 12 to 16 knots.

Liquefied gas carriers
The bulk transport of natural gases in liquefied form began in 1959 and has steadily increased since then.[16] Specialist ships are used to carry the

various gases in a variety of tank systems, combined with arrangements for pressurizing and refrigerating the gas. Natural gas is released as a result of oil-drilling operations. It is a mixture of methane, ethane, propane, butane and pentane. The heavier gases, propane and butane, are termed 'petroleum gases'. The remainder, largely methane, are known as 'natural gas'. The properties, and behaviour, of these two basic groups vary considerably, requiring different means of containment and storage during transit.

Natural gas

Natural gas is, by proportion, 75–95 per cent methane and has a boiling point of –162°C at atmospheric pressure. Methane has a critical temperature of –82°C, which means it cannot be liquefied by the application of pressure above this temperature. A pressure of 47 bar is necessary to liquefy methane at –82°C. Liquefied natural gas carriers are designed to carry the gas in its liquid form at atmospheric pressure and a temperature in the region of –164°C. The ship design must protect the steel structure from the low temperatures, reduce the loss of gas and avoid its leakage into the occupied regions of the vessel.

Tank designs are either self-supporting, membrane or semi-membrane. The self-supporting tank is constructed to accept any loads imposed by the cargo. A membrane tank requires the insulation between the tank and the hull to be load bearing. Single or double metallic membranes may be used, with insulation separating the two membrane skins. The semi-membrane design has an almost rectangular cross section and the tank is unsupported at the corners.

A liquefied natural gas carrier utilizing semi-membrane tanks is shown in Figure 12.7. The cargo carrying section is divided into five tanks of almost rectangular cross-section, each having a central dome. The liquid holding tank is made of 9 per cent Ni steel while the secondary barrier is made of stainless steel. These two are supported and separated from the ship's structure by insulation which is a lattice structure of wood and various foam compounds.

The tank and insulation structure is surrounded by a double hull. The double bottom and ship's side regions are used for oil or water ballast tanks whilst the ends provide cofferdams between the cargo tanks. A pipe column is located at the centre of each tank and is used to route the pipes from the submerged cargo pumps out of the tank through the dome. The accommodation and machinery spaces are located aft and separated from the tank region by a cofferdam. Liquefied natural gas carriers exist in a variety of sizes up to about 130 000 m³. Speeds range from 16 to 19 knots.

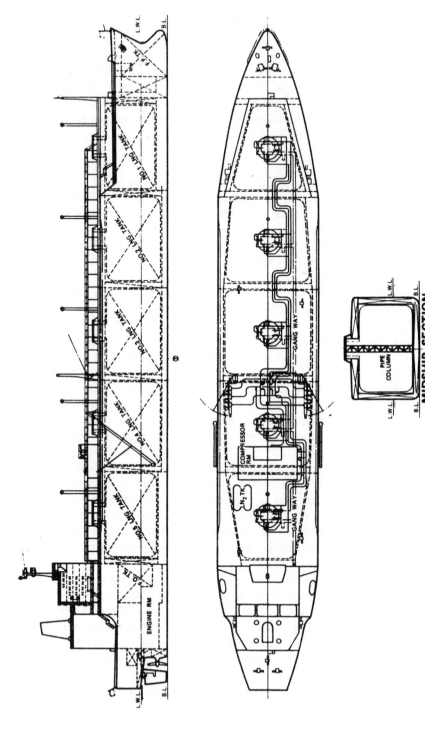

Figure 12.7 Liquefied natural gas carrier

Petroleum gas

Petroleum gas may be propane, propylene, butane or a mixture. All three have critical temperatures above normal ambient temperatures and can be liquefied at low temperatures at atmospheric pressure, normal temperatures under considerable pressure, or some condition between. The design must protect the steel hull where low temperatures are used, reduce the gas loss, avoid gas leakage and perhaps incorporate pressurized tanks. Tanks are either pressurized, semi-pressurized and partially refrigerated or fully refrigerated at atmospheric pressure. The fully pressurized tank operates at about 17 bar and is usually spherical or cylindrical in shape for structural efficiency. The tanks usually penetrate the upper deck.

Semi-pressurized tanks operate at a pressure of about 8 bar and temperatures in the region of $-7°C$. Insulation is required and a reliquefaction plant is needed for the cargo boil-off. Cylindrical tanks are usual and may penetrate the deck. Fully refrigerated atmospheric pressure tank designs may be self-supporting, membrane or semi-membrane types as in liquefied natural gas tankers. The fully refrigerated tank designs operate at temperatures of about $-45°C$. A double-hull type of construction is used.

A liquefied petroleum gas carrier utilizing semi-membrane tanks is shown in Figure 12.8. The cargo carrying section is divided into five tanks. Tanks 1 and 5 are used for the exclusive carriage of liquid butane with the remainder being used for either butane or propane. The butane-only tanks are self-supporting whereas the butane/propane tanks are of the semi-membrane type. The tank insulation uses polyurethane foam and the propane carrying tanks also employ a lattice structure of wood. The propane tanks are refrigerated to about $-45°C$ and the butane tanks to about $-10°C$. At these lower temperatures the inner hull is employed as the secondary barrier.

The double hull construction, cargo pumping arrangements, accommodation and machinery location are similar to a liquefied natural gas carrier. A reliquefaction plant is, however, carried and any cargo boil-off is returned to the tanks. Liquefied petroleum gas carriers exist in sizes up to around $95\,000\,m^3$. Speeds range from 16 to 19 knots.

Passenger ships

Passenger ships can be considered in two categories, the cruise ship[17] and the ferry. The ferry provides a link in a transport system and often has roll on/roll off facilities in addition to its passengers. Cruise ships, Figure 12.9, provide luxurious transport between interesting destinations in pleasant climates. The passenger is provided with a superior

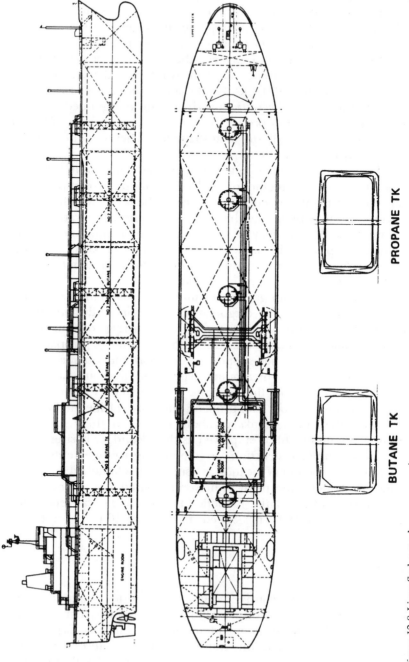

Figure 12.8 Liquefied petroleum gas carrier

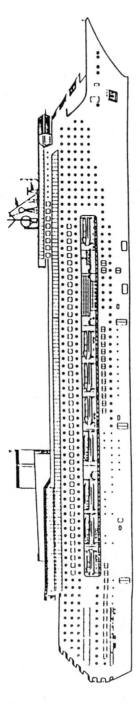

Figure 12.9 Cruise liner (courtesy RINA)

standard of accommodation and leisure facilities. This results in a large superstructure as a prominent feature of the vessel. The many tiers of decks are fitted with large open lounges, ballrooms, swimming pools and promenade areas. Aesthetically pleasing lines are evident. Stabilizers are fitted to reduce rolling and bow thrusters are used to improve manoeuvrability. Cruise liners range in size up to passenger-carrying capacities of around 2400 (gross tonnage about 75 000). Speeds are usually in the region of 22 knots.

Ocean-going ferries are a combination of roll on/roll off and passenger vessel. The vessel has three layers, the lower machinery space, the car decks and the passenger accommodation. A large stern door and sometimes also a bow door provide access for the wheeled cargo to the various decks which are connected by ramps. The passenger accommodation varies with length of the journey. For short-haul or channel crossings public rooms with aircraft-type seats are provided and for long distance ferries cabins and leisure facilities. Stabilizers and bow thrusters are usually fitted to improve manoeuvring. Size varies according to route requirements and speeds are usually around 20 to 22 knots.

Tugs

Tugs perform a variety of tasks and their design varies accordingly. They move dumb barges, help large ships manoeuvre in confined waters, tow vessels on ocean voyages and are used in salvage and firefighting operations. Tugs can be categorized broadly as inland, coastal or ocean going. Put simply, a tug is a means of applying an external force to any vessel it is assisting. That force may be applied in the direct or the indirect mode. In the former the major component of the pull is provided by the tug's propulsion system. In the latter most of the pull is provided by the lift generated by the flow of water around the tug's hull, the tug's own thrusters being mainly employed in maintaining its attitude in the water.

The main features of a tug, Figure 12.10, are an efficient design for free running and a high thrust at zero speed (the *bollard pull*), an ability to get close alongside other vessels, good manoeuvrability and stability.

Another way of classifying tugs is by the type and position of the propulsor units.

(1) *Conventional tugs* have a normal hull, propulsion being by shafts and propellers, which may be open or nozzled, and of fixed or controllable pitch, or by steerable nozzles or vertical axis

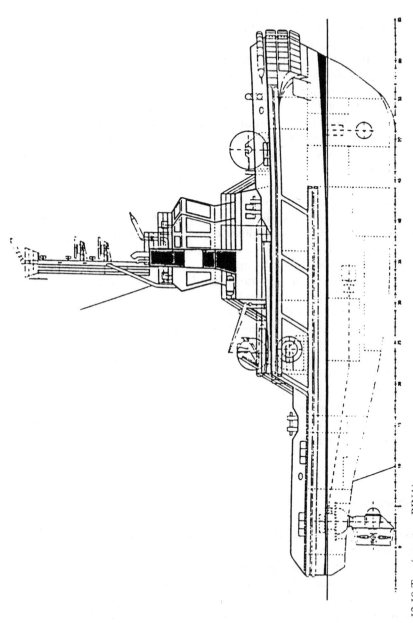

Figure 12.10 Tug (courtesy RINA)

propellers. They usually tow from the stern and push with the bow.

(2) **Stern drive tugs** have the stern cut away to accommodate twin azimuthing propellers. These propellers, of fixed or controllable pitch, are in nozzles and can be turned independently through 360° for good manoeuvrability. Because the drive is through two right angle drive gears these vessels are sometimes called Z-drive tugs. They usually have their main winch forward and tow over the bow or push with the bow.

(3) **Tractor tugs** are of unconventional hull form, with propulsors sited under the hull about one-third of the length from the bow, and a stabilizing skeg aft. Propulsion is by azimuthing units or vertical axis propellers. They usually tow over the stern or push with the stern.

In most tug assisted operations the ship is moving at low speed. Concern for the environment in the event of a spillage of oil from a tanker, or any other hazardous cargo has led to the concept of the escort tug. In this concept[9] the assisted ship may be moving at 10 knots or more. Success depends upon the weather conditions and the proximity of land or underwater hazards, as well as the type and size of tug. Some authorities favour a free-running tug so as not to endanger ship or tug in the majority (incident free) of operations. In this case the tug normally runs ahead of the ship. It has the problem of connecting up to the ship in the event of an incident. For this reason other authorities favour the tug being made fast to the escorted ship either on a slack or taut line.

The direct pull a tug can exert falls off with speed and indirect towing will be more effective at higher speeds. Tugs can be used as part of an integrated tug/barge system. This gives good economy with one propelled unit being used with many dumb units.

High speed craft

A number of hull configurations and propulsion systems are discussed here, each designed to overcome problems with other types or to confer some new advantage. Thus catamarans avoid the loss of stability at high speed suffered by round bilge monohulls. They also provide large deck areas for passenger use or deployment of research or defence equipment. Hydrofoil craft benefit from reduced resistance by lifting the main hull clear of the water. Air cushion vehicles give the possibility of amphibious operation. The effect of waves on performance is minimized in the *Small Waterplane Area Twin Hull* (SWATH)[18] concept. Some craft are designed to reduce wash so that they can operate at higher speeds in restricted waters. The choice of design depends upon the intended service. In some cases a hybrid is used. Although most applications of these concepts have been initially to small craft some are now appearing in the medium size, especially for high speed ferry services.

Monohulls

Many high speed small monohulls have had hard chines. Round bilge forms at higher speeds have had stability problems. Hard chine forms with greater beam and reduced length give improved performance in calm water but experience high vertical accelerations in a seaway. Their ride can be improved by using higher deadrise angles leading to a 'deep vee' form. Current practice[19] favours round bilge for its lower power demands at cruising speed and seakindliness, with the adoption of hard chines for Froude numbers above unity for better stability. One advantage of the round bilge form in seakeeping is that it can be fitted more readily with bilge keels to reduce rolling.

Surface effect vessels

In SEVs the weight is mainly, or totally, supported by an air cushion created by blowing air into a space under the craft and contained by a skirt. In some craft side walls remain partially immersed when the craft is raised on its cushion and the skirt is limited to the ends. The sidewalls mean that the craft cannot negotiate very shallow water but they do improve handling characteristics in winds and enable water propellers to be used for propulsion. Propulsion is often, but not necessarily, by means of airscrews.

The effect of the air cushion is to reduce the resistance to the motion through the water so that higher speeds are possible for a given power. The SEV is employed as a passenger ferry on a variety of short-haul routes. For the cushion craft shown in Figure 12.11 the passenger seating is located above the central plenum chamber with the control cabin one deck higher. Ducted propellers and rudders are located aft to provide forward propulsion. Centrifugal lift fans driven by diesel engines create the air cushion. Air jet driven bow thrusters are provided to improve manoeuvrability.

Early SEVs were relatively high cost, noisy and needed a lot of maintenance. As a result of experience with the early, mainly military craft later versions are considerably improved in all these respects. They are contenders for a number of commercial applications.

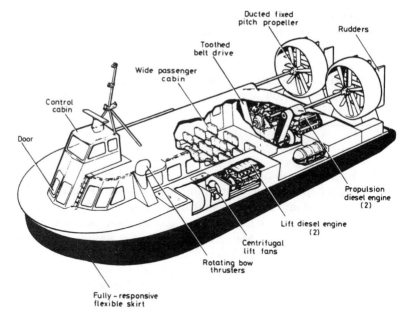

Figure 12.11 Air cushion vehicle

Hydrofoil craft
Hydrofoil craft make use of hydrodynamic lift generated by hydrofoils
attached to the bottom of the craft. When the craft moves through the
water a lift force is generated to counteract the craft's weight, the hull
is raised clear of the water and the resistance is reduced. High speeds
are possible without using unduly large powers. Once the hull is clear
of the water and not, therefore, contributing buoyancy, the lift required
of the foils is effectively constant. As speed increases either the
submerged area of foil will reduce or their angle of incidence must be
reduced. This leads to two types of foil system:

(1) Completely submerged, incidence controlled. The foils remain
completely submerged, reducing the risk of cavitation, and lift is
varied by controlling the angle of attack of the foils to the water.
This is an 'active' system and can be used to control the way the
craft responds to oncoming waves.
(2) Fixed surface piercing foils. The foils may be arranged as a
ladder either side of the hull or as a large curved foil passing
under the hull. As speed increases the craft rises so reducing the
area of foil creating lift. This is a 'passive' system.

Foils are provided forward and aft, the balance of area being such as to provide the desired ride characteristics. The net lift must be in line with the centre of gravity of the craft. Like the SEV, the hydrofoil has been used for service on relatively short-haul journeys. Both types of craft have stability characteristics which are peculiarly their own.

Multi-hulled vessels

These include sailing catamarans, trimarans,[20] offshore rigs, diving support vessels and ferries. Catamarans are not new as two twin hulled paddle steamers of about 90 m length were built in the 1870s for cross channel service. The upper decks of catamarans provide large areas for passenger facilities in ferries or for helicopter operations. In comparing monohulls and catamarans it is important to establish the basis of comparison, equal length, displacement, or carrying capacity. The greater wetted area of the catamaran leads to increased frictional resistance but their relatively fine hulls can have reduced wave resistance at higher speeds, perhaps assisted by interference effects between the two hulls. A hull separation of about 1.25 times the beam of each hull is reasonable. Manoeuvrability is good.

High transverse stability and relatively short length mean that seakeeping is not always good. This has been improved in the wave piercing catamarans developed to reduce pitching, and in the SWATH designs where the waterplane area is very much reduced and longitudinal motions can be reduced by using fins or stabilizers.

Multi-hull designs have a relatively high structural weight and often use aluminium to preserve payload. Wave impact on the cross structure must be avoided or minimized so high freeboard is needed together with careful shaping of the undersides. SWATH ships are very sensitive to changes in load and its distribution so weight control is vital.

Rigid inflatable boats (RIBS)

Inflatables have been in use for many years and, with a small payload, can achieve high speeds. The Royal National Lifeboat Institution make use of rigid inflatables in which the rigid lower hull is shaped to make the craft more seakindly and the inflatable principle safeguards against sinking by swamping.

Comparison of types

All the types discussed in this section have advantages and disadvantages. For a proper comparison, design studies of each prospective type to meet the requirement are needed although some requirements may point directly to one form. For instance, a craft capable of running up on to a hard surface suggests an air cushion vehicle. Many of these types of craft in use today are passenger carrying. SEVs with speeds of over 40 knots are commonplace, and can compete with air transport on some routes. Hydrofoils enjoy considerable popularity for passenger carrying on short ferry routes because of their shorter transit times. Examples are the surface piercing Rodriguez designs and the Boeing Jetfoil with its fully submerged foil system. Catamarans are used for rather larger high speed passenger ferries.[21]

WARSHIPS

Some very interesting problems attach to the design of warships.[10] A fighting ship needs to carry sensors to detect an enemy and weapons to defend itself and attack others. It must be difficult for an enemy to detect and be able to take punishment as well as inflict it. Its ability to survive depends upon its *susceptibility* to being hit and its *vulnerability* to the effects of a striking weapon. Susceptibility depends upon its ability to avoid detection and then, failing that, to prevent the enemy weapon hitting.

Stealth

A warship can betray its presence by a variety of *signatures*. All must be as low as possible to avoid detection by an enemy, to make it more difficult for enemy weapons to home in and to prevent the triggering of sensitive mines. The signatures include:

(1) *Noise* from the propulsor, machinery or the flow of water past the ship. An attacking ship can detect noise by passive sonars without betraying its own presence. Noise levels can be reduced by special propulsor design, by fitting anti-noise mountings to noisy machines and by applying special coatings to the hull. Creating a very smooth hull reduces the risk of turbulence in the water.

(2) *Radar cross section.* When illuminated by a radar a ship causes a return pulse depending upon its size and geometry. By arranging the structural shape so that the returning pulses are scattered over a wide arc the signal picked up by the searching ship is much weaker. Radar absorbent materials can be applied to the outer skin to absorb much of the incident signal.

(3) *Infra-red* emissions from areas of heat. The reader will be aware that instruments are used by rescue services to detect the heat from human bodies buried in debris. The principle is the same. The ship is bound to be warmer than its surroundings but the main heat concentrations can be reduced. The funnel exhaust

can be cooled and can be pointed in a direction from which the enemy is less likely to approach.

(4) **Magnetic.** Many mines are triggered by the changes in the local magnetic field caused by the passage of a ship. All steel ships have a degree of in-built magnetism which can be countered by creating opposing fields with special coils carrying electrical current. This treatment is known as *degaussing*. In addition the ship distorts the earth's magnetic field. This effect can be reduced in the same way but the ship needs to detect the strength and direction of the earth's field in order to know what correction to apply.

(5) **Pressure.** The ship causes a change in the pressure field as it moves through the water and mines can respond to this. The effect can be reduced by the ship going slowly and this is the usual defensive measure adopted.

It is impossible to remove the signatures completely. Indeed there is no need in some cases as, for instance, the sea has a background noise level which helps to 'hide' the ship. The aim of the designer is to reduce the signatures to levels where the enemy must develop more sophisticated sensors and weapons, must take greater risk of being detected in order to detect, and to make it easier to seduce weapons aimed at the ship by means of countermeasures. Enemy radars can be jammed but acts such as this can themselves betray the presence of a ship. Passive protection methods are to be preferred.

Sensors

Sensors require careful siting to give them a good field of view and to prevent the ship's signatures or motions degrading their performance. Thus search radars must have a complete 360° coverage and are placed high in the ship. Hull mounted sonars are usually fitted below the keel forward where they are remote from major noise sources and where the boundary layer is still relatively thin. Some ships carry sonars that can be towed astern to isolate them from ship noises and to enable them to operate at a depth from which they are more likely to detect a submarine.

Weapon control radars need to be able to match the arcs of fire of the weapons they are associated with. Increasingly this means 360° as many missiles are launched vertically at first and then turn in the direction of the enemy. Often more than one sensor is fitted. Sensors must be sited so as not to interfere with, or be affected by, the ship's weapons or communications.

Own ship weapons

Even a ship's own weapons can present problems for it, apart from the usual ones of weight, space and supplies. They require the best possible arcs and these must allow for the missile trajectory. Missiles create an efflux which can harm protective coatings on structure as well as more sensitive equipment on exposed decks. The weapons carry a lot of explosive material and precautions are needed to reduce the risk of premature detonation. Magazines are protected as much as possible from penetration by enemy light weapons and special firefighting systems are fitted and venting arrangements provided to prevent high pressure build up in the magazine in the event of a detonation. Magazine safety is covered by special regulations and trials.

Enemy weapons

Most warships adopt a policy of layered defence. The aim is to detect an enemy, and the incoming weapon, at the greatest possible range and engage it with a long range defence system. This may be a hard kill system, to take out the enemy vehicle or weapon, or one which causes the incoming weapon to become confused and unable to press home its attack. If the weapon is not detected in time, or penetrates the first line of defence, a medium range system is used and then a short range one. Where an aircraft carrier is present in the task force, its aircraft would usually provide the first line of defence. It is in the later stages that decoys may be released. The incoming weapon's homing system locks on to the decoy and is diverted from the real target although the resulting explosion may still be uncomfortably close. The shortest range systems are the *close in weapon systems*. These essentially are extremely rapid firing guns which put up a veritable curtain of steel in the path of the incoming weapon. At these very short ranges even a damaged weapon may still impact the ship and cause considerable damage.

Sustaining damage

Even very good defence systems can be defeated, if only by becoming saturated. The ship, then, must be able to withstand at least some measure of damage before it is put out of action completely and even more before it is sunk. The variety of conventional attack to which a ship may be subject is shown in Figure 12.12.

The effects on the ship will generally involve a combination of structural damage, fire, flooding, blast, shock and fragment damage. The ship must be designed to contain these effects within as small a

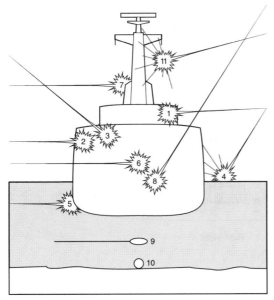

Low capacity, contact

1   cannon shell,
    HE and AP

High capacity, contact

2   HE shell
3   HE bomb
4   HE bomb, near miss
5   contact torpedo
    or mine

Medium capacity, contact

6   missile, sea skimming,
    and SAP shell
7   missile, high level
8   medium case bomb

High capacity, non-contact

9   magnetic-fuzed
    torpedo
10 ground mine
11 proximity-fuzed missile

Figure 12.12 Conventional weapon attack (courtesy RINA)

space as possible by *zoning*, separating out vital functions so that not all capability is lost as a result of one hit, providing extra equipments (redundancy) and protection of vital spaces. This latter may be by providing splinter proof plating or by siting well below the waterline.

An underwater explosion is perhaps the most serious threat to a ship. This can cause whipping and shock as was discussed under shock in Chapter 11.

Types of surface warship

Warships are categorized by their function, for instance the aircraft carrier.[22] Frigates[23] and destroyers tend to be maids of all work but their main function is usually anti-submarine or anti-aircraft. Their weapon and sensor fits and other characteristics will reflect this, Figure 12.13. Usually the main armament is some form of missile system designed to engage the enemy at some distance from the ship. The missile may be guided all the way to the target by sensors in the ship or may be of the type 'fire and forget'. In this case having been directed in the general direction of the target the weapon's own sensors acquire the target and control the final stages of attack. This latter type leaves the ship free to engage other targets.

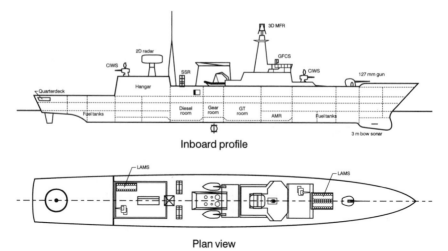

Figure 12.13 Frigate (courtesy RINA)

Mine countermeasure ships may be either sweepers or hunters of mines, or combine the two functions in one hull. Modern mines can lie on the bottom and only become active when they sense a target with quite specific signature characteristics. They may then explode under the target or release a homing weapon. Since sweeping mines depends upon either cutting their securing wires or setting them off by simulated signatures such mines are virtually unsweepable. They need to be hunted, detection being usually by a high resolution sonar, and then destroyed by placing a small charge alongside the mine to trigger it. The charge is usually laid by a remotely operated underwater vehicle. Because mine countermeasure vessels themselves are a target for the mines they are trying to destroy, the ship signatures must be extremely low and the hulls very robust. Nowadays hulls are usually made from glass reinforced plastics and much of the equipment is specially made from materials with low magnetic properties.

Submarines

The submarine has many unique features. It is dealt with here under warships because to date all large submarines have been warships. Some smaller commercial applications are discussed later but submarines are not economic for general commercial work. Although designed to operate primarily at depth, their behaviour on the surface must also be considered.

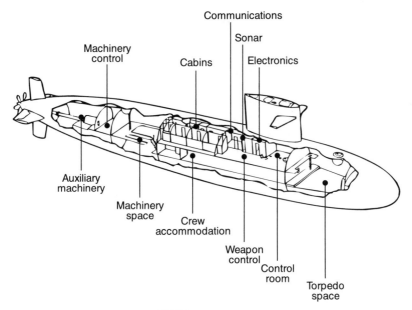

Figure 12.14 Submarine (courtesy RINA)

The layout of a typical submarine is shown in Figure 12.14. Its main feature is a circular pressure hull designed to withstand high hydrostatic pressure. Since it operates in three dimensions the vessel has hydroplanes for controlling depth as well as rudders for movement in the horizontal plane. Large tanks are needed which can be flooded to cause the ship to submerge or blown, using compressed air, for surfacing. Propulsion systems are needed for both the surfaced and submerged conditions. For nuclear submarines, or those fitted with some other form of *air-independent propulsion* (AIP), the same system can be used but usually diesels are provided for surface operations. 'Conventional' submarines use electric drive, powered by batteries, for submerged work. An air intake pipe or 'snort' mast is fitted to enable air to be drawn into the boat at periscope depth and periscopes are provided for the command to see the outside world.

Clancy,[24] describes in some detail *USS Miami* (SSN-755) and *HMS Triumph* (S-93) plus the ordering and build procedures, roles and missions. The reference includes the weapons and sensors fitted, dimensions, diving depths and speeds. Diagrammatic layouts of these submarines (and sketches of others) are given. Anechoic tiling and radar absorbent materials, to improve stealth are mentioned.

The hydroplanes can only exert limited lift so the submarine must be close to neutral buoyancy when submerged and the longitudinal centres of buoyancy and weight must be in line. Since there is no waterplane, when submerged the metacentre and centre of buoyancy will be coincident and BG will be the same for transverse and longitudinal stability. On the surface the usual stability principles apply but the waterplane area is relatively small. The stability when in transition from the submerged to the surfaced state may be critical and needs to be studied in its own right. The usual principles apply to the powering of submarines except that for deep operations there will be no wave-making resistance. This is offset to a degree by the greater frictional resistance due to the greater wetted hull surface.

The pressure hull must be able to withstand the crushing pressures at deep diving depth. Design calculations usually assume axial symmetry of structure and loads. This idealization enables approximate and analytical solutions to be applied with some accuracy. Subsequently detailed analyses can be made of non axi-symmetric features such as openings and internal structure. The dome ends at either end of the pressure hull are important features subject usually to finite element analysis and model testing. Buckling of the hull is possible but to be avoided. Assessments are made of *inter-frame collapse* (collapse of the short cylinder of plating between frames under radial compression); *inter-bulkhead collapse* (collapse of the pressure hull plating with the frames between bulkheads) and *frame tripping*.

The design is developed so that any buckling is likely to be in the inter-frame mode and by keeping the risk of collapse at 1.5 times the maximum working pressure acceptably small. The effects of shape imperfections and residual stresses are allowed for empirically. Small departures from circularity can lead to a marked loss of strength and the pressure causing yield at 0.25 per cent shape imperfection on radius can be as little as half that required for perfect circularity.

Batteries are being constantly improved to provide greater endurance underwater and much effort has been devoted to developing air-independent propulsion systems to provide some of the benefits of nuclear propulsion without the great expense. Closed-cycle diesel engines, fuel cells and Stirling engines are possibilities.[25] The systems still require a source of oxygen such as high-test peroxide or liquid oxygen. Fuel sources for fuel cell application include sulphur-free diesel fuel, methanol and hydrogen.

Having given a submarine a propulsion capability for long periods submerged, it is necessary to make provision for better control of the atmosphere for the crew. The internal atmosphere can contain many pollutants, some becoming important because they can build up to dangerous levels over a long time. A much more comprehensive system of atmosphere monitoring and control is needed than that fitted in earlier conventional submarines.

So far commercial applications of submarines has been generally limited to submersibles some of which have been very deep diving. Many are unmanned, remotely operated vehicles. Most of these applications have been associated with deep ocean research, the exploitation of the ocean's resources, rescuing the crews of stricken submarines[25] or for investigations of shipwrecks.[26] This last reference lists a range of submersibles. A growing use is in the leisure industry for taking people down to view the colourful subsurface world. In some types of operation the submersible may be the only way of tackling a problem such as the servicing of an oil wellhead in situ which is too deep for divers.

A possible use for commercial submarines would be to facilitate operations under ice, perhaps to exploit minerals on the ocean floor or to obtain access to areas normally cut off by extensive ice fields. Such vessels would need to use some form of air-independent powering.

SUMMARY

The way in which a design is initiated and then progressed has been reviewed. Some of the main factors a naval architect has to consider and the compromises to be made have been outlined to illustrate why certain kinds of ship have developed the way they have. The impact of computers on the whole process of design, build and operation has been touched upon. Finally the main characteristics of a number of merchant ship and warship types have been described to show the end result of the naval architect's endeavours.

It has only been possible to touch briefly on many interesting topics but it is hoped that the reader has obtained an overview of what is involved and will be motivated to read more widely on this fascinating subject.

References

1. Andrews, D. (1992) The management of warship design. The MOD warship project manager's perspective. *TRINA*.
2. Goss, R. O. (1982) *Advances in maritime economics*. UWIST Press.
3. Gilfillan, A. W. (1969) The economic design of bulk cargo carriers. *TRINA*.
4. Rawson, K. J. (1973) Towards economic warship acquisition and ownership. *TRINA*.
5. Raper, R. G. (1970–71) Designing warships for a cost-effective life. *TIMarE*.
6. Goss, R. O. (1967) The economics of automation in British shipping. *TRINA*.
7. Aldwinkle, D. S. and Pomeroy, R. V. (1982) A rational assessment of ship reliability and safety. *TRINA*.
8. BS 5760: 1981. Reliability of system equipment.

9. International conference with the Nautical Institute. (1993) *Escort tugs; design, construction and handling – the way ahead.* RINA.
10. Brown, D. K. and Tupper, E. C. (1989) The naval architecture of surface warships. *TRINA.*
11. Greenhorn, J. (1989) The assessment of surface ship vulnerability to underwater attack. *TRINA.*
12. Snaith, G. R. and Parker, M. N. (1972–3) Ship design with computer aids. *TNECIES.*
13. Buxton, I. L., Hills, W., Robertson, A. J. S. and Sen, P. (1992) Offshore patrol vessel selection: A decision support system. *Warship '92. Affordable warships – extending and enhancing maritime capabilities.* RINA.
14. Thornton, A. T. (1992) Design visualization of yacht interiors. *TRINA.*
15. *Significant ships of 1994.* Annual publication of the RINA.
16. Ffooks, R. (1979) Natural gas by sea. Gentry Books.
17. Payne, S. M. (1992) From Tropicale to Fantasy: a decade of cruiseship development. *TRINA.*
18. RINA Symposium (1985) *SWATH ships and advanced multi-hulled vessels.*
19. Dorey, A. L. (1989) High speed small craft. The 54th Parsons Memorial Lecture. *TRINA.*
20. Pattison, D. R. and Zhang, J. W. (1994) Trimaran ships. *TRINA.*
21. RINA Symposium (1993) *Fast passenger craft – new developments and the Nordic initiative.*
22. Honnor, A. F. and Andrews, D. J. (1981) HMS Invincible: the first of a new genus of aircraft carrying ships. *TRINA.*
23. Ferreiro, L. D. and Stonehouse, M. H. (1994) A comparative study of US and UK frigate design. *TRINA.*
24. Clancy, T. (1993) *Submarine.* Harper Collins.
25. RINA (1988, 1991, 1993) *International symposia on naval submarines.*
26. Garzke, W. H., Yoerger, D. R., Harris, S., Dulin, R. O. and Brown, D. K. (1993) Deep underwater exploration vessels – past, present and future. SNAME Centennial Meeting.

Appendix: Units, notation and sources

The text of this book is based on widely accepted international units and notation.

UNITS

The units in common use in the United Kingdom are those endorsed by the International Organisation for Standardisation, the *Système International d'Unités* (SI)[1]. The base units and some derived and supplementary units are given in Tables A.1 and A.2. Whilst this book is based mainly on SI units, reference is also made, where appropriate, to the older Imperial units. Readers should find this useful when using data or documents produced before SI units were adopted or produced by countries not yet using them. To assist in an understanding of both sets of units some equivalences are listed in Table A.3.

Table A.1 SI base units

Quantity	Unit name	Unit symbol
Length	metre	m
Mass	kilogram	kg
Time	second	s
Electric current	ampere	A
Thermodynamic temperature	kelvin	K
Amount of substance	mole	mol
Luminous intensity	candela	cd

Table A.2 Some derived and supplementary units

Quantity	SI unit	Unit symbol
Plane angle	radian	rad
Force	newton	$N = kg\ m/s^2$
Work, energy	joule	$J = N\ m$
Power	watt	$W = J/s$
Frequency	hertz	$Hz = s^{-1}$
Pressure, stress	pascal	$Pa = N/m^2$
Area	square metre	m^2
Volume	cubic metre	m^3
Density	kilogram per cubic metre	kg/m^3
Velocity	metre per second	m/s
Angular velocity	radian per second	rad/s
Acceleration	metre per second squared	m/s^2
Surface tension	newton per metre	N/m
Pressure, stress	newton per square metre	N/m^2
Dynamic viscosity	N sec per metre squared	Ns/m^2
Kinematic viscosity	metre squared per second	m^2/s
Thermal conductivity	watt per metre kelvin	$W/(m\ K)$
Luminous flux	lumen (lm)	cd.sr
Illuminence	lux (lx)	lm/m^2

Table A.3 Some equivalent values

Quantity	UK unit	Equivalent SI unit
Length	foot	0.3048 m
	mile	1609.34 m
	nautical mile (UK)	1853.18 m
	nautical mile (International)	1852 m
Area	sq. ft	$0.0929\,m^2$
Volume	cub. ft	$0.0283\,m^3$
Velocity	ft/s	0.3048 m/s
	knot (UK)	0.514 77 m/s
	knot (International)	0.514 44 m/s
Standard acceleration, g	32.174 ft/s^2	$9.806\ 65\,m^2/s$
Mass	ton	1016.05 kg
Pressure	lbf/in^2	6894.76 N/m^2
Power	hp	745.7 W

NOTATION

This book adopts the notation used by the international community, in particular by the International Towing Tank Conference and the International Ships Structure Congress. It has been departed from in some simple equations where the full notation would be too cumbersome.

Where there is more than one meaning of a symbol, that applying should be clear from the context.

Where a letter is used to denote a 'quantity' such as length it is shown in *italics*. For a distance represented by the two letters at its extremities the letters are in italics. Where a letter represents a point in space it is shown without italics.

Symbols

a	resistance augment fraction
A	area in general
B, b	breadth in general
b	span of hydrofoil or aerofoil
C	coefficient in general, modulus of rigidity
D, d	diameter in general, drag force, depth of ship
E	modulus of elasticity, Young's modulus
f	frequency
F	force in general, freeboard
F_n	Froude number
g	acceleration due to gravity
h	height in general
I	moment of inertia in general
J	advance number of propeller, polar second moment
k	radius of gyration
K_Q, K_T	torque and thrust coefficients
K, M, N	moment components on body
L	length in general, lift force
m	mass
M	bending moment in general
n	rate of revolution, frequency
p	pressure intensity
p, q, r	components of angular velocity
P	power in general, propeller pitch, direct load
Q	torque
R, r	radius in general, resistance
R_n	Reynolds' number
S	wetted surface

t	time in general, thickness, thrust deduction factor
T	draught, time for a complete cycle, thrust, period
u, v, w	velocity components in direction of x-, y-, z-axes
U, V	linear velocity
w	weight density, Taylor wake fraction
W	weight in general, external load
x, y, z	body axes and Cartesian co-ordinates
X, Y, Z	force components on body
α	angular acceleration, angle of attack
β	leeway or drift angle
δ	angle in general, deflection, permanent set
θ	angle of pitch, trim
μ	coefficient of dynamic viscosity
ν	Poisson's ratio, coefficient of kinematic viscosity
ρ	mass density
φ	angle of roll, heel, list
ω	angular velocity, circular frequency
V, ∇	volume
Δ	displacement force
η	efficiency in general
σ	cavitation number, direct stress
Λ	tuning factor

Subscripts

Much of the notation above is qualified by a subscript in particular applications. The subscripts used are:

B	block
D	developed (area), drag, delivered (power)
E	effective (power), encounter (waves)
F	frictional (resistance), Froude
H	hull
L	longitudinal, lift
M	midship section
O	open water (propeller)
OA	overall
P	longitudinal prismatic
PP	between perpendiculars
Q	torque
R	residuary (resistance), relative rotative (efficiency), rudder
S	shaft
T	transverse, total, thrust
VP	vertical prismatic

W	waterline, waterplane, wave-making
WP	waterplane
y	yield (stress)
Θ	pitching, trimming
φ	rolling, heeling
ζ	wave elevation

SOURCES

Learned societies

Many references are to the papers of learned societies, published either in their transactions or in reports of conferences. Membership of a learned society is recommended as a means of keeping abreast of the many new developments in the discipline as they occur and also for the opportunity to meet like-minded people. Additionally there is the status associated with membership of a recognized body with the possibility, in the UK, of being able to register as a member of the Engineering Council. Corresponding bodies exist in other countries. It is likely that such membership will become more important in future as an aid to obtaining particular posts in industry.

The principal societies, with their abbreviated titles, whose papers have been cited in this book are:

The Royal Institution of Naval Architects: RINA (INA before 1960).
Institution of Engineers and Shipbuilders of Scotland: IESS.
The Society of Naval Architects and Marine Engineers: SNAME.
The Society of Naval Architects of Japan: SNAJ.
The Institute of Marine Engineers: IMarE.

Many of the references are for papers presented to the RINA. These are used because they are of high quality and are widely available. The RINA has a division in Australia and many joint branches, with the IMarE, throughout the world.

Most learned societies produce journals on a regular basis, discussing recent developments of interest. The journal of the RINA is called *The Naval Architect* and is published ten times a year.

References

References are given at the end of each chapter to assist the reader in following up various aspects of the subject in more detail. In turn these references will provide information on the sources used and further references for additional reading if required.

Where the papers quoted are contained in the transactions of a learned society they are referred to as, for instance, *TRINA, TSNAME*, etc., plus year of publication. For references to articles in the *Naval Architect* the abbreviation *NA* is used.

Other references are taken from the published papers of research organizations, classification Societies, the British Standards Institute (BSI) and government organizations.

Reference

1. BS 5555: 1993; ISO 1000: 1992. SI Units and recommendations for the use of their multiples and certain other units.

Index

At Butterworth-Heinemann we are determined to provide you with a quality service. To help supply you with information on relevant titles as soon as it is available, please fill in the form below and return to us using the FREEPOST facility. Thank you for your help and we look forward to hearing from you.

What title have you purchased? _____

Where was the purchase made ? _____

When was the purchase made? _____

Name (Please Print): _____

Job Title: _____

Street: _____

Town: _____

County: _____ Postcode: _____

Country: _____ Telephone: _____

Company Activity: _____

Signature: _____ Date: _____

```
(FOR OFFICE USE ONLY)




```

BUTTERWORTH
HEINEMANN

Butterworth-Heinemann Limited – Registered Office: Michelin House, 81 Fulham Road, London, SW3 6RB. Registered in England 194771.
VAT number GB: 240 242902.

Direct Mail Department
Butterworth-Heinemann

FREEPOST

OXFORD

OX2 8BR

UK